PRAISE FOR *TURNING LEARNING INTO*

"In *Turning Learning into Action* Emma takes a practical and common sense approach to addressing one of the most pressing needs in training and development today: ensuring learning transfer. She effectively describes what needs to happen in the post-instructional period to ensure business results. This thoughtful and readable book is highly recommended."
Andrew Jefferson and Roy Pollock, co-authors of *The Six Disciplines of Breakthrough Learning*

"With *Turning Learning into Action*, Emma tackles the thorny issue of change after learning. Learning and development managers know that evaluation and measurement of learning is an important part of training design. Now they are realizing that learning transfer is essential too. This book makes a significant contribution to the transfer of learning to the job, with a practical approach of how real business results can be delivered."
Jack and Patti Phillips, founders of the ROI Institute and authors of over 30 books on measurement and evaluation

"The Turning Learning into Action methodology has made a concrete difference to our training results over the last eight years. A must to read and implement!"
James Harper, previously Training Manager, BMW Group Australia, now Training Manager, BMW Group Japan

"Emma's dedication to learning outcomes has made a real contribution to the success of our entrepreneurs since 2009. Great work Emma in getting into print what you truly believe in."
Tracey Webster, CEO, Branson Centre of Entrepreneurship, Johannesburg, South Africa

"LIW has used the Turning Learning into Action methodology with global clients for the last four years. It has become a crucial part of our approach to delivering measurable business impact for our clients – I highly recommend it!"
Pia Lee, CEO, LIW

TURNING LEARNING INTO ACTION

A proven methodology for
effective transfer of learning

EMMA WEBER

KoganPage

LONDON PHILADELPHIA NEW DELHI

First published in Great Britain and the United States in 2014 by Kogan Page Limited

2nd Floor, 45 Gee Street
London EC1V 3RS
United Kingdom
www.koganpage.com

1518 Walnut Street, Suite 1100
Philadelphia PA 19102
USA

4737/23 Ansari Road
Daryaganj
New Delhi 110002
India

© Emma Weber, 2014

The right of Emma Weber to be identified as the author of this work has been asserted by her in accordance with the Copyright, Designs and Patents Act 1988.

ISBN   978 0 7494 7222 1
E-ISBN   978 0 7494 7223 8

British Library Cataloguing-in-Publication Data

A CIP record for this book is available from the British Library.

Library of Congress Cataloging-in-Publication Data

CIP data is available.

Library of Congress Control Number: 2013049650

Typeset by Graphicraft Limited, Hong Kong
Print production managed by Jellyfish
Printed and bound by CPI Group (UK) Ltd, Croydon, CR0 4YY

Contents

PART TWO
THE LEARNING TRANSFER SOLUTION 77

Turning Learning into Action® 79

Preparation – setting expectations 99

Preparation – creating the TLA plan 109

PART THREE
MAKING LEARNING TRANSFER HAPPEN AND THE BENEFITS BY STAKEHOLDER 199

How to roll out TLA successfully 201

The benefits of TLA by stakeholder 218

Conclusion 231

About the author

Emma Weber is the founder of Lever Learning and developer of the Turning Learning into Action® methodology.

Born in England, now carrying an Australian passport, in 2002 Emma left a successful corporate career in London to start her own business in Australia, following her passion for coaching and learning.

Emma's firm belief, and the platform on which she has built her successful global business, is that the key aim of learning in the workplace is to create tangible business benefits. She established Lever Learning to help organizations and their employees convert learning to effective action back on the job.

Under her guidance Lever Learning now delivers Turning Learning into Action® programmes throughout 16 countries and in 11 languages.

A recognized authority on the transfer of learning, Emma has been a guest speaker on learning effectiveness at conferences in Australia, New Zealand and the USA.

Fostering entrepreneurship is Emma's other keen interest and for the last three years she has co-facilitated training at the Branson Centre of Entrepreneurship in Johannesburg, South Africa. She is also an active supporter of Club Kidpreneur, a foundation that helps children unlock their passion and potential for business.

In her spare time Emma salsas, sings and enjoys the beautiful Sydney coastline. In 2013 she cycled 800km (500 miles) across regional Thailand, raising funds for Hands Across the Water, Australia's fastest growing charity.

Contact Emma on **emma@leverlearning.com**

- Follow Emma's blog at **http://leverlearning.com/blog/**
- Connect on LinkedIn at **au.linkedin.com/in/emmaweber/**
- Follow on Twitter **https://twitter.com/emmaweber**
- Watch on YouTube **http://www.youtube.com/user/EmmaWeber1**

Acknowledgements

Like all books, this one was not a solo effort.

First, my thanks to the amazing Karen McCreadie without whose help this book would not have got past 26,000 words. Karen you have kept this project on track and moving forward. Thanks for your skill, talent and persistence. A word architect to be recommended. Thanks also to Jack and Patti Phillips from the ROI Institute who have allowed me to reference their evaluation work and research. You are true inspirations in the Learning and Development field.

The book has also been developed with the unknown help of many hundreds of participants who have attended training and then worked one-on-one either with my team or myself. You have helped us identify the patterns that occur back in the workplace that create the learning transfer dilemma and more importantly, allowed us to shape the methodology that solves that dilemma as quickly and effectively as possible. Thank you.

A huge thank you to my team for their unwavering support and enthusiasm for all things learning transfer! Thanks for trusting the process and doing outstanding work day after day with such expertise, grace and care. Thank you for supporting people to grow through learning, and helping them to deliver business results in the process. Maree McKeown, Alison Williams, Theresa Hackett, Deb King, Hilary Chatterton, Phenella Lill, Pam Solberg-Tapper, Anna Marshall, Cindy Biggs, Florence Divet, Gulruh Turhan, Jennifer Arnold-Levy, Esther Goette, Sogut Zengingonul, Halka Balackova, Coen Hamming, Ivana Klepaczova , Sheryl Pope, Keke Quei – you know you all ROCK!

A special mention to the back office geniuses of Madhura Bhagwat, who keeps the Lever Learning machine running smoothly and Juliet Hammond our evaluation specialist, both of whom enable me to do the work I love. Thanks for being such legends.

Going back to the very beginning, thank you to David Williams and James Harper, formerly of BMW Australia, who gave me my first big corporate break after I had left the world of the employee and travelled 17,000 km to start my own business. Your belief and trust in me and my process started this ball rolling.

This work wouldn't have been taken to the world without the belief and enthusiasm of our partners – Stuart and Renata at Diversity Consulting, Jeremy at Blue Sky Development, Kevin, John , Paul and Ros at JBA Design – thank you for choosing to partner with us and having our methodology support your great work. Teamwork gets the results. A special thank you to our strategic partner LIW, specifically Pia, Dan. Dan, Charlie, Rob, Sue, Alan, Sharon, Mark, Kerry and Mel who have taken us global – to countries I never dreamed would demand my learning transfer methodology! You have my deepest respect and gratitude for letting us do great work with your clients.

Lever Learning is the vehicle that allows me to take my learning transfer work to the widest audience possible. It thrives under the guidance of an amazing team of mentors – Jenni Smith, David Powell, Peter Finlayson and Cimone-Louise Fung. Heartfelt thanks. A special thank you must go to mentor extraordinaire Creel Price, whose entrepreneurial genius keeps us growing from strength to strength.

Thanks sincerely to my friends who have supported me through my book journey and my business journey. I feel incredibly blessed to have the best people in my life.

To my wonderful family – Mum, Helen, Phil, Charlie and the gorgeous James and Thomas – thank you for your love, support and trust as I live on the other side of the world following my dream.

And finally, to you the reader, thanks for not only picking up this book but for being inspired to read it. Thank you for allowing me the flexibility to start my sentences with 'and', sharing my passion with you along the way!

My hope is that you will take this book and turn your learning into action and join with me in allowing Learning Transfer to make a real difference in our workplaces.

Enjoy *Turning Learning into Action* and let me know how you go.

Emma
emma@leverlearning.com

Introduction

When it comes to corporate learning there is a very old, very large elephant in the room. In training there is often a Grand Canyon-sized gulf between what we know and what we do with what we know. And if we look at the research regarding transfer of learning the depth of this crisis is shocking: 80–90 per cent of all training programmes and initiatives are never implemented into the daily activity of the business.

In 1988 *Personnel Psychology* published 'Transfer of training: a review and directions for future research', which is considered one of the earliest and most detailed examinations of the learning transfer problem. Authors Baldwin and Ford noted that: 'American industries annually spend more than $100 billion on training and development, not more than 10 per cent of the expenditure actually results in transfer to the job.' These findings were then reconfirmed by Ford and Weissbein in 1997 in 'Transfer of training: an updated review and analysis', published in *Performance Improvement Quarterly*. In Broad and Newstrom's book *Transfer of Training: Action-packed strategies to ensure high payoff from training investments*, the authors wrote: 'Most of the investment in organizational training... is wasted because of the knowledge and a skill gained (well over 80 per cent by some estimates) is not fully applied by these employees on the job.' So not only do we know that there is a transfer of learning problem – we have actually known about it for a long time.

In the late 1980s Harold D Stolovitch wrote a book called *Telling Ain't Training*. It was published by the American Society of Training and is still considered a classic today. Stolovitch told us that what happens before and after the training is every bit as important as the training itself. That was over 30 years ago. Then in 1992 Broad and Newstrom wrote about the nine barriers to learning transfer.

Dusty training folders still litter company offices. They might have been re-labelled and now no longer contain pearls of wisdom about communication skills but instead the profit and loss statements for 2005 or job applications for the new apprenticeship scheme. The more substantial training folders often double as a doorstop or bookend! Or they are simply stuffed into a cupboard in a back office or under an unused desk so that the owner doesn't have to be reminded of their failure to implement a single idea from the course.

In fact this became a mantra for training for many years. I have lost count of the times I've heard the Learning and Development (L&D) Manager or the CEO come into a training programme before it begins and enthusiastically tell the participants that if they take just one thing away from the course they will have improved. I'm sorry but no one has the time to give up two days of their life to learn just one thing out of many! Besides, what the participants actually hear is, 'I need to *remember* one thing. That way when I meet the L&D Manager or CEO in the cafeteria or corridor I can give the appropriate spiel about the "one thing" I learnt and everyone will be happy!'

Anyone can remember one thing. And even if they can't there's always Google! We live in a time of unprecedented access to information. Without leaving the house we can read articles in *Harvard Business Review* or digest research papers from some of the smartest minds on the planet. Lack of information is not to blame for dismal training results. The problem, as we all know, is the gap between what we know and what we do with what we know.

When L&D managers and CEOs buy training they are not buying it so that the participants can have a nice day out of the office and source a new door-stop. They are buying the training because they have a problem that needs to be solved and they are seeking real-world behavioural change back in the workplace. Learning is a pathway to a different outcome – whether that is improved sales, better leadership or better performance. If that different outcome never materializes then the training has failed.

Training doesn't work in its current format because there is nowhere near enough support *after* the training to help participants make the changes to their behaviour in the working environment.

The purpose of this book is to address that situation. It is relevant to anyone who is involved in designing, sourcing, delivering, facilitating, participating or buying learning programmes – especially if those learning solutions involve the transfer of knowledge to an individual for the express purpose of altering behaviour in the workplace.

Part One explores the challenges we face and what has caused this problem in the first place. We will unpack the cornerstone of training design – the ADDIE model – to appreciate its strengths whilst also exposing its key limitations and how those limitations have unintentionally created this universal failure in corporate learning. We will identify the missing link in learning and ask why that link has remained missing for so long. And we will explore what people are currently doing to try to solve the problem – and why those solutions are largely ineffective.

Part Two presents a detailed explanation of our tried and tested solution – Turning Learning into Action® (TLA). TLA has already been successfully used by some of the world's most recognized companies, including high-end automotive, technology and innovation, electronics, financial services, insurance and fast-moving consumer goods (FMCG) companies. Whatever the type of business or industry, and whatever the type of training – if we *want the training to matter* we need to impose a structured process to ensure that the learning is transferred back to the workplace. TLA is that structured process.

TLA ensures that training *does* work and it always works when transfer of learning is a major priority in the acquisition of that training. I will therefore encourage you throughout this book to consider that perhaps *less* training is the answer, not more. Why waste time investing in training without transfer of learning methodologies, when experience and research already proves that it simply doesn't work? Why risk alienating our people on yet another training programme when there is no structured process to ensure that the skills and knowledge they learn are effectively translated into the behavioural change we originally sought? Wouldn't it be better to reduce the amount of training and increase the transfer so that the training we *do* invest in makes a measureable difference to performance and results?

We'll never get 100 per cent of the people transferring 100 per cent of the learning, but this book introduces a methodology that will transform training results *without* having to radically change training plans. We don't need to start from scratch or source a new type of training or find new training suppliers. We just need to shift our perspective a little to include a transfer of learning methodology so that we get the most bang for our buck.

Finally, Part Three explores TLA from the various stakeholder perspectives. No one stakeholder group is solely responsible for transfer of learning. Everyone from the CEO, the L&D professionals, trainers and participants have conspired, albeit often unknowingly, to create the dismal results of the past and must also collectively conspire to create the successful results of the future. Part Three explains the role of each stakeholder to ensure success. If everyone does a little then huge gains are possible and we can finally reap the rewards that training has promised but failed to deliver for too long.

Part One
THE LEARNING TRANSFER CHALLENGE

01
The evolution of training

Faced with a business need, problem or opportunity that can be solved by training most businesses go through a process described by the ADDIE model (Figure 1.1). The source of the ADDIE model is fairly obscure although it is thought that it was developed for the United States armed forces in the mid-1970s. Today there are an estimated 100 variations and it is referred to in a variety of different ways such as Instructional Systems Design (ISD), Instructional Systems Design & Development (ISDD), Systems Approach to Training (SAT) or Instructional Design (ID). But almost all the current instructional design models used in business today are variations of the original ADDIE model and I believe that this fact lies at the very heart of the learning transfer shortfall. Let me explain why...

FIGURE 1.1   The instructional design process as indicated by ADDIE

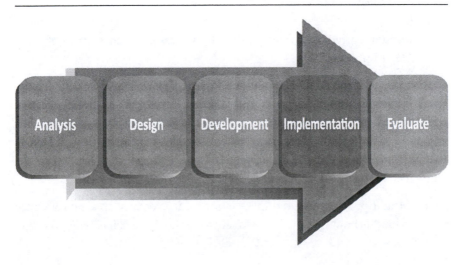

Analysis   Design   Development   Implementation   Evaluate

According to Wikipedia (2013) the definition of each element is as follows:

- *Analysis* – 'The analysis phase clarifies the instructional problems and objectives, and identifies the learning environment and learner's existing knowledge and skills.'

- *Design* – 'The design phase deals with learning objectives, assessment instruments, exercises, content, subject matter analysis, lesson planning and media selection. The design phase should be systematic and specific. Systematic means a logical, orderly method of identifying, developing and evaluating a set of planned strategies targeted for attaining the project's goals. Specific means each element of the instructional design plan needs to be executed with attention to details.'

- *Development* – 'In the development phase, instructional designers and developers create and assemble content assets blueprinted in the design phase. In this phase, the designers create storyboards and graphics. If e-learning is involved, programmers develop or integrate technologies. Testers debug materials and procedures. The project is reviewed and revised according to feedback.'

- *Implementation* – 'The implementation phase develops procedures for training facilitators and learners. Training facilitators cover the course curriculum, learning outcomes, method of delivery, and testing procedures. Preparation for learners includes training them on new tools (software or hardware) and student registration. Implementation includes evaluation of the design.

  'This is also the phase where the project manager ensures that books, hands-on equipment, tools, CD-ROMs, and software are in place, and that the learning application or website functions.'

- *Evaluation* – 'The evaluation phase consists of two parts: formative and summative. Formative evaluation is present in each stage of the ADDIE process.'

On the face of it the ADDIE model is a logical, dynamic and flexible framework for instructional designers and training developers to build effective training and performance solutions. Whilst it is incredibly useful and has advanced training effectiveness considerably since its inception, I believe that the model has created an unintended consequence that has led to the inefficiencies in corporate training.

As it is traditionally presented there is rarely, if ever, any specific reference to behavioural change or the idea of transfer of learning. That's the problem.

Consider for a moment that ADDIE refers to a training timeline – before, during and after the training. We will now look at each of these processes in turn.

Before the training

If we look at the ADDIE model from the perspective of timing it is easy to appreciate that the first three stages – analysis, design and development – are all concerned with how that training is created. It is therefore focused on what happens *before* the training.

During the analysis phase the instructional problem is clarified to ensure that training is actually the best solution. If it is, then the training designer will establish the specific learning problem that needs to be resolved, and sets business goals and performance objectives for the learning solution. Analysis needs to take into account the audience's need, existing knowledge, timelines and the learning environment. It must also address any learning constraints. Most companies and L&D professionals are already familiar with tools such as training needs analysis (TNA) and are therefore already proficient in training analysis and get it right 80 per cent of the time.

The design phase is focused on the learning objectives, lesson planning, delivery selection, exercises, subject matter, content and means of assessment. Design involves creating a clear vision for accomplishing the roles and objectives of the training.

The development phase is taking the agreed design elements and fleshing them out with the actual content and learning material. The programme is essentially put together and tested ready for implementation.

In our drive to improve and perfect design and development we have come a long way in our understanding of how people learn best. American educational theorist David A Kolb published his adult learning model in 1984 (Figure 1.2). Kolb's learning theory sets out four distinct stages in the learning cycle and builds on the work of Kurt Lewin, Carl Jung, Carl Rogers, John Dewey and Jean Piaget.

This model is universally acknowledged as one of the most important in explaining how adults learn effectively. It is therefore the blueprint for instructional design and has ensured that learning is designed with role play exercises and skills practice sessions to improve effectiveness.

FIGURE 1.2   Kolb adult learning principles

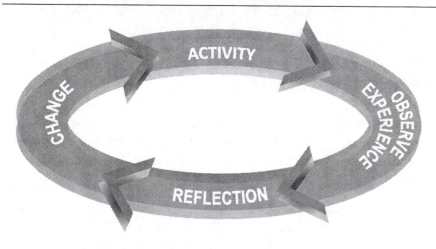

As a result of Kolb's influence training also began to incorporate adequate time for reflection so that participants had time to think about what they were learning and relate it back to their own experiences and into the workplace. Trainers have become very skilled at incorporating reflection into the learning process and are keen to help participants to apply the learning to their own working situation – at least theoretically.

Reflection is recognized as a vital component to adult learning as it encourages the learner to assimilate the information and make it personal and relevant to their own life and work situation. It is this reflection stage that helps to facilitate change. If an individual is taught leadership skills but the information remains abstract and one dimensional, and the individual doesn't have an opportunity to practise those skills or role-play them so they can get an experience of the difference between the new approach and their old approach, then the information remains just that – information. If, on the other hand, they are encouraged to apply that information to a real situation in their working lives, or imagine how they would apply the information to a real situation, then they are better able to see how it can actually help them personally. And if they can do *that* then change is at least possible.

Before ADDIE, and the insights into adult learning provided by Kolb, corporate training used to be 'chalk and talk'. A trainer or teacher would stand up at the front of the room with a blackboard, flip chart or whiteboard and talk at his or her students, who would scribble down the occasional note. Improved understanding into the way that adults learn together with a powerful instructional design framework took training from 'chalk and talk' to a whole new level of effectiveness. The industry pushed away from lecturing towards facilitation, it ensured that experiential learning and time for reflection was included so that the participants could gain more realistic understanding of the material and have time to consider how the information affected them personally. Today reflection is a recognized part of training design and development and this insight alone has massively improved training.

Generally speaking, instructional designers, companies and training organizations are already really good at design and development. They know how to effectively teach adults and how to incorporate the various elements to improve results. Consequently I've seen some outstanding training programmes with rich, original content, interesting and interactive exercises and innovative delivery – and it is clear that most organizations are already getting design and development right 85 per cent of the time.

During the training

Implementation is concerned with everything that happens *during* the training.

If we were to look at ADDIE in its purest form or best intention, implementation was probably intended to cover more than just the delivery of the material. Certainly I've read articles and books over the years that clearly articulate that the fourth stage of the ADDIE model is more than implementing a two-day training programme or other learning event – it is about implementing the whole learning experience. This would certainly imply a process to ensure that learning is transferred into the workplace. But the reality is that over the years implementation has come to focus largely on the delivery of the information in the training event.

The Wikipedia definition for implementation clearly shows that implementation is considered to be almost entirely about the delivery of the training material to participants, making sure that the person delivering the material is properly trained and making sure that the material that has been developed is distributed to the students. By this definition, which is the standard industry definition, most companies are also very good at implementation.

We've known for a long time that different people learn in different ways and that the development of technology now allows trainers the ability to combine a variety of learning media in any one programme so as to cater to each style.

Traditional old school 'chalk and talk' training catered mainly to the audio and visual learner who would absorb information by hearing it and seeing a presentation. Both mediums have been improved by technology, which can bring the information to life through audio or video footage and graphics – all delivered in stunning high definition. For kinaesthetic learners who learn best by experiencing the information, training is now vastly improved by the incorporation of role play, practical experiences, video examples and interactive online quizzes.

In truth everyone learns using all three learning styles, and improved technology and the easy access to computers, smartphones and the internet has certainly revolutionized the delivery and implementation of training. Big bulky folders have been replaced by smaller workbooks; technological flexibility has allowed instructional designers unlimited opportunities to implement learning solutions that truly allow participants to plug into their preferred delivery channel to reinforce learning and get the most out of the learning event.

As a result we are already very proficient at implementation and have become very adept at honing the transfer of information from the trainer to the individual. I've seen some brilliant training programmes with superb content and a vibrant delivery style, and where the participants love the training. The vast majority of courses and learning solutions are more than adequate for delivering the results they were designed for. As a result we are already getting it right about 85 per cent of the time.

After the training

In the ADDIE model, evaluation deals with what happens *after* the training and certainly it is the hot topic in learning and development. HR and learning professionals are being increasingly challenged to demonstrate that the money invested in training is paying dividends. Again we are already very proficient at *some* evaluation and we'll explore the various parts in the next chapter.

The challenge with evaluation as it is often described in the context of ADDIE is that it is retrospective – focusing on assessing how successful the knowledge transfer has been to the participant rather than how successful that participant has then transferred that knowledge to the workplace through behaviour change.

Clearly both are important as it is impossible for the learner to apply what he or she has learned unless that knowledge transfer process has been effective. Looking back at the training and evaluating how effectively the knowledge has been transferred to the participant is therefore an essential first step – and we are already very good at this type of evaluation. What we are not so good at is looking back several months after the training event in order to evaluate how effectively the participant is using that new knowledge in the workplace. It is this transfer of learning evaluation that is so often missing.

It is worth noting that there is a huge difference between compliance-based information training and soft-skills training before, during and after the training. Today businesses are required, often by law, to train employees in relation to health and safety issues. This type of training is often focused on compliance and protection – both for the employee and the employer. In this case there is no choice about change – people must comply. Evaluation in this context is therefore often straightforward.

This is not the case with soft-skills training. The term 'soft skills' refers to training such as leadership, sales, communication and negotiation skills. More often than not these programmes are delivered in a face-to-face setting and are already delivered and taught very well. The problem is that soft-skill training is often seeking to change the habitual ways we do things, relate to others and generally show up in the world so as to improve performance in the workplace. That is not easy and it won't happen automatically with-out some follow-up transfer of learning methodology and evaluation that goes beyond assessing knowledge. Without this additional step participants of soft-skills training can often 'get away with' not changing – so they don't change. And that's a real tragedy because it's soft-skills training that can really transform a business. The only way to successfully transfer soft skill to the participant and genuinely change real world behaviour over the long term is by a transfer of learning follow-up process so that behaviour change – not just knowledge uptake – can be evaluated.

Instructional design checklist

One of my first jobs in Britain after leaving university was as a financial merchandiser. I worked with the retail buyers and it was my job to get the right product, at the right price, in the right place at the right time. If a customer goes into a store and they have run out of a dress or shirt in their size then it is the merchandiser's fault: having the product available is a basic requirement of the process. Likewise when we are talking about training there are basic requirements that ensure we get the right people to the right programme in the right place at the right time.

It is also very important to get instructional design right because it will affect the outcome of the training. If we wanted to bake a beautiful birthday cake we wouldn't start with rotten eggs, out-of-date flour and a bashed-up baking tin. The same is true of instructional design, so getting the basic principles right is essential. Learning can be enhanced at each stage of the ADDIE process but the biggest win will be after the training programme. Tweaking what we do within ADDIE might help learning transfer, but make no mistake that unless the period *after* the training is tackled the benefits will be minimal.

Whilst this book is not about instructional design, below is a quick assessment summary of each of the ADDIE elements.

Analysis

Conduct a training needs analysis, often known as a TNA. Interview key stakeholders such as senior executives, leaders, participants, managers of participants and any other affected parts of the business to minimize assumption and ensure that existing knowledge is taken into account.

Questions that drive this process include:

- What are the businesses needs driving this training project?
- What are the goals and objectives for this training project?
- How will we define success for both the learner and the project?
- How will we measure that success?
- Who is the intended training audience?
- What do the members of the learning audience already know?
- What do they need to learn?
- What resources are already available?

This stage concludes with the development of the learning objectives that should be aligned with the business outcomes. To maximize learning transfer at this stage:

- Ensure everyone is clear about the required business outcomes and what specifically the business would like done differently as a result of the training.

- Ensure that the only people who attend are people within the organization who will benefit from the training and who are in a position to action what they have learnt.

Design

The instructional designer creates a blueprint or design for the training programme in much the same way as architects will draw up plans for a house as a blueprint for construction. The design should include:

- Plans for pre-work.
- How the programme will be communicated to the audience.
- How to get the learner engaged.
- The run sheet for the programme with detailed activities and frames to be covered.
- How the programme will be evaluated.
- The look and feel of the programme materials and graphics.

To maximize learning transfer at this stage:

- Confirm how the manager will be involved in the process.
- Include the key stakeholders in the design of the programme.
- Consider what is the process for embedding the learning so that it is easy to recall and remember, ie mnemonics.
- Gain buy-in for the process that inspires and engages the participants so they are prepared and keen to learn.
- Create a balance between practical, experiential learning activities and lecture-style learning – this aids future behaviour change at the earliest stage possible. Make sure there is a higher proportion of practical exercises to theory so that people can actually trial the processes while they are at the event. That way, they will have an experience of it rather than just technical understanding of it.

Development

During development the materials for the programme are created. This will include workbooks, learning aids, graphics and materials for exercises and activities within the programme.

To maximize learning transfer at this stage: ensure that the workbooks, materials and activities are attractive to different learning styles – visual, auditory and kinaesthetic.

Implementation

The more thorough the analysis, design and development stages the easier the implementation phase will be. To maximize learning transfer at this stage:

- Engage the learners.
- Create relevance to the participant role.
- Capture clear actions and commitments during the process.

In an ideal world the implementation phase will also include a learning transfer strategy to take effect after the learning intervention.

Evaluation

In terms of ADDIE the typical evaluation process is often limited to the participant's evaluation of the programme that they have attended, this is a basic requirement but does nothing for learning transfer.

To maximize learning transfer at this stage evaluation needs to be scheduled for two to three months after the programme so that the impact of the training can be accurately measured in terms of what benefits have been realized as a result of the training.

For more on instructional design best practice and how this can influence learning transfer I strongly recommend *The Six Disciplines of Breakthrough Learning: How to turn training and development into business results* (2010) by Calhoun Wick, Roy Pollock and Andy Jefferson.

70/20/10 is not the answer either

Before exploring the real problem with learning – why it is historically so ineffective and how to fix it – it is important to acknowledge one of the latest models in the learning and development community – the 70/20/10 model.

Based on research by Michael M Lombardo and Robert W Eichinger for the Center for Creative Leadership, the 70/20/10 model is a framework around how people learn, which is now guiding L&D investment and focus. Essentially what the 70/20/10 model states is that:

- 70 per cent of learning and development occurs through on-the-job experience, projects, tasks and problem solving in real time.
- 20 per cent of learning and development occurs through feedback, conversations and social interaction.
- 10 per cent of learning and development occurs through formal training programmes.

This model is gathering momentum in L&D circles and it is really easy to see why. If training facilitators, designers, managers, L&D professionals, HR executives, CEOs and leaders already know that all the research proves that 80–90 per cent of all training programmes and initiatives are never implemented into the daily activity of the business, then the 70/20/10 model allows everyone to breathe a collective sigh of relief. If only 10 per cent of all learning occurs in formal training anyway, then perhaps the fact that the participant never uses what they learn is not such a disaster after all!

The wholesale adoption of the 70/20/10 framework is effectively giving companies a huge reason to slash their training budget by saying that they only want 10 per cent of learning to happen through formal training. In effect, the industry is simply finding another reason to ignore the transfer of learning shortfall. Instead of solving that problem, the 70/20/10 approach simply lets businesses and L&D professionals off the hook by saying – 'Hey, in formal training people only learn 10 per cent of what they need to do their job anyway so these awful training statistics don't matter!'

The problem, of course, is that this argument completely misses the point – people are still not doing what they should be doing and they are not changing their behaviour through on-the-job experience, projects, tasks and problem solving (the 70 per cent) any more than they are changing their behaviour and incorporating learning from feedback (the 20 per cent) or formal training (the 10 per cent).

How the learning is acquired is irrelevant – what is relevant is whether the person receiving the learning is then applying that learning to change their behaviour and improve performance. Regardless of whether we agree with the 70/20/10 model or not there is still a shortfall in the application of learning, so there is still a missing link.

The missing link

ADDIE has been the hallmark of good training for decades. We have sought to understand how adults learn and have universally incorporated those elements into design and development – and yet training still fails. We have elevated content creation and delivery to an art form and implemented outstanding training and yet training still fails. We have collected 'happy sheets' or invested in complex return on investment (ROI) calculations in our effort to evaluate training and yet training still fails. The only difference now is that we can quantify the failure. If ADDIE is effectively mastered and training effectiveness has still remained largely unchanged for decades then clearly something is missing. If we have almost perfected each element of the instructional design process and the vast majority of training is still a colossal waste of time and money then clearly there *has* to be something missing.

If we have embraced the 70/20/10 model and slashed our formal training budget but the 70 per cent of learning that takes place through on-the-job experience, projects, tasks and problem solving is still not converting into business solutions and improved performance then there *still* has to be something missing.

There is. What is missing is a proven transfer of learning process.

The adherence of ADDIE in one form or another has meant that everyone is trying to design a process that delivers learning rather than a process that delivers change. And for the record, as a tool to deliver learning ADDIE is extremely good, but as a tool to deliver change it is not. There are two distinct parts to effective training. The first is the transfer of learning to the participant. The second is the transfer of learning from the participant into the workplace, as evidenced by behaviour change. ADDIE facilitates the first part brilliantly but it skips the second part almost entirely.

The 70/20/10 model may redistribute where learning occurs in a business but it does nothing to address whether that learning is being applied in the business. There is and always will be new ideas and frameworks being developed, because people are constantly drawn to the illusion of the easy solution, some magical switch that once flicked will miraculously close the gap between knowledge and application. There is no magic switch. We need to embrace the fact that helping people change is a very different process from helping them learn, and uploading the learning is a very separate process from downloading the learning.

Remember that when someone is commissioning a learning programme they don't want the learning per se, they want the change that the learning is going to give the participants and the subsequent improvement that learning will deliver to the business. People may enjoy training and expect it as part of their remuneration package but the purpose should always be to help people to change their behaviour and improve their performance from A to B, because it is that improvement that will ultimately help move the business from A to B and beyond.

Behaviour change is the key to massively improving results. ADDIE is devoted to delivering learning outcome rather than changes in performance or performance outcomes. Even when it comes to evaluation the only level of evaluation that truly focuses on the measurement of performance outcomes is level three – behaviour – and it is largely ignored (more on this later).

If the accepted training design model allows us effectively to ignore performance outcomes in favour of learning outcomes then it is hardly surprising that training fails to deliver real-world change on a consistent basis. And creating a new and innovative model about where that learning comes from won't solve the issue either. Without the necessary focus on performance outcomes, transfer of learning has no universally applied strategy, there is no ownership of the process and the 'solutions', as we will see in Chapter 3, are piecemeal, ad hoc and largely ineffective.

Just think about it... training is created because of a business need (see Figure 1.3). What follows are analysis, instructional design and delivery of the 'solution'. Every business wants that training to impact performance in some way. But it is not happening – and it is not happening because of the distribution of training ownership.

Traditionally the L&D department owns half of the training cycle and the other half of the training is owned by the business. Once the need has been jointly discussed between the business unit and the L&D department, L&D will design and deliver the programme. Then they pass implementation, transfer of learning and result back to the business, either through performance appraisals, manager intervention or some other business unit initiative. If, as the 70/20/10 model would suggest, 70 per cent of learning occurs on the job, then the manager is even more responsible for the learning results. And yet considering the statistics of failed training this learning loop is clearly not working.

FIGURE 1.3   The current formal learning loop

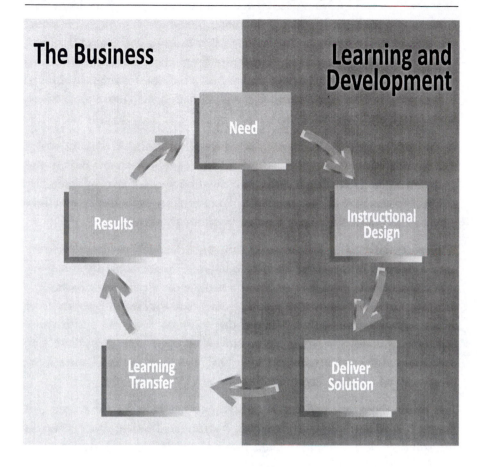

Collectively we need to shift the ownership of learning transfer so that L&D are much more involved in the results that the business is getting (see Figure 1.4). Not only would it mean that learning transfer was effective but it would also increase the visibility of learning and development.

If we want the business to own learning transfer now or in the future then we must give the people in the business the time and the skills to do it. In most companies, that would require a huge cultural change within an organization, and a significant change in job description for most managers. In my experience managers at all levels are already working at capacity. To add the responsibility for learning and learning transfer to the manager's plate without sufficient support is unfair and likely to damage business results. It may be the utopian vision to have managers own learning completely but it is much more realistic to have L&D make a step change to take more

FIGURE 1.4 The revised formal learning loop

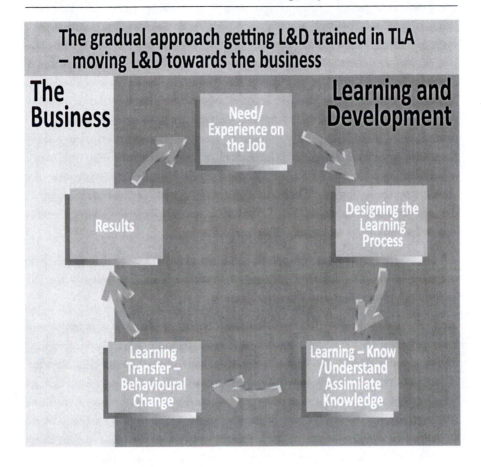

ownership of learning transfer and results, so that from the bottom up L&D can demonstrate to the business just what learning can *really* achieve. The rest of the business may then start to get very inspired by learning.

In the end it doesn't actually matter how brilliantly we analyse our learning need. It doesn't matter if the design of the solution was flawless and the development divine. And it doesn't matter how brilliantly the learning was implemented. It doesn't even matter if the learning was classroom-based or on the job. If the implementation phase does not include an ongoing process to help participants or employees to make behavioural change back in the workplace, then chances are our brilliant initiative will become another statistic in the legacy of failed organizational training. And that is a tragedy.

The tragedy is that 'implementation' in the context of ADDIE has simply been the implementation or delivery of the skills and knowledge *to* the individual and not necessarily the delivery of those skills and new knowledge *to* the business. When people exit the implementation phase they probably do know what to do – and through practice and role play in the learning solution they have an experiential appreciation that they can do it. They may even feel competent and confident, but without support to transition those skills and new knowledge back into the workplace the result is almost always the same. The learning disappears into the 'learning black hole'. Back in the day-to-day environment, with deadlines to meet, e-mails to answer and meetings to attend, good intentions give way to daily work pressures and the learning is forgotten or put off. People tell themselves, 'I'll try it the new way next week when I've got a bit more time' or 'I'll use the new system when everyone else uses it but not before' or 'There's nothing wrong with the old way anyway'. Or, my personal favourite, 'Yes, I think that was really interesting or useful but it doesn't apply to me/us – I/we are different.'

All that happens is that the people who attended the learning have their negative opinion of training galvanized. And that's such a waste – for the individual, the trainer and the organization.

And just in case you're thinking that this doesn't apply to you because you have adopted the 70/20/10 model so formal training isn't that important anyway, consider this: the first activity often touted as a '70 per cent activity' is 'opportunities to apply new learning and skills in real situations'. But, as we already know, we can give people opportunities to apply their new skills and learning till the cows come home and most people won't embrace those opportunities unless someone 'holds their feet to the fire' and makes them accountable for applying new learning and skills in a real situation.

Another '70 per cent activity' is often stated as 'opportunities to reflect and learn from projects'. Again, giving someone the opportunity to do something on a project basis doesn't mean they will adopt it as part of their day-to-day business behaviour. Projects finish. They have an end point and once the project is done often the learning stays with the project. That is why training fails. So whether the training occurs on the job, or through feedback or in formal training, what transforms that information into action that alters behaviour and improves performance is accountability. The simple reality is that the 70 per cent of learning isn't happening either. And, until it is, business can't just slash the 10 per cent and think that the problems they sought training to solve in the first place are going to miraculously disappear.

ADDIE transformed the learning experience beyond recognition and greatly improved the transfer of learning to the participant. It encouraged learning that is a world away from the 'chalk and talk' days of old, yet whilst it facilitated huge strides in the right direction it is not enough. So don't waste precious time and resources perfecting the ADDIE process. Good instructional design, where the basics are done well together with a potent transfer of learning strategy, will always outperform perfect instructional design with no transfer of learning strategy.

For training to be truly effective it must adhere to ADDIE, be owned by the L&D department *and* incorporate a proven transfer of learning strategy. Effective learning transfer is the missing link and it is just as relevant to on the job '70 per cent learning' initiatives as it is to the formal '10 per cent learning' initiatives. If business is seeking a solution to a business problem or seeking sustained employee performance improvement then a proven learning transfer process is the only viable solution.

Summary of key points

- Almost all the current instructional design models used in business today are variations of the original ADDIE model.
  - Analysis
  - Design
  - Development
  - Implementation
  - Evaluation
- Analyse, design and development are all concerned with how that training is created. It is focused on what happens *before* the training. Improved understanding into the way adults learn together with a powerful instructional design framework has taken training from 'chalk and talk' to a whole new level of effectiveness.
- Implementation is concerned with everything that happens *during* the training. We are already very proficient at implementation and have become very adept at honing the transfer of information from the trainer to the individual.

- Evaluation deals with what happens *after* the training. However, it usually focuses on evaluating how successful the knowledge has been transferred to the participant rather than how successful that participant has transferred that knowledge to the workplace through behaviour change.

- 70/20/10 is not the answer either. People are still not doing what they should be doing and they are not changing their behaviour through on-the-job experience, projects, tasks and problem solving (the 70 per cent) any more than they are changing their behaviour and incorporating learning from feedback (the 20 per cent) or formal training (the 10 per cent).

- How the learning is acquired is irrelevant – what is relevant is whether the person receiving the learning is then applying that learning to change behaviour and improve performance.

- ADDIE has been the hallmark of good training for decades, but if we have almost perfected each element of the instructional design process and the vast majority of training is still a colossal waste of time and money then clearly there *has* to be something missing.

- If we have embraced the 70/20/10 model and slashed our formal training budget but the 70 per cent of learning that takes place through on-the-job experience, projects, tasks and problem solving is still not converting into business solutions and improved performance then there *still* has to be something missing.

- There is – and what is missing is a proven transfer of learning process.

- Behaviour change is the key to massively improving results. ADDIE is devoted to delivering learning outcomes rather than changes in performance or performance outcomes.

- If the accepted training design model allows us to effectively ignore performance outcomes in favour of learning outcomes then it is hardly surprising that training fails to deliver real-world change on a consistent basis.

- Without the necessary focus on performance outcomes, transfer of learning has no universally applied strategy, there is no ownership of the process and the 'solutions' are piecemeal, ad hoc and largely ineffective.

- In the end it doesn't actually matter how brilliantly we analyse our learning need. It doesn't matter if the design of the solution was flawless and the development divine. And it doesn't matter how brilliantly the learning was implemented. It doesn't even matter if the learning was classroom based or on the job. If the implementation phase does not include an ongoing process to help participants or employees to make behavioural change back in the workplace then our brilliant initiative will become another statistic in the legacy of failed organizational training.

- ADDIE transformed the learning experience beyond recognition and greatly improved the transfer of learning to the participant. It encouraged learning that is a world away from the 'chalk and talk' days of old, yet whilst it facilitated huge strides in the right direction it is not enough.

- For training to be truly effective it must adhere to ADDIE, be owned by the L&D department *and* incorporate a proven transfer of learning strategy.

02
Learning's missing link – why it has been missing for so long

The fact that we have almost mastered instructional design in terms of the individual elements of the ADDIE model, but that training still fails, means that there must be a missing link in learning. That missing link is the transfer piece where the participant of the training event, loaded up with new knowledge and skills, then goes back to his or her place of work and uses the new knowledge and skills to change their behaviour and improve performance as a result.

There are, I believe, five reasons why the missing link has remained missing for so long:

1 no ownership;
2 wrong objective;
3 obsession with content;
4 obsession with evaluation;
5 focus on learning not on change.

No ownership

Each of the individual component parts of the ADDIE model is discrete. Often they are executed by different people. The analysis of the training challenge is usually done by a training professional or someone inside the business. The finish line for that person is to accurately identify the business problem, research the challenge and come up with a proposal about how that problem can be fixed through training. Once they have successfully identified the problem and provided a suggested solution they have done their job.

The next discrete part of the process is the design and development of the training event. The finish line for this component is the creation of the training event or the sourcing of the right learning solution. The designer and developer will consider their job complete when the training is ready to be implemented.

The next discrete stage is the implementation. Sometimes this is done with in-house staff or the training is delivered by external training providers. Either way their objective or finish line is to implement the programme and make sure the participants leave the course having learned some new information, gained new knowledge or acquired a new skill. That is their goal. Even if the design and development has allowed for role play and exercises, so that the participants have an opportunity to connect the dots and apply the new information to their working environment, it is still conceptual. Most trainers are extremely aware of the need for reflection in the training process and will make sure that participants take the time to apply what is being taught to their own situations back in the workplace. But even with the best will in the world that reflection and role playing is always confined to the training event itself – there is no way to guarantee transfer or learning and behaviour change in the workplace while in a training event. The only way to do that is to involve the participants *after* the training event and hold them to account for what they say they will do in the workplace. As this can't really be assessed in the training event, implementation is most often considered successful if feedback at the end of the programme is good, or the participants test well on their new knowledge. Neither of these, however, have any relevance to whether or not the individual will *use* what they learnt when they return to work. But as far as the person who has implemented the programme is concerned – they have finished their task and succeeded.

The next stage is evaluation. The finish line for evaluation is to establish whether or not the training was effective – but we already know that it is not so coming up with novel new ways to establish that doesn't seem relevant. The goal of evaluation is not to make sure that training was effective, it is to measure whether it is being applied or not.

I am still genuinely shocked by how many learning and development departments I've come across where the departmental key performance indicators (KPIs) are 'bums on seats' or 'spend per capita' or 'training days delivered' or some other attendance-based measure. If the objective of training is to ensure that a certain number of people attend a particular learning solution over any given period then is it really any wonder that training is failing to deliver meaningful measureable results to business?

And the really sad part is that attendance-based measures are very common. I'm sure that measuring training attendance figures was initially a fairly logical and simple way to monitor the success of training in an organization but it is absolutely the wrong measure.

If the gauge regarding training 'success' starts and ends at who walks through the door then chances are we won't even realize how much time and money we are needlessly wasting on training. Being able to point to high attendance figures – as though that alone 'proves' that training initiatives are successful – is flawed.

Recall the learning loop in Figure 1.3. When there are too many people or interest groups involved in the training process, even if each is doing their bit perfectly there is no ultimate responsibility. If the buck doesn't stop with one person or business unit then there is not enough ownership to shepherd the process to fruition.

Ultimately, too many organizations are focused on the wrong finish line. And this misdirection is resulting in nothing more than cleverly constructed arguments in order to justify not changing. 'Training failure? No, not this company. Our training is a roaring success. We've put 56 people through our training in just six months.' So what? We could put our entire workforce through it and tick all the boxes but it won't make any difference to our bottom line. KPIs and success measures need to move away from rudimentary attendance indicators and instead focus on what really matters. The only genuine finish line for any training is when behaviour has changed and there is a measureable change to performance and effectiveness as a result.

Too often the finish line for training depends on which part of the ADDIE model is being focused on and there is a different finish line for each stage. As such, the real purpose of the learning event – to transfer learning back to the workplace by changed behaviour – falls between the cracks of the individual ADDIE components. Everyone is so focused on delivering their piece of the puzzle that they have not considered the training as a whole unit. Those involved in training have missed the fact that whilst the individual elements of ADDIE have been successful the training as a whole has still failed.

And if everyone has different finish lines, then even if they did wonder if the training objectives were actually being delivered it was always considered someone else's problem. As such there is no ownership for the transfer of learning. And without ownership nothing gets done.

Just consider the mundane experience of shopping in a supermarket. Over the tannoy a voice will announce, 'Will someone please go to fresh food.' A customer could wait all day at fresh food and no one would come. If on the other hand the message over the tannoy stated, 'Will John Butler please go to fresh food', the customer would meet John Butler within a few minutes. Without ownership nothing gets done. Everyone assumes someone else will do it, so no one does it. And that's what happens in transfer of learning. The transfer of learning from the participant back to the workplace is not clearly articulated in the ADDIE framework, even though it probably did originally belong in implementation. Because there is no place for it, no one remembers it and it falls through the cracks. If it's not in the framework then it's not on the agenda, as everyone instead turns their attention to delivering learning instead of delivering genuine behaviour change.

Added to this, training can be confined to a particular individual or department or can be company-wide, which also makes it challenging to assign ownership. The participant often just wants to get it over with so they can get back to their 'proper job'. Even if they are happy to be in the training and are enthusiastic about making change to improve performance, without ongoing encouragement and support it is unlikely.

The L&D manager's ownership stops and starts in the sourcing and execution of the training – all he or she wants to do is to prove that enough people are being trained in the organization. And the CEO or senior manager believes that they did their bit when they signed the cheque. All he or she wants is to feel that action is being taken to solve issues and improve performance.

The training professional wants to deliver top-notch content and close out the day with happy participants and glowing feedback. As far as they are concerned they've done their job and the transfer piece is now down to the individual and their manager.

In the end there are simply too many stakeholders who have different agendas and, as there is no single agreed consensus regarding the finish line or the objective of the programme, no one takes ownership of the transfer of learning process. Instead each stakeholder skews the measurement protocol to suit their own objectives so that their segment appears successful. Whether that training is translated into real business results is and always has been secondary. Without focus on the missing link and genuine ownership of the outcomes it is easy to see how it has been missing for so long.

Wrong objectives

In business, training is used or created to solve a challenge. Companies would not invest in training if it was not thought that the training would deliver a particular performance improvement outcome that would justify the time and expense. That is obvious. There is therefore always an objective to training, whether that is implicit or explicit. In the last section we explored the issue of changing finish lines and the fact that this creates limited ownership in the training as a whole process.

For instructional designers the objective of the training has traditionally been to create and deliver good training that allows participants to demonstrate understanding, skills or knowledge in a new topic. To be fair, this is valid and logical but it assumes that the objective of training is to deliver new information and ensure that the people receiving the information understand it and will use it. As we all already know there is, however, a vast difference between what people know and what they do.

The real objective of training is to change what people do, not just impact on what they know. And yet up to now the objective of training has been limited to identifying what people intend to do and whether or not they can demonstrate proficiency in whatever has just been taught. By the way, both are important but they are not the only necessary components for successful training.

In their book *Beyond Learning Objectives* authors Jack and Patti Phillips identify five levels of objectives:

1 reaction objectives;

2 learning objectives;

3 application objectives;

4 impact objectives;

5 ROI objectives.

- *Reaction objectives*

  If the purpose of a training programme is to ensure that participants perceive it as valuable and to work out what the participants *intend* to do with the training, then we need reaction objectives. Think of these reaction objectives as a useful indicator of participants' willingness to do what we want them to do.

  Reaction objectives are useful but the typical 'smile sheet' is not. Typical reaction objectives include whether participants enjoyed the training or how well different components of the training enabled knowledge acquisition. Reaction objectives that can contribute to learning transfer in some way indicate the relevance of the content and whether the participant intends to use what they have learnt. This is helpful in the transfer of learning process in that measures of relevance and intent to use can highlight potential challenges. But they don't describe those challenges, or provide opportunity to influence changes that can improve learning transfer.

- *Learning objectives*

  If the purpose of a training programme is to ensure that participants acquire new knowledge, skills, or information and demonstrate their ability to use the material then we need learning objectives. Think of learning objectives as indicators of participants' ability to do what we want them to as a result of the training.

  Learning objectives are not new to learning and development professionals. They want to be able to report that the participants on, for example, an objection handling course, could either demonstrate effective objection handling at the end of the course or *know how to* effectively handle objections. It is important in the early stages of a programme to be aware of how well participants know the content. Without the ability to apply, they can't apply. But knowing is not doing. And it is the doing that will ultimately drive results.

- *Application objectives*

  If the purpose of a training programme is to ensure that participants actually use the material back in the workplace then we need application objectives. Think of application objectives as indicators that people are doing what we want them to do as a result of the programme.

At the very least the objective of any training, established at the outset of instructional design, is to ensure that the participants use their new skills back in the workplace. Where a learning objective may state that the participants can *demonstrate* objection handling, an application objective would state that all participants are *using* the objection handling technique to deal with work situations 80 per cent of the time or more. That is a very different objective and it is always going to deliver a very different result.

Often L&D professionals are reluctant to set application objectives because they don't feel they have control over the application. But they do have influence; and, in the end, it is the L&D professional who has to account for the success of a programme. Establishing application objectives directs designers, developers and facilitators to focus on the *use* of knowledge and skill, not just the *acquisition* of knowledge and skill.

- *Impact objectives*
  If the purpose of a training programme is to improve business measures, then impact objectives are necessary. Think of impact objectives as defining the consequence of people doing what we want them to do. Impact objectives answer the 'So what?' question often asked when application objectives are met.

  This sort of objective seeks to identify what the training will mean to the business and asks – 'So what?' For example, the business impact objective of the objection handing training could increase sales and decrease the sales cycle, therefore increasing sales and productivity.

- *ROI objectives*
  If the purpose of the training is to improve business measures, and there is interest in knowing how the improvement in those measures (programme benefits) compare to the cost of the programme, then we need a return on investment (ROI) objective.

  ROI objectives take the impact objectives two steps further so as to financially quantify what that increased sales or productivity would mean to the bottom line. By converting the improvement in impact measures to money, and comparing that value to the cost, a learning professional can see the ultimate, economic contribution of the programme. Sometimes the objective of the training may just be to break even, but an ROI objective would allow the CEO to monitor that. Using the example above, the increased level of sales and therefore profit could be calculated and this could be compared to the cost of the training, therefore creating an ROI.

In my experience writing the learning objectives is, by far, the most underrated part of the instructional design process and has the biggest impact on learning transfer. If the objective is to get the participant to the end of the training programme then transfer of learning beyond that point is unlikely.

The outcome of the training, ie the objectives that are set for that training, will always have a profound impact on what is achieved. If, at the very start our objectives are to gauge what people intend to do and what they can demonstrate, then there is no way that transfer of learning will occur because it is not even an objective of the training and we will never hit a target that we don't aim at!

The sad fact is that the objective of most training programmes languishes at level one (reaction) and two (learning objectives) and, as such, training is not planning to get behaviour change and application of knowledge. If we are not at least aiming for behaviour change then we won't get it.

If the objective of training is to measure intention and demonstration of skill in the training environment then it is hardly surprising that the importance of transfer of learning has been missed for so long. If few people are setting out to create training that will be considered successful only when application objectives or above have been attained then everyone can sit back, put their feet up and bask in their reflective glory at another 'successful' training programme. The problem – as the horrendous learning statistics affirm – is that these objectives do not constitute success at all. They are simply milestones on the way to success.

From the start instructional designers must expand their objectives for the training to include application objectives – at the very least – and as such they need to deliver training using ADDIE *and* a transfer of learning strategy.

Although impact and ROI objectives can be useful, I believe it is application objectives that are the key to success. Most managers are more than happy with the outcome when they can see the learning demonstrated in the workplace by the participants on a regular basis. For more on objectives and how to really make them work in the instructional design process I strongly recommend *Beyond Learning Objectives: Develop measureable objectives that link to the bottom line*, by Jack and Patti Phillips. When I'm involved in setting objectives for training this is my practical, easy-to-read bible.

Obsession with content

The third reason why the missing link has been missing for so long is our obsession with content. Francis Bacon once said 'Knowledge is power' and it is. But there is a caveat – you actually have to use it for it to be genuinely powerful. We are obsessed with information and the internet has certainly facilitated our access to information in a way unimaginable in Bacon's time. But information is not enough. Just have a cursory glance at your bookshelf – be honest about how many of those books you have read from start to finish. More importantly, of all the knowledge in those books, what have you implemented?

For years we have been so intoxicated by information, technology and delivery opportunities in training programmes that we have failed to appreciate that training effectiveness still hasn't improved that much. Content and delivery are red herrings when it comes to transfer of learning.

When the opportunities to present and deliver material opened up and technology swung the door of possibility wide open most people heralded this technological advancement as the long-sought answer to training effectiveness. The assumption was that all these new delivery channels would help solve the implementation problem. And to be fair it was a reasonably logical assumption. If someone didn't enjoy reading or didn't enjoy classroom-style learning then they may prefer e-learning or completing online learning modules in their own time. These new delivery methods are great for making learning more accessible and potentially more engaging to a wider audience but they do not address the transfer of learning issue. It may make the transfer of information to the individual easier and more enjoyable but it does nothing for the transfer of that learning into the workplace. As I said earlier, no behaviour is being changed by these new delivery channels. How the training is delivered makes very little difference to whether or not people will use that training in their daily working lives.

Training professionals could and do argue that this is incorrect. They will tell us enthusiastically that it is now possible to slice up the training content in new innovative ways so that it can be delivered after the training and be used to remind the participants to implement change. But all the theory and the evidence regarding adult learning already proves that we can't *remind* people about implementing change. So creating a 'follow-up programme' where the facilitator sends video clips, text messages, PowerPoint slides, and online links and intranet access codes at various intervals after the main event does not actually solve the problem. The barrage of post-learning content reminders does not compensate for this major training omission. People don't change by being reminded to change. In fact reminding them to change could have the opposite effect.

Just think about it for a moment. Say we announce to our respective partners that we want to join the local gym and lose a bit of weight. But we never quite get around to it. The gym is never open when we want to visit or we just seem to find other things that are more important. This is something that we *want* to do. But what happens when our partner starts reminding us that we were going to join the gym? Is that a happy discussion that inspires us to take action or is it more likely to leave us feeling pressured into joining the gym and end in an argument? In the end we feel as though we are being nagged into compliance and are consequently more likely to rebel and refuse to go to the gym at all.

Reminding a participant of what they learnt in the training event – regardless of how innovatively that reminder is delivered – will not illicit change.

Most people in the learning arena have heard the phrase 'Learning needs to be a process not an event'. And yet our preoccupation with content and delivery means that all we are really doing is bulking out the event, either by finding new additional ways to deliver the same content or simply adding more content. Training solutions can now be delivered in a vast array of options, with expandable levels of detail to suit everyone from the skim readers to the detail freaks. There are millions of brilliant courses out there being delivered really well by seasoned and passionate learning professionals, and yet those brilliant courses are not converted into change in the workplace. How the training is delivered makes very little difference to whether or not participants will use that training in their daily working lives.

All that technology has done is allow us to kid ourselves just a little bit longer that if we just improve the content or deliver that content slightly differently, slightly more innovatively, then the participants receiving it will miraculously change their behaviour. Getting super excited about how to deliver more content or remind people into making change doesn't actually address the underlying issue. People need to be supported to make behaviour change over the long term, they need to be held accountable for what they say they want to achieve and they need time to reflect upon what they have learned so that they can apply it to their own life and situation.

This obsession with content also often ends up squeezing reflection out of the training event, which is disastrous considering that it is reflection that can really make a different to learning transfer. It is easy for a trainer to fall in love with their content – especially if they designed the course themselves. Often they are justifiably proud of their material and are enthusiastic about sharing it and finding innovative ways to slice it up and deliver it. I've seen training, for example, where the trainer has hired actors to role-play customers and facilitate discussions. The problem, however, is that all this focus on delivery means that the trainers don't always allocate enough time to the art of reflection.

When a trainer is wedded to their content, even when their intentions are honourable and they genuinely want to deliver maximum value they can end up packing the training event with *too much* content. In a quest to deliver all that content they don't allocate enough time to allow the participants to personalize the learning through reflection and decide what they intend to do with the learning back in the workplace.

Reflection is already a recognized part of the training event but the importance of reflection doesn't stop in the training. It is especially important to the transfer of learning process. Participants also need time to reflect on their activity when they get back to their workplace so that they can assess, review and fine tune their understanding of the information in a real work situation occurring in real business time rather than just the controlled training environment. Reflection is therefore crucial for behavioural change but it must happen during the training *and* in a structured regular way after the training.

Content has also become synonymous with quality and the courses that are packed with information are often viewed more favourably by those who hold the training budget. The downside is that the facilitator is then under pressure from the start to deliver all that material in the allotted time. And if they fall behind for whatever reason and are forced to drop either content or the action planning session at the end of a programme they will almost always drop the action planning.

Instead the facilitator will tell the participants to fill in the action plan themselves when they get home, or back at work, but of course that never happens. Alternatively they may squeeze it in at the very end. But by then it is too late, participants are tired and the last thing they want to do is engage in reflection about how they will use the information when they get back to the workplace. In effect, the training professional has left one of the most important parts of the training to the time when people are too tired to do anything other than think about what they want for dinner.

Without proper engaged reflection and personalization of the material to the participants' own situation – and the transference of those observations into a concrete action plan to put in motion as soon as the individual is back at work – nothing will change. And even then it is just the start of that transfer process. Unfortunately, content obsession has clouded the issue for too long.

Obsession with evaluation

Evaluation represents the Holy Grail of learning and development. Although clearly a necessary part of the learning and development process it does not *create* change it just measures the extent of the change.

Donald Kirkpatrick wrote about evaluation in a series of articles for the *American Society for Training and Development* (ASTD) journal back in 1959. His interest in training evaluation came about following his experience as a teacher and he recalls, 'I was teaching and I thought to myself as long as I'm running seminars why don't I evaluate them?' Kirkpatrick humbly admits that all he really wanted to do, to begin with, was to evaluate the reaction. 'I found though this wasn't enough, I wanted to know if they'd learned anything but then that didn't seem enough either. I needed to know if they'd taken anything back to their jobs, whether they changed their behaviour and got positive results.' It was this thinking that led to the creation of his evaluation model and it forms the basis of evaluation to this day. Kirkpatrick's model consists of four distinct evaluation levels: reaction, learning, behaviour and results. A fifth evaluation level – ROI – was added later by other authors.

Level one: reaction

Level one evaluation is interested in what the participant thinks and feels about the training. Reaction-based evaluation is easy and is already done well in most learning interventions. The trainer is easily able to establish participant's reaction to the training through the distribution of feedback forms or 'happy sheets' at the end of the training programme.

Level two: learning

The second level of evaluation is seeking to establish whether or not there has been an increase in knowledge or capability from the training intervention.

This occurs through some form of test or exam. Participants may have to demonstrate their new skill while being observed or complete a question-naire to demonstrate knowledge. Learning-based evaluation is also easy and is already done well.

Level three: behaviour

The third level is focused on evaluating the extent of behaviour change and whether capability improvement is being utilized and applied in the workplace. I believe that behaviour-based evaluation holds the secret to eradicating train-ing ineffectiveness. This is also the level that is most frequently missed.

Level four: results

Level four evaluation seeks to establish the effects of the training on the business or environment. Results-based evaluation seeks to establish the results that can be seen in the business as a consequence of the training. At level four HR professionals are seeking to establish the effects on the business or environ-ment resulting from the trainee's altered performance.

Level five: ROI and the ROI methodology

There have been modifications to Kirkpatrick's evaluation model by various authors, the most well known being Jack and Patti Phillips. The Phillips' model not only redefines the levels so that they are applicable beyond the learning environment, but also adds new theory, a process model, and a set of standards to ensure reliable implementation. The new theory is the theory of cost-benefit analysis, which leads to ROI. Steps in cost-benefit analysis include identifying the benefits of a programme (level four – results, or, as the Phillips's refer to level four – impact), converting those benefits to money, com-paring the monetary benefits to costs, and calculating either the benefit–cost ratio or the ROI percentage. Additionally, the Phillips model includes a step to isolate the effects of the programme, providing evidence that the improve-ment in impact measures is actually due to the programme – a step ignored in Kirkpatrick's four steps.

The ROI methodology was originally developed by Jack Phillips in the 1970s. Since 1992 Jack and Patti Phillips have run the ROI Institute, which focuses on research, consulting and education around the ROI methodology. This methodology is designed to allow HR professionals to compare business impact results to the overall cost of training in order to quantify the ROI of training as well as generate information that stakeholders can use for improving programmes and processes.

Being able to prove training results is certainly a valid exercise because it provides L&D managers with a means of justifying and negotiating training budgets – and that is an important reason for establishing ROI. Additionally, prior to investing in a programme one can forecast the ROI to establish the potential success of the programme – that is if all conditions are met. They key is to ensure that all conditions are met.

Unfortunately, learning professionals tend to swing toward the extremes. Either they place too much emphasis on 'happy sheets' or they place too much focus on ROI. Unless the right questions are asked, 'happy sheets' are a waste of time. They may be needed to check that the facilitator hasn't made any huge errors in the delivery of content, and offer the trainer some insight into how to improve their programme, but they make no difference to the participant. If a training professional cannot get more than 80 or 90 per cent satisfaction following a one- or two-day programme then there is something seriously wrong with the programme or approach.

Testing someone's knowledge via exam or questionnaire is important, but it limits the opportunities for improving a programme and the environment that is intended to support implementation of the programme. HR managers and L&D professionals get excited because they send out a questionnaire and participants get it right. Sadly, all that this proves is that people have remembered the information or report that they can apply the information. It is certainly a necessary first step in the transfer of learning process as the individual must first gain the new knowledge and information, but the real question is whether or not participants are using the information that they remember on a regular basis back at work.

At the other end of the evaluation scale we have the Rolls-Royce of evaluation – ROI. But even the Phillips team who developed the methodology, and who are the undisputed thought leaders in the field of ROI evaluation, estimate that only 5 to 10 per cent of all training initiatives need to be evaluated to ROI level. That is not to say they think that 5 to 10 per cent of all training needs to be effective, just that it needs to be analysed and evaluated to such a high level – and this acknowledges the time and resources it takes to evaluate to ROI successfully.

At the time of writing there were around 7,000 people worldwide accredited in ROI evaluation, of whom I am one. Whilst I am a huge fan of Jack and Patti's work on ROI, by their own admission it is not for everyone and it is certainly not necessary for every training programme.

Case studies and success stories

If 'happy sheets' are too easy and ROI too complex the alternative trend is the creation of case studies or success stories. The case study evaluation method popularized by Robert Brinkerhoff suggests that if the participants can write up case studies of their successes and how they have used what they learnt then it is a simpler way to establish if someone is using the learning. The key question that Brinkerhoff proposes in his book – *The Success Case Method: Find out quickly what's working and what's not* – is 'Were you able to use something you learned to achieve a concrete, positive result?'

It's a great question but just because one or two people from the training programme have successfully changed their behaviour doesn't mean that everyone in the training has successfully changed their behaviour. As a result, case studies can often make the training look more effective than it really is.

Following a training event the L&D manager will commission interviews with participants and those stories are written up as case studies to demonstrate the success of the programme, but if we take the laws of probability alone there is always a few people on every course who love it and use the learning immediately. It is therefore very easy to find those people who will then wax lyrical about how fabulous the course was and how they have changed as a result. Some people are just better than others at translating an idea or learning into action.

Plus if we consider the stages of change documented by Prochaska, Norcross and DiClemente in their classic book *Changing for Good* (1998), people will always be at different stages in the change process: from pre-contemplation through contemplation, preparation, action, maintenance and finally termination. There will always be certain people on any course who are already at the action stage and are ready for the information. They will already be prepared for change and will simply use the training as a catalyst.

Using case studies to demonstrate success is no more effective or definitive than happy sheets or tests. Unless case studies are backed up by data on performance improvements across the training programme then the 'successful' people can simply be cherry picked to tell their story, which then acts as a measure of success that is not indicative of the rest of the group. Besides, even Brinkerhoff reports in his book that without some structured transfer of learning process following the training event only 15 per cent of people who attend training can answer his question with specific examples.

Interestingly, when Wick, Pollock and Jefferson (at the time with the Fort Hill Company) asked learning leaders what percentage of trainees apply what they have learnt – long enough and well enough to improve their performance – they too indicated a fairly dismal 15 per cent. But even if it is 15 per cent we can quite easily find those people and have them complete glowing case studies to indicate success, when in reality the vast majority of attendees make zero change following the training.

Missing the mark

The reason everyone wants to be able to evaluate training in a clear and definitive way is because they are keen to prove that training is working. They want to be able to show senior management that the learning interventions are adding real value to the business. But training in its current format – without emphasis on transfer of learning – doesn't work so trying to establish a definitive way to prove results doesn't actually solve the problem. If anything the quest for the ultimate evaluation tool is a bit like the L&D industry shooting itself in the foot.

At best our preoccupation with complex evaluation is a handy distraction from really dealing with the key issue of assessing and supporting real-world behaviour change *after* the learning event when participants are back in the workplace.

The only really essential part of evaluation for the vast majority of training interventions is to evaluate whether there has been effective behavioural change and whether the learning is being applied back in the workplace. And yet the ADDIE model focuses on evaluation without clearly articulating the type of evaluation that could really have an impact on effectiveness – measuring application or behaviour change. Consequently people busy themselves with measuring the extent that the participant has enjoyed the programme or can remember the information. Or they get lost in the complexity of ROI.

When it comes to L&D and the evaluation of that activity I believe we have actually lost sight of the real objective of training. We are now so consumed by methodologies or theories that help us to qualify and quantify small or discrete parts of the training experience that we've forgotten why the training intervention was undertaken in the first place. Tell me, which is more important – the ability to evaluate and measure training or being able to physically see the behaviour changes and performance improvements back in the workplace?

Let's consider weight loss as an analogy to the training and development industry. If John is overweight he will eventually come to the realization that something has to change. Perhaps his car broke down and he had to walk home and realized how horribly unfit he really was. Perhaps the doctor gave him the 'do something or die' speech. Whatever prompted the desire to change, John knew that change was needed to solve the problem.

To get a real handle on what he was up against he probably stepped cautiously onto the scales to ascertain his start point and get an idea of how much weight he was aiming to lose. But beyond that John doesn't actually really care about the measurement. After several weeks, John starts to feel better, his trousers are fitting better. After a couple of months he is out playing football with his son, he can fit into his favourite pair of jeans again and everyone is commenting on how much younger he looks. Does John care whether he has lost 4.2 kilos or 3.8 kilos? Does he brag about his new reduced weight to anyone who will listen or does he just enjoy the fact that he feels and looks better?

Is it the outcome or the effects of the outcome that are exciting? Sometimes we can get so focused on measuring the outcome that we lose sight of why that outcome was important in the first place. What matters to John is that his effort is observable – to him when he looks in the mirror and to others who compliment him on how much weight he has lost. His friends, family and work colleagues are unconcerned as to whether he has lost 4.2 kilos or 3.8 kilos. In reality observing change is much more important than simply measuring it. The measurement may help us quantify our start point or increase our motivation to change but ultimately it is the outcome that is important.

The same is true in training. The outcome of training is to provide information to encourage a change in skills, behaviour or attitude so that individuals can improve their day-to-day performance. That's it. As a manager when we send our team on communication training – do we really care what the ROI is or are we just thrilled when the individuals start using the skills on a daily basis and we can see training participants talking more constructively about solutions or having more effective meetings?

The whole point of learning interventions is to provide skills and knowledge so as to facilitate real-world behaviour change in the workplace. Most people who are sent on soft-skill training initiatives are already pretty good at those skills but just need a tweak here and there to lift performance still further. Do managers care whether the participants of training programmes got 100 per cent in their follow-up quiz or would he or she rather observe the shift in attitude and behaviour at work that the training was commissioned to solve in the first place?

Several times in my career I have sold ROI projects into companies and each time, as soon as they trial the transfer of learning methodology that I share in part two and start to actually see the behaviour change, they no longer want to pay for the ROI analysis. They know it is working because they can see the change in behaviour within the organization, so why pay for the analysis when the results speak for themselves?

All too often our obsession with evaluation is used as a distraction from the main event – behaviour change. I would much rather people stop worrying about quantifying the effects of the training and focus their attention on learning transfer. If we do *that* properly we won't need a 20-page report full of statistics and assumptions to establish if our learning interventions are working or not. The results will be observable on a daily basis as people actually use their new skills in the workplace. Behaviour change is what managers want and KPIs need to change to reflect this. We need to shift the emphasis of evaluation towards what really matters – observable behaviour change back in the workplace after the learning event.

Focus on learning not on change

The combined effects of these issues have served to disguise, fudge or allow people to effectively ignore the missing link of learning for decades. Each new obsession takes the industry merrily down another interesting diversion and delays the consistent application of a genuine solution to training failure. Millions of hours may be poured into the advancement of content and the creation of innovative ways to deliver that content, we may even invest thousands of hours evaluating outcomes, but when the majority of evaluation is focused on the learning outcomes and not the performance outcomes then little will change.

This brings us to the final culprit. The final reason why the missing link has stayed missing for so long is because the industry has been primarily focused on strategies to facilitate learning instead of strategies to facilitate change.

We have a brilliant instructional design model in ADDIE and people have pretty much mastered it. We have brilliant minds applied to the detail of adult learning. We have already discussed Kolb and his model for adult learning and most training programmes already incorporate the recognized principles of adult learning.

The other giant in this area is Malcolm Knowles. Knowles was an American adult educator who is most famous for his adoption of the theory of andragogy – a term initially coined by German teacher Alexander Kapp. Andragogy is essentially how to best create an environment where adults will learn effectively. According to Knowles:

- Adults need to be involved in the planning and evaluation of their instruction.
- Experience (including mistakes) provides the basis for learning activities.
- Adults are most interested in learning subjects that have immediate relevance to their job or personal life.
- Adult learning is problem-centred rather than content-oriented.

Again, most trainers worth their salt know this stuff and are doing a really good job alongside instructional design to create really brilliant programmes. And yet training still fails to deliver.

Why? Because effective learning transfer is not just about learning it's about change. There can be little doubt that with the ADDIE model and the focus on effective adult learning the training programmes that are being developed and delivered are good enough to illicit learning. But unless we set out to create change from the training and appreciate the intricacies of personal behavioural change then nothing much will ever happen. It's not that people are lazy, unmotivated or difficult, it's that personal behavioural change is not automatic or easy. Nor is there a one-size-fits-all approach to personal transformation.

According to Charles Jennings at the 2012 AITD (Australian Institute of Training and Development) conference, there are certain dynamics that support learning. He states that they are:

- experience (formal or informal);
- conversations/socializing;
- practice;
- reflection (debrief).

Building on this, I believe, we need to consider the dynamics that support change and learning transfer, which are:

1 reflection (debrief);

2 making a decision to change;

3 accessing the iceberg – getting under the behaviour to feelings thoughts, values belief, fears and needs;

4 self-accountability.

The quickest way to support change is to help someone access what is causing their behaviours in the first place rather than the behaviours themselves. It is therefore important to unpack behaviours so as to access the thoughts, feelings, beliefs, values, needs and fears that an individual has around those behaviours. That simply does not happen in a traditional learning environment. Good training already facilitates most of the dynamics that support learning. Transfer of information to the individual is therefore already happening fairly effectively in most cases.

But no one is then helping those learning participants after the event to reflect on the information they received, make a decision to change and help them to understand why they currently do the things they do so that they can appreciate the need for change and embrace self-accountability to make the necessary alterations. And that's why behaviour doesn't change.

Donald Kirkpatrick came the closest to really nailing this issue when he presented his evaluation model. According to Kirkpatrick, level three evaluation was about assessing how much a participant's behaviour had changed as a result of the training. Assuming we commissioned training to solve a particular challenge, behaviour change was the desired outcome so it stands to reason that measuring whether that was successful or not would be a step in the right direction. But identification of this level of evaluation is not enough.

In 2011 Jim Kirkpatrick (Donald's son) referred to level three behaviour evaluation as the underappreciated 'missing-link' between learning and results. In the article 'The Kirkpatrick new world level 3' (2011), co-authored with his wife Wendy (both training professionals in their own right), the Kirkpatricks suggested that Donald Kirkpatrick's level three is at best underutilized and is, in most cases, completely skipped (see **www.trainingzone.co.uk**).

I agree completely and it is this insight that is at the heart of learning transfer. There is too much emphasis on measuring the learning outcome rather than measuring changes in behaviour and, therefore, performance. The only level that effectively measures performance outcomes is level three – behaviour or application depending on whose model is being referred to.

The problem is that managers frequently shy away from behaviour change because it is perceived as being too hard – they know from their own experience that it is difficult to change the way one communicates, leads or sells, as in most cases these are habitual behaviours, practised over time. Plus, perhaps equally importantly, managers and leaders do not fully appreciate the process of individual change because all the theory that is presented in relation to effective training is learning theory not change theory. They have never been taught to effectively facilitate change.

In most businesses the decision to embark on training or learning initiatives is taken by management. More often than not that decision is made without consultation or involvement of the people who will undergo the actual training programme. This is fairly normal in that managers may recognize business issues that could potentially be solved or improved by behaviour change and they set about trying to fix those shortcomings through training. Although typical, this means that the impetus to change comes from an external source and so when managers announce that everyone is to be put through a training programme it is rarely met with enthusiasm.

In short, managers are trying to encourage people to change their behaviour through training but we already know that it is extremely difficult to *make* someone change. In their book *First Break all the Rules* authors Marcus Buckingham and Curt Coffman detailed the result of two huge research studies undertaken by the Gallup Organization over a 25-year period. The studies gave voice to over 1 million employees and 80,000 managers and one of the findings was that, 'People don't change that much. Don't waste your time trying to put in what was left out. Try to draw out what was left in – that's hard enough!'

The only really effective way to change people is to encourage them and support them to want to make the changes themselves. And yet a great deal of training is 'inflicted' on individuals who don't necessarily want to be in the training or don't understand why they are in the training. Making lasting change from that starting point is therefore extremely difficult.

We cannot force someone to change, we cannot ask them to change and we cannot plead with them or cajole or punish them to change. We cannot give them information and expect that they will automatically connect the dots and change work habits and processes that they have probably been using for years. And we certainly cannot remind people to change simply by bombarding the participant with an endless stream of content delivered in a variety of novel or innovative ways. Change is not the result of some magic bullet or fairy dust sprinkled over participants at the end of the course – it is a process, a measured and managed process. In fact the only similarity amongst the leading change methodologies is that everyone agrees that change *is a process* and that it occurs over a period of time. It is not an event. And self-change is infinitely more potent than administered change.

Understanding motivation

For hundreds of years academics and scientists believed that there were two main motivational drives. The first is the drive to survive, or the biological imperative. This is an intrinsic motivational drive because it comes from within and motivates us to eat, breathe, drink, rest and breed. As a motivational tool the biological imperative is blunt and it is not very useful in a business setting. Sure, we could threaten an individual that if they don't change they will lose their job – and such a threat to their survival may indeed illicit a short-term burst of activity and effort. But it is not an effective long-term solution. Once the immediate threat of losing their job passes they will revert to old behaviour. All we will ever get is reluctant compliance.

The second recognized motivational drive is reward and punishment. Reward and punishment are known as extrinsic motivational tools because the impetus to change is coming from external sources. According to these motivational forces the only way we can get people to change or to meet deadlines or deliver on objectives is to reward them when they do something positive and punish them when they do something negative. These motivational tools (carrot and stick) have been used in business for centuries but they are also blunt and ineffective when it comes to motivating people to change – especially for soft-skills training.

In Daniel Pink's brilliant book *Drive: The surprising truth about what motivates us*, he discusses the many drawbacks of reward and punishment in a business environment. Scientific research and social science studies have proven time and time again that reward and punishment don't work that well and have a number of very toxic side effects:

- Rewards actively diminish motivation by turning something enjoyable into a chore.
- Rewards often reduce creativity.
- Rewards can diminish results.
- Rewards often foster bad behaviour.

- Rewards actively inhibit good behaviour.

- Rewards are addictive.

- Rewards are expensive to administer because it costs the business more and more to maintain the same results. People get used to rewards and become complacent.

- Punishing unwanted behaviour can actually increase the unwanted behaviour.

Pink gives many compelling examples as to the ineffectiveness of reward and punishment. For example, Edward Deci, Professor of Psychology and Gowen Professor in the Social Sciences at the University of Rochester, and director of its human motivation programme, along with two colleagues went back over 30 years of research assessing 128 experiments on motivation and they concluded that, 'tangible rewards tend to have a substantially negative effect on intrinsic motivation'. The long-term damage caused by offering short-term rewards is one of the most robustly proven findings in social science and yet it is constantly ignored.

The Federal Reserve Bank in the United States commissioned research into the effectiveness of rewards on performance and commissioned four economists from MIT, Carnegie Mellon and the University of Chicago to investigate and report on their findings. They concluded that: 'In eight of the nine tasks we examined across three experiments, higher incentives led to worse per-formance.' The London School of Economics also confirmed these findings after analysing 51 studies of corporate reward schemes. They reported that: 'We find that financial incentives... can result in negative impact on overall performance.'

In the case of punishment, social scientists have found that imposing a punishment or penalty will very often bring about *more* of the unwanted behaviour not less. In one study, economists Uri Gneezy and Aldo Rustichini studied a child care facility over the course of 20 weeks. Open at 7.30 am, parents were expected to collect their children by 4 pm. In the first four weeks the researchers monitored how many people picked up their kids late. Prior to the fifth week all parents were notified that the child care facility was cracking down on late collection and parents collecting their children late would have to pay a fine. By the end of the study period almost twice as many parents were late to collect their children. Imposing a punishment for bad behaviour increased the instances of the very behaviour they were seeking to eradicate.

We cannot scare people into changing and we cannot reward them into changing. These extrinsic motivational tricks may work in the short term but they are not sustainable. If people are only doing what we want them to do because they are scared of the consequences if they don't, or they have been promised a big fat bonus, then as soon as the bonus has cleared the bank or the danger is passed they will revert to type.

The reason that behaviour change is considered so difficult is because so far we have relied on the second motivational drive in the form of rewards and punishments (carrot and stick). Neither work very well when it comes to changing behaviour and improving performance. What we need to do is to understand that there is a third motivational drive and tap into that.

This third motivational drive may be more fragile than either the first or second motivational drives and it certainly requires more skill to elicit but it is extremely potent. The third motivational drive is intrinsic and inspires people to do things just for the love of doing those things. US psychologist Harry F Harlow first hinted at this third motivational drive in the 1940s after he conducted experiments on rhesus monkeys. The monkeys were given puzzles to solve. And what he found was that the monkeys solved the puzzles without reward or punishment. He reported at the time that: 'The behaviour obtained in this investigation poses some interesting questions for motivation theory, since significant learning was attained and efficient performance maintained without resort to special or extrinsic incentives.' Harlow suggested that there must be something missing from the accepted understanding of motivation but he was largely ignored.

In 1960, MIT Management Professor Douglas McGregor wrote a book called *The Human Side of Enterprise*. He too challenged the idea that we are only driven by the need to survive and by reward and punishment. McGregor believed that business was missing a major opportunity because of false assumptions about human nature. He argued that command and control-style management actively stifled motivation.

Abraham Maslow, one of Harlow's former students, also questioned the standard view of motivation and he introduced the world to Maslow's 'hierarchy of needs' theory and later developed humanistic psychology in the 1950s.

And in the mid-1980s Edward Deci and Richard Ryan proposed self-determination theory (SDT), which seemed to plug the gaps in our understanding about motivation. It also helps to explain just how hard it is for people to change their behaviour through training – unless they are specifically supported to do so over the longer term.

Deci and Ryan suggested that the most powerful motivation of all is intrinsic motivation, which is 'activated' in the presence of three human needs:

- autonomy;
- competence;
- relatedness.

Autonomy

In 1976 Dr Ellen Langer and her colleague at the time Judith Rodin conducted a famous study in a nursing home. The purpose of the experiment was to make residents more mindful of their day-to-day activities and help them engage with life more fully.

In one group, the elderly participants were encouraged to find ways to make more decisions for themselves such as when to welcome visitors and when to watch TV. In addition each participant was asked to choose a house plant that they would look after and be responsible for. The participants in the second group did not have the same autonomy over their choices, and although they were given a house plant they did not choose it for themselves and they were told that the nurses would look after it.

A year and a half later the resident were re-tested against a variety of tests they had taken at the start of the experiment and the first group was found to be more cheerful, active and alert. They were also healthier. Less than half as many residents from the first group died over the term of the experiment compared to the group who could not exert any autonomy over their day-to-day lives.

In short, we need to feel some measure of control over our situation in order to feel motivated and engaged. And yet just think about the change that is expected after training: we are by definition asking people to give up that control. They are being asked to move from a task or way or operating over which they have control and understanding to a way that they do not recognize. This makes them feel uneasy and it is why the motivation to return to old habits is so strong.

Competency

It was Hungarian psychologist Mihaly Csikszentmihalyi who gave us a greater understanding of high performance when he discovered 'flow'. Flow is often talked about in relation to sport or artistic endeavour but it is relevant in all areas of work and is characterized by a complete absorption in the task where the individual loses all track of time.

Csikszentmihalyi calls these moments 'autotelic experiences', from the Greek *auto* meaning self and *telos* meaning goal or purpose and he suggests that when we are in flow the reward for the task is the task itself. We are able to display a level of competence and progress towards mastery.

He even conducted a series of experiments to demonstrate just how critical a feeling of competence is to well-being. Having identified areas where individuals experienced flow and a sense of competence the participants were directed to remove flow from their daily lives. And the results were almost immediate. People became sluggish, began complaining of headaches and had difficulty concentrating. Csikszentmihalyi noted that: 'After just two days of deprivation... the general deterioration in mood was so advanced that prolonging the experiment would have been unadvisable.'

In other words, without an opportunity to demonstrate competence in anything, even something trivial, we begin to exhibit symptoms that are remarkably similar to a serious psychological disorder such as depression.

Have a think about training in this context. We are asking people to relinquish their own feelings of competence in the workplace. It may feel okay in the controlled and safe environment of the training programme but as soon as the individual returns to the workplace they are taken out of their comfort zone. Is it really any wonder that, without any support to transfer the learning, the individual will be strongly motivated to revert to the old behaviour and the old habits just so that they can reconnect to that feeling of flow or competence?

Relatedness

People need other people, they feel motivated when they are related to others and this can be seen in most working environments where teams and colleagues work closely together. When we are connected to other people that we like, respect or care about we are intrinsically motivated.

Again, think of this in terms of training. Often people are taken away from their group or they are split up, or their roles start to shift and they suddenly feel threatened. Their relatedness to their colleagues makes it much easier to ignore the training and maintain the status quo.

When people are able to express autonomy, competence and relatedness and their needs are met they are intrinsically motivated and are more likely to be creative, enthusiastic and productive. When these needs are inhibited our intrinsic motivation plummets.

Seen from this perspective it is easy to see why training can actively demotivate people. On the whole it is chosen for individuals without their consent or involvement. They are asked to actively move away from tried and tested skills and abilities that they are in control of and are able to demonstrate a high level of competence in and they are often asked to alter the working dynamics to those around them. All these components make change incredibly uncomfortable and confrontational. The easiest solution, therefore, is to ignore the training and go back to the old way of doing things.

The reason that training can fail to change behaviour is because the transfer of learning is difficult. As such it is often missing and the methods that managers use to try and compensate for that don't work. Remember, we can't remind someone to change. In the traditional training model all we are really doing is slicing up content and delivering that content at appropriate intervals after the training event. We assume that this will be enough to transfer the knowledge into real-world behavioural change, but it isn't. In fact reminding our way to change can so easily become counterproductive. There is nothing more demotivating than someone constantly reminding us that we need to do something differently or make some sort of change. Even when that reminder is done well or sensitively it is still often perceived as negative and unhelpful.

Threatening people with punishment or encouraging them with reward is not going to be much better when trying to motivate people to change. The most potent form of motivation is intrinsic motivation, which comes from within the individual and is fostered when that person can feel autonomous, competent and related to others. When we can create a learning environment where we can get the participants to want to change – and support them to hold themselves to account to make those changes whilst recognizing that it will not happen overnight – then we have a real opportunity to turn learning into action.

Without this understanding it is easy to see how managers and leaders have ignored behaviour change. They either assume it is impossible so don't see the point of trying. Or they have such low expectations about transfer of learning that they genuinely believe that if 10 or 20 per cent of participants do something with the training that's a good result! It's not.

Effective learning transfer is actually very simple but it is not best achieved in a group setting. Change is an individual and personal process and it is only possible one-on-one, which leads us to the final reason that transfer of learning has been ignored for so long. Managers assume it must be expensive. It is easy to justify a training programme when 20 people across many divisions are attending. This one-to-many approach is often perceived to be cost-effective. So much so that many organizations regularly send people on training to learn skills that have no bearing whatsoever on their daily activities. The logic is simply that if the training has been purchased anyway and can accommodate 20 people then the manager might as well find 20 people to attend. So they send payroll on sales courses because 'it can't hurt'. In Harold Stolovitch's book *Telling Ain't Training* (2002) he estimated that 30 per cent of participants in corporate training are totally unsuitable for what they are to be taught. And the reason is that the manager thought that 'it might be useful' or 'nothing else is available' or 'a colleague enjoyed it so it's worth a try'. Clearly this is not helping learning transfer. If participants won't ever come across a situation in their day-to-day working life where they will be called upon to use the skills they have just spent two days learning then learning transfer is actually impossible.

Wouldn't it be more useful to make sure that people are only trained in areas that are directly useful to them and then invest in transfer of learning to make sure they actually use it to change their behaviour and improve performance?

The reality is that the corporate world is spending billions on training but there is minimal investment in the transfer of that training to ensure that the effort delivers the intended business result. This book is an invitation to consider that a change of thinking is required about how to spend the training budget. We need to be more discerning about the training we choose, cut back on the amount of training and instead invest in learning transfer so that the training we do undertake delivers the behaviour change and real-world results we seek.

Summary of key points

- The fact that we have almost mastered instructional design in terms of the individual elements of the ADDIE model, but that training still fails, means that there must be a missing link in learning – transfer of learning.

- There are five reasons why the missing link has remained missing for so long:

  - No ownership: too often the finish line for training depends on what part of the ADDIE model the stakeholder is focused on and there is a different finish line for each stage. As such there is no ownership. The real purpose of the learning event – to transfer learning back to the workplace by changed behaviour – falls between the cracks of the individual ADDIE components.

  - Wrong objectives: the outcome of the training, ie the objectives that are set for that training, will always have a profound impact on what is achieved. If at the very start the objective is to gauge what people intend to do and what they can demonstrate then there is no way that transfer of learning will occur, because it is not even an objective of the training and it is impossible to hit a target without aiming at it.

  - Obsession with content: for years we have been so intoxicated by information, technology and delivery opportunities that we have failed to appreciate that training effectiveness still hasn't improved that much. All that technology has done is allow us to kid ourselves just a little bit longer that if we just improve the content or deliver that content slightly differently or slightly more innovatively then the participants receiving it will miraculously change their behaviour. They won't – content and delivery are red herrings when it comes to transfer of learning.

  - Obsession with evaluation: evaluation represents the Holy Grail of learning and development. Although clearly a necessary part of the L&D process it does not *create* change it just measures the extent of the change. Too often our obsession with evaluation is used as a distraction from the main event – behaviour change.

  - Focused on learning not on change: effective learning transfer is not just about learning strategies it is about change strategies. There can be little doubt that with the ADDIE model and the focus on effective adult learning the training programmes that are being developed and delivered are good enough to illicit learning. But unless we set out to create behaviour change from the training then nothing much will ever happen. It's not that people are lazy, unmotivated or difficult, it is that personal behavioural change is not automatic or easy.

- The reality is that the corporate world is spending billions on training but there is minimal investment in the transfer of that training to ensure it delivers the intended business result. We need to be more discerning about the training we choose, cut back on the amount of training and instead invest in learning transfer so that the training we do undertake delivers the behaviour change and real-world results we seek.

03
Learning's missing link: the solutions so far

Most people in the learning and development industry are fully aware of training's dismal record in affecting behavioural change and there is a growing recognition that this missing link is transfer of learning.

In 2011 the American Society for Training and Development (ASTD) for the first time dedicated an entire conference to learning transfer. At the Annual Expo, breakout sessions devoted to the transfer of learning were packed out and the ASTD realized that this was a topic worthy of greater attention, stating that: 'They want to address the growing recognition that learning without transfer is incomplete.' This is a clear indicator that transfer of learning is an idea whose time has come. People are finally coming round to the fact that they need to take this issue seriously and talk about the elephant in the room. CEOs, L&D leaders and other people investing in learning are really starting to ask questions about learning transfer, which is beginning to change the way that learning is viewed within organizations. Business needs to be efficient regardless of the economic weather. Everyone needs to drive towards sustainability and waste minimization, and all business functions are under increasing scrutiny – including training.

In 2010 Michael Leimbach conducted a major investigation into transfer of learning techniques, involving the analysis of 32 individual studies (all within the previous two years) to establish the potency of each technique. The resulting report, 'Learning transfer model: a research-driven approach to enhancing learning effectiveness', published by the Emerald Group, stated that individual transfer of learning initiatives could improve training effectiveness by up to 20 per cent and should a business employ several techniques they could achieve training performance improvements in excess of 180 per cent.

Not only is that an impressive and potentially game-changing indication of just how important transfer of learning really is, but it also clearly illustrates that whilst we may not always know why training is ineffective we are constantly searching for answers.

Assuming that organizations have the basics correct – that the right people are on the course in the first place, the training is truly relevant to their role and they will be able to use the training back in their working life – there are nine popular tactics that are frequently used to facilitate learning transfer. These nine approaches are what people are currently doing to address the training effectiveness shortfall and some are clearly better than others. CEOs, senior managers and leaders, when pressed, believe they are addressing transfer of learning issues and I frequently hear at least one of these nine responses:

1 'Our managers conduct training follow-up.'

2 'We facilitate training follow-up discussion groups.'

3 'We run half-day training refresher/follow-up sessions.'

4 'We have executive coaching.'

5 'We use action learning.'

6 'We use blended learning solutions.'

7 'We create a social media community.'

8 'Participants must present their learning back to their workgroup.'

9 'We ensure everyone is properly prepared for the learning.'

Let's explore these tactics in more depth and weigh up the merits of each proposed solution...

'Our managers conduct training follow-up'

In my observation of what is actually happening in business, this approach is certainly one of the most popular. And it is little wonder when you consider that L&D managers and business leaders already believe they are addressing the transfer of learning issue because they have charged the participants' manager to do the training follow-up and ensure that the skills learnt in the training are embedded into the business.

Personally I believe this is a fundamental error and one of the major reasons why genuine transfer of learning is so poor. Remember the learning loop (Figure 1.3, page 20) – traditionally half the training is owned by the L&D department and the other half by the business. When push comes to shove, however, it is the manager who is almost always assumed to own the 'business' part of the training. Once the need has been jointly discussed between the business unit and the L&D department, L&D will either design and deliver the programme or outsource it. Once the training event has taken place any transfer of learning expectations are passed over to the business, or more specifically – the managers of the participants of the programme. This current learning loop is not working, as evidenced by the dismal training results and lack of real learning.

Let's take a moment to consider why. It is unusual for managers to attend the training and as such they often feel ill-equipped to take ownership of the process. Plus, transfer of learning is a very specific skill and assuming managers will take ownership without support or training in those critical skills is naive. To add insult to injury, the adoption of the 70/20/10 model is heaping even more pressure on the already beleaguered manager. If 70 per cent of an individual's learning needs are supposedly taken care of on the job then it is the manager who is ultimately responsible for ensuring that happens.

There can be little doubt that the manager plays a crucial role in transfer of learning but I believe that role is fundamentally misunderstood. The importance of the manager is not down to that individual's ability to facilitate transfer of learning but in their effective management of the transfer environment. Numerous studies have shown a strong correlation between how much (or otherwise) the manager supports the training and how much of that training is then successfully transferred to the workplace.

According to American Express researcher Dr Paul Leone this 'transfer climate' is the extent to which factors in a participant's immediate work environment either help or hinder the transfer of learning back to the job. And clearly the manager's attitude to the training, both before and after, will have an effect on learning transfer. If a participant's manager is supportive and enthusiastic about the training prior to and after the intervention then that support sends a very clear message of importance and relevance to the individual. As such the participant is far more likely to pay attention and implement what they have learnt than if the manager is indifferent. If the manager is openly dismissive or even hostile towards the training then – even if it is great material and the participants love it and see its relevance – there are few employees who would deliberately go out of their way to implement it when they know that doing so is going to meet with hostility and disdain from their manager. These factors alone will greatly influence transfer of learning.

Unfortunately this transfer climate argument has been somewhat hijacked by those who use it as validation that the manager is therefore the right person to manage the transfer process. Making sure that the managers are on board and appreciate the relevance of the training, and have communicated their enthusiasm and support for the training in order to create the optimal transfer environment, is *very* different, however, from expecting those managers to hold their training participants' feet 'to the fire' and take full responsibility for the actual transfer of learning process. Remember, transfer of learning is a change process not a learning process, and people rarely change without accountability that makes it very uncomfortable or difficult for them *not* to change.

Expecting the managers to be able to create this accountability is unrealistic – certainly without the proper training in a proven transfer of learning methodology. But it is a different issue to helping to positively influence the transfer climate. I interviewed Roy Pollock, co-author of *The Six Disciplines of Breakthrough Learning*, who, at the time, was at the Fort Hill Company. In the interview he stated that the manager's role is to create a positive transfer climate by:

- Having a brief discussion beforehand about the importance of the training and the expectation for its use.
- Facilitating undistracted attendance by arranging for others to cover the participants' work and minimize interruptions.
- Following-up with the learner afterwards about his/her goals for application.
- Recognizing or rewarding application of new learning and expressing disappointment at non-use.

These management expectations are valid and logical, but to expect more than this is, in my opinion, a mistake. Plus it is unfair because supporting someone to change their behaviour and transfer learning into their working lives is a very specific skill. The assumption is that follow-up conversations are easy and straightforward. They are not – and unless the manager has been taught a specific transfer of learning methodology then most managers don't have the skills or the tools to actually make that transfer possible. Instead they are having the occasional casual conversation so they can tell their superiors that they followed up with the participant, which is very different from what is actually needed.

At the 2012 AITD (Australian Institute of Training and Development) conference Dr Jay Cohen talked about how leaders needed to become 'leaders of learning'. His central message was that managers shouldn't be managers unless they take learning seriously and that managing learning in their team should be their main task as a manager. It is an attractive idea. And it could certainly close the gap in transfer of learning – but it is so far away from the reality of what most people experience in business that it's hard to see how managers would make the transition in one fell swoop.

Look at health, for example: I *know* that if everyone on the planet ate more fresh fruit and vegetables, less processed and junk food, became more physically active, stopped drinking so much alcohol and stopped smoking then the medical problems that we collectively face would be slashed. The world knows this. Science and research has proven it beyond a shadow of a doubt. Does this information make any difference, however, to the reality of what is actually happening? No.

The same applies to training. We might think that the transfer of training shortfall can be narrowed or even eradicated if the mangers just get on board and take responsibility for it but that doesn't alter the fact that currently they are not getting on board and taking responsibility for it because they are already under pressure to perform across umpteen other criteria and they don't have the tools, time or training to make it a reality.

It is true that many managers have been trained to coach the individuals in their team and yet manager-led learning transfer is still not happening. To coach effectively we need to change pace and put on the 'coaching hat'. Considering that most managers are already working flat out it is virtually impossible for them to change their pace for two or three minutes in the hope that they may participate in a 'coaching moment'. The effective 'coaching moment' is a myth. I'm a full-time professional coach and I coach all day long and yet I rarely switch into coach mode in an instant with my team. There are no 'coaching moments' – we have to change hat, drop the gears and dive into a deep coaching conversation if we want to illicit change and that simply does not happen when a manager is already running around at 100 miles per hour.

Certainly creating 'leaders of learning' and expecting all managers to become transfer of learning experts is an attractive and convenient solution. The trainer, once they have delivered the material and finished the learning event, is happy to relinquish responsibility to the manager. Trainers are usually outside contractors so this approach certainly appears to make sense. The L&D manager is happy to abdicate responsibility to the manager because they are busy sourcing new training for other departments. And the CEO can feel reassured that things are progressing in the right direction. Meanwhile, the manager is already busy and probably doesn't have the skills to ensure the transfer actually happens.

As a result managers feel overwhelmed, especially when they have not been on the training programme and therefore think that it's going to be hard for them to support the people who have. If they are equipped with the right methodology this isn't true, but this common misconception can actively put them off having the follow-up conversations. Often, even if they do have a follow-up conversation it is tacked on to the end of another agenda or conducted informally 'in passing'.

The follow-up conversation might therefore sound a little like this:

> Manager: 'How did you do on the training programme?'
> Participant: 'Oh, yes, I really enjoyed it.'
> Manager: 'Great, what was your biggest take away from the course?'
> Participant: 'That I really need to plan out my day before I start work so I know what I'm trying to achieve each day.'
> Manager: 'Great, glad it was useful.'

That's it! And believe it or not, that would be considered to be a pretty good follow-up. The manager in question would probably be applauded for remembering to have the conversation in the first place. Certainly the manager engaged with the participant in a one-on-one dialogue and found out what that person thought was the most beneficial part of the training, but is that exchange going to change the participant's behaviour? Does the fact that the participant now realizes the importance of planning the day's activities and objectives mean that he or she will actually take the time to make those plans and pursue those objectives consistently? No, it does not. All it means is that the participant can remember a key point from the training and the manager can be comforted that the training was worthwhile.

This can be demoralizing for any manager because they know it doesn't work. More often than not they will have enough follow-up conversations to allow them to report that activity to their superior so that the transfer of learning box can be ticked, but everyone involved knows that nothing much has actually changed. No one is happy about this situation but no one is really sure how to change it.

Assuming we can miraculously convert managers into 'learning leaders' is an ideal that may be worth striving for but it is far removed from what is actually happening in businesses right now. It's like expecting a 40-stone smoker to climb Mount Everest with just one week to prepare for it. It's just not going to happen, and trust me I'm not being negative. I love the idea of having leaders of learning, but wishing it would happen and thinking how great it might be if it did happen is a world away from what is actually happening. So let's stop pretending or hypothesizing about what we would like to happen in an ideal world. Let's stop blaming the managers and embrace a step change instead. Let's take small manageable steps towards a lasting solution so that perhaps one day in the future managers will be genuine leaders of learning and the transfer of learning failure that currently plagues the industry can be assigned to history.

We need to remember that the issue is not whether managers are having follow-up conversations – as these *are* sometimes happening. The real issue is whether managers have a methodology for behavioural change so that the follow-up conversation facilitates a genuine change of behaviour or performance improvement from the participant. Do managers really understand how to hold other people to account without dictating to them or nagging them? Most managers don't, because they've never been taught or the framework they have been taught is so broad and loose that they find it impossible to apply.

Even if managers have been given some type of coaching training the emphasis is usually on asking questions and not telling the individual what to do. Instead they are encouraged to ask questions until the individual comes up with their own answers. But most managers find that quite disempowering because they still don't know how to hold that person to account on the agreements they make and really 'hold their feet to the fire'. The coaching skills may encourage flexibility so that the participant comes up with their own solutions, but unless we have the tools and skills to transfer that flexibility into a proven process for change then the follow-up conversation is nothing more than a nice chat. The participant may feel engaged and the discussion may be more interactive but it still probably won't result in behaviour change or performance improvement.

As a consequence, manager-led transfer of learning is notoriously poor and the manager is blamed. But it is not the manager's fault. Perhaps it is about time that we cut managers some slack and become open to the possibility that they may not be the best person to facilitate transfer of learning – at least not unless they have been thoroughly trained in an effective learning transfer methodology.

'We facilitate training follow-up discussion groups'

Another popular 'solution' to ensure that learning is transferred from the training event to the workplace is follow-up discussion groups.

The idea is that after the learning intervention participants meet regularly back in the workplace to discuss the training, reflect on the learning and review progress. I remember meeting a major electronics manufacturer whose transfer of learning strategy was follow-up discussion groups where people got together after the training to discuss what they were doing. These groups did nothing to change behaviour and became nothing more than a talk-fest. They took place a couple of times after each learning intervention and then fizzled out. And this company was spending millions every year on corporate training.

Again, in theory, this approach makes sense because it allows the people who took part in the training an opportunity to meet, review, reflect, ask questions and check in with one another on progress. It provides an opportunity to raise concerns, compare notes and get re-engaged with the change if necessary.

In practice, however, discussion groups rarely facilitate or improve transfer of learning. They may be better than nothing but they don't make much difference. They may allow people to exchange views and discuss the material but they can too easily be viewed as a convenient 'break from work' or a forum to vent and complain rather than a constructive place to solve ongoing implementation issues and resolve challenges. Plus there is rarely any accountability in a group session. Having an opportunity to personalize the training and reflect on how the new information and skills could help an individual is key to transfer of learning and yet this process does not happen in groups.

In a study by Marilyn Wood Daudelin, as detailed in her article 'Learning from experience through reflection', published in the journal *Organizational*

Dynamics (1996), a group of 48 managers from a Fortune 500 company was divided into four groups. Each group was to engage in a one-hour reflection session where they were encouraged to think about what they had learnt. The first group, labelled the 'individual group', was asked to reflect on their own. The second group labelled the 'helper group' was asked to reflect with the help of a coach. The third group known as the 'peer group' was joined by three or four other people from the study and asked to reflect together. And the fourth group was the control group who did not engage in any reflection. Each group was asked to follow the same four-stage reflection process and use the same reflection questions.

As expected, the individual group and helper group achieved more learning than the control group, who did not engage in any reflection activity. What was surprising, however, was that the peer group did not show a statistically significant improvement. The reason for this was put down to three things. First, the peer group focused on finding similarities between each other's experiences, which actually prevented them from personalizing the training and assimilating the learning more fully than groups one and two. The need to discuss a number of different topics prevented the group from going into useful depth about any one issue and, because there were more people in the group, it was much less structured. None of these peer groups followed the reflection process or asked the reflection questions, whereas those who reviewed the material alone or in one-on-one groups did.

Involving co-workers and creating a way for participants to encourage and support each other is all part of a successful learning transfer environment or transfer climate – but in and of itself this involvement does not automate transfer of learning. If everyone is supportive and enthusiastic they can encourage the application of new skills in the workplace, but if they are not or if there are cynical elements in the group then application will almost always give way to time wasting and complaining.

Discussion groups fall into the peer group format and as such are ineffective in the transfer of learning because there is no personal ownership for the transfer. Topics are often only discussed superficially so as to give everyone a chance to speak rather than reflecting on the genuine value of the training to each individual personally. It is this personalized reflection that is key to the transfer of learning and it is this exact personalized reflection that is so often missing in follow-up discussion groups. Also, because these sessions are held internally by the participants themselves they are the first thing to get cancelled when the workload increases or people get busy.

'We run half-day training refresher/follow-up sessions'

This approach is often instigated by the trainer or training company delivering the learning intervention as an 'answer' to the transfer of learning shortfall. Often the proposition of half-day training refreshers/follow-up sessions is part of the sales pitch to convince learning purchasers that the trainer appreciates the learning transfer issue and is taking steps to address it.

Their training solution will therefore include the learning intervention *and* a half-day follow-up programme delivered several weeks later. If this process were to include reflection and review and offered participants the opportunity to ask questions and raise concerns then it would certainly be a useful addition to the learning process. If participants were asked to bring back examples of how they had used the learning in their working environment since the initial training then it would certainly encourage people to make at least some effort to use the training. Unfortunately these half-day refresher/follow-up programmes are usually just an opportunity to review the content again with no real provision for accountability. Participants simply get together again to go through the content that was previously delivered, which makes it incredibly easy for participants to 'hide' – they may attend the follow-up session but when there is only enough time for a limited number of people to share their experiences it is easy to look engaged in the discussion but not be.

If the participants know that the refresher will recap on the existing content then all they need to do is look back over their notes so that they can regurgitate a few salient points. If they can do this, then the assumption is that they must be using the training. Chances are they are not. When the focus is on making sure the participants can demonstrate that they remember or understand the information, rather than on whether or not they are using that information, then it's very easy to consider a half-day follow-up to be a success. But remembering the content of the training or being able to give a single example of when it was used does not automatically ensure that what is remembered is used on a daily basis or has become a positive habit. Having half-day follow-up programmes may illicit a tiny amount of change – as someone is reminded that a piece of information was actually quite useful – but the difference between having a half-day follow-up and not having one is negligible.

Getting back into a training room to cover previously covered information doesn't make any difference to whether or not that information has been translated into action and on-the-job performance improvements.

'We have executive coaching'

Increasingly the top-end leadership training programmes include some form of executive coaching as part of the training process. However, it is almost always offered as face-to-face coaching, which means that it is often impossible to roll out across a large organization and is likely to be extremely expensive.

In addition, most of the training commissioned by organizations does not involve executives and senior managers. In any business most of the training is directed at department employees or front-line personnel. The transfer of learning to the workplace is every bit as important for those people as it is for executives and yet traditionally there is no coaching option for them.

The other major problem with executive coaching is that often the coaching conversations are being conducted by the trainer who did the initial training. The skills required to design and deliver a compelling training programme and the skills required to support individuals to convert that information into action are very different. When the trainer conducts the coaching conversation they are probably fairly wedded to their content and will simply spend the coaching time redelivering that content rather than getting ideas from the participant about how they intend to action those ideas and create behaviour change.

I firmly believe that after the content has been delivered, when it comes to behavioural change the further away we can get from the content the better. What matters post-learning is what people actually do, what behaviours change and what action they take following the intervention. If the coach is attached to the content of the training it is very hard to put that aside and focus on the participant. Behaviour change requires that we focus on the participant not the information.

'We use action learning'

Often when I ask CEOs and learning professionals how they ensure that their training initiatives transfer into the business they will tell me that they use action learning protocols.

According to the Worldwide Institute of Action Learning (WIAL) Action Learning can be used to solve complex problems, develop leaders, build teams and expand corporate capability. Their corporate website states:

'Action Learning has become a dynamic process that assists organizations to challenge the status quo, and to develop creative, flexible and successful strategies. Action Learning positions inquiry at the core of organizational behaviour, develops critical thinking and creates mutual respect among employees at all levels.'

Wikipedia describes action learning as: 'an educational process whereby the participant studies their own actions and experience in order to improve performance'.

The idea is that learning is transferred and made real through action, repetition and fine-tuning rather than through traditional instruction. Again, in theory this sounds much more relevant to transfer of learning because it suggests that participants use the information they learn in training and fine tune their approach and, therefore, their knowledge through trial and error. In practice, however, action learning seems to focus more on problem solving than on transfer of learning.

Action learning involves small groups called action learning sets, which often include people from diverse parts of the organization who are brought together to solve a problem. In theory, working in these groups leverages adult learning principles because the groups enable each person to reflect on what they learn in the process, so they can take it back to their own areas and spread the word. However, as we have just established, reflection in a group setting is not effective because no one really takes ownership of the learning and personalizes it sufficiently to impact their own situation.

Action learning is usually initiated on a project-by-project basis. The problem with this approach is that as soon as the learning is transferred into a project the completion of the project becomes the aim. The participant splits out what he or she does on the job from what they do in their action learning project. The theory is that once the individual starts to use the new behaviour in the project they will automatically transfer that insight or learning into their daily activity but that doesn't necessarily happen. Once the action learning project is finished then those new behaviours that made it possible are also finished and the individual soon reverts back to the old way of working. The participants are not being deliberately difficult – it is just that the process of splitting their everyday work from their action learning project separated the two things and each individual will not automatically transfer the learning to their everyday work after the action learning project is complete.

The most effective way to use action learning projects is to make sure they are directly linked to the individual's daily activity so that they have the opportunity to transfer the behaviour to their day-to-day role.

'We use blended learning solutions'

This 'solution' is another really popular response to the question of learning transfer, especially since the acceleration of technology. Blended learning is the term used to describe the mix of content delivery channels, which range from face-to-face instruction to interactive computer-based programmes and the use of the emerging electronic media. The idea is to provide the learner with realistic and practical ways to access the learning in a way and time that best suits them and as such it is often touted as the solution to transfer of learning. Trainers and course designers create the training intervention using a variety of content types and delivery methods and they then pull out key messages and find novel ways to deliver those key messages at various stages after the event. A participant may, for example, receive flashcards, text messages, access to online tutorials and refresher material. There may be smartphone applications and audio or video clips from the training event.

Again this may sound effective. If someone prefers to do their learning when they have time alone in their car on the way to work then being able to download the content via a podcast to their iPhone would be really useful. If someone works on computers all day then probably the last thing that they will want to do is watch a webinar. If someone has a short attention span then they may prefer to complete one online training module every day. The way that content can now be delivered and disseminated has radically changed the ability to deliver quality content and improve knowledge transfer but, as we discussed in the previous chapter, the knowledge is not the problem. Businesses and training organizations are already very skilled in delivering knowledge in the form of learning. Bombarding participants with additional content or reminding them of the key messages from the original training event – regardless of how cleverly that is delivered – won't change behaviour.

Blended learning may improve how the content is delivered and it may allow the participant to tap into their own preferred learning style but it makes absolutely zero difference to whether or not that information is used to alter behaviour and improve performance.

'We create a social media community'

Another popular response regarding how organizations are addressing the transfer of learning shortfall is the belief that the creation of online social-media-driven communities are finally going to solve the problem.

The idea here is very similar to facilitating follow-up discussion groups only this time it's done online through a company intranet or a social media site/community such as Facebook or Twitter. Rather than meeting regularly face to face, participants simply join an online forum where they can 'meet' other participants, discuss problems and share progress.

Using forums in this way can be great for keeping the training in mind. It can increase the bond between the participants who can therefore help and support each other. But like discussion groups it can turn into a handy work distraction where participants can endlessly discuss the problem without seeking resolution or improvement. People are far more 'honest' online than they ever would be face to face and this is not necessarily a good thing when seeking behaviour change. The forum can often be a great place to air views but without accountability nothing changes. Plus these sorts of initiatives may appeal to the younger demographic but are unlikely to engage older employees.

Learning is made possible by reflection and personalizing the training to each participant's work activity and the best way to achieve that is alone or with one-on-one support, not peer support. Social media forums therefore facilitate the same ownership and accountability issues as discussion groups.

As a tool this type of online community can be a great addition to the training strategy but alone it will be little more than a discussion opportunity with no real accountability to implement the learning. The social interaction and ability to keep the training alive is really powerful but there also needs to be a way to hold people to account. As such it is a support strategy rather than a transfer of learning strategy.

'Participants must present their learning back to their workgroup'

One of the best ways to know if someone has really understood something is to ask them to teach it to others. This is the premise behind this learning transfer tactic and it is the reason why plenty of managers and leaders consider this approach as a valid method for ensuring training is understood and transferred.

I am often told that a business has a transfer of learning strategy and the manager will enthusiastically explain that the participants of training must present their learning back to their team or workgroup, thus ensuring that they have learnt the material and were paying attention. But as we've already established, understanding something and using something are two entirely different things.

This tactic is useful because it requires the participant to review their notes and engage with the material so that they can come up with the best way to present it to their colleagues. But, again, presenting back to a group demonstrates that a participant understands the material but it does not demonstrate they are using that new knowledge to change behaviour and improve performance. It may encourage participants to pay attention and foster good comprehension but all it really establishes is whether the participant has a good understanding of the content and how good their presentation skills are. It doesn't predict whether or not the individual can or will apply the information he or she presents to the group.

'We ensure everyone is properly prepared for the learning'

The theory about how to improve learning effectiveness has been around for decades. Stolovitch wrote his landmark text *Telling Ain't Training* in the 1980s and was very clear that pre-learning and post-learning were more important than the training itself.

Part of effective pre-learning is to make sure that the people who are attending the training have the right attitude towards it. It is important that they feel confident that the training will make a positive impact and they are capable of learning what they are being asked to learn.

There is little doubt that pre-learning conversations or group sessions to encourage the right attitude for the training can help the process, but what happens after the training has a much bigger impact on learning transfer than what happens before.

It is certainly helpful to have the right transfer climate and focused and enthusiastic participants, but this is not an indicator for success. I've seen enthusiastic participants transfer little, and deeply cynical participants transfer a great deal, so preparation is not the precursor for successful learning transfer that it is often hailed to be. What really matters is what happens after the training.

The focus on pre-learning and 'learner readiness' is a bit of a red herring too. While it is helpful to try to get this right and encourage the right attitude and environment it doesn't alter the fact that the gaping hole in transfer of learning is what happens *after* the training – and that's what this book is all about. As mentioned earlier, we have spent decades making the various parts of the ADDIE process very professional and yet the reality is that these improvements have not made a great deal of difference to the effectiveness of learning transfer. Therefore it would logically follow that whilst important, if we are hunting for genuine learning transfer then we need to shift our focus to what happens once everyone is back in the workplace.

Let's face it – whilst learner readiness or the various elements of instructional design have vastly improved the transfer of knowledge to the participant they have made negligible difference to the transfer of learning: where that participant then uses the knowledge in their daily working life.

The dangers of a faulty premise

By far the most popular solutions put forward by companies in their attempt to remedy the transfer of learning challenge are to assume that the manager is responsible. And it is little wonder when we consider that the most widespread and best-known transfer of learning model or theory comes from Broad and Newstrom. In 1992 Mary Broad and John Newstrom proposed that there were three critical stages (before, during and after training) and three critical stakeholders (manager, trainer and trainee) of learning transfer. According to Broad and Newstrom's research the top three most critical roles and time frames in the transfer of learning process are:

1 The manager *before* the training.
2 The trainer *before* the training.
3 The manager *after* the training.

However, when this premise is investigated in detail Broad and Newstrom themselves confirm that the data collection – although extensive – was based on the perceptions of where trainers felt the biggest impact on learning transfer could be made. This thinking was never empirically tested, and indeed the authors call for more research in the area, yet it is still widely followed today and is, I believe, part of the problem not part of the solution. For a start, it puts far too much emphasis on the manager, which conveniently lets everyone else in the training process off the hook. Yes the manager is critical in creating the right transfer environment but they are not automatically responsible for the actual transfer of learning. Plus we already know that relying on the manager to facilitate transfer of learning is completely ineffective. Most managers already have enough on their plate without being expected to be change agents too – often with little support or training for this role.

Plus Broad and Newstrom don't adequately acknowledge the role of the learner in their own change process. In their book *Transfer of Training* (1992) Broad and Newstrom detail 79 transfer strategies – 41 of which they believe the managers should drive, 24 the training should drive and only 14 that the learner owns. However, Knowles was very clear that when it comes to adult learning the learner needs to feel involved in the planning and evaluation of their learning. They want an opportunity to draw on their experience and past mistakes and they want to ensure that the learning is problem-focused and directly relevant to their job.

In short, for adults to learn effectively they have to exert some control over the process of learning. Yet the first time the trainee is mentioned by Broad and Newstrom regarding the importance of stakeholders is fifth out of a possible nine:

1   The manager *before* the training.

2   The trainer *before* the training.

3   The manager *after* the training.

4   The trainer *during* the training.

5   The trainee *during* the training.

6   The trainee *after* the training.

7   The trainee *before* the training.

8   The manager *during* the training.

9   The trainer *after* the training.

Transfer of learning is by definition a process that happens after the learning has taken place, so realistically how can what happens before and during the programme possibly be more important than what happens after?

Obviously the training needs to be appropriate to the participants or they won't transfer it and it needs to be good otherwise there is nothing to transfer. And yes, the attitude of the participant coming into the training is important but it is not pivotal to success. It is easier to teach happy, positive and engaged individuals who want to be in a training programme but I've seen enough examples of the opposite to know that effective training and transfer of learning is possible regardless of attitude. We've done amazing things with people who have got to the end of the programme and still thought the training was useless – we've turned them around and got them to transfer the learning. Of course it helps if the participants are enthusiastic but, certainly in my experience, it is not the predictor of successful learning transfer that Broad and Newstrom suggest it to be.

Transfer of learning is about successful application of the learning. It is about change and about helping participants to make the necessary be-haviour modifications to improve performance in the workplace. Everyone who has ever tried to change people will confirm that it is very hard to do: they have to want to change themselves. An important part of this is to encourage them to see the advantages of change, support them through that process and instil enough accountability so as to make it difficult or uncomfortable not to change. But we can't force people to change, so it just doesn't make sense that the manager is the most important person in the transfer of learning process.

The most important person in the transfer of learning process is the person who has received the training and what *they* do *after* the training – and yet according to Broad and Newstrom the trainee after the training is the third *least* important person in the process. To me that just doesn't seem right. Do, though, consider having a thorough read of the data documented in Broad and Newstrom's *Transfer of Training – Action-packed strategies to ensure high payoff and training*, and come to your own conclusions on whether it is indeed, as I believe, a faulty premise.

Time for the real solution

There is no doubt that people are aware of training ineffectiveness. Everyone connected to corporate training – from the participants to the facilitators to the designers and the L&D professionals and CEOs authorizing the train-ing – know that it doesn't work very well. Research conducted by Saks and Belcort (2006) showed that on top of the initial challenge of learning transfer there is a steady decline in the use of those new skills over time. So even if people do initially use the learning they receive only 35 per cent of those skills will still be in use 12 months later.

There are countless tactics currently employed by business in an attempt to improve training effectiveness and this is testament to the fact that people recognize the problem and are focused on genuinely finding a solution. In the report 'Learning transfer model: a research-driven approach to enhancing learning effectiveness' mentioned earlier, author Michael Leimbach identified 66 individual learning transfer activities across the 32 studies he analysed. Of the 66 separate activities the author was able to classify them into just 11 different activities across three primary categories:

- Learner readiness:
  - motivation to learn;
  - intent to use;
  - career goal alignment;
  - self-efficacy.
- Learning transfer design:
  - practice and modelling;
  - goal setting;
  - application review.
- Organizational alignment:
  - manager support;
  - peer support;
  - job connection;
  - learning culture.

Leimbach suggested that taken alone most of the 11 learning transfer activities would improve performance by about 20 per cent over training alone. And taken together they could enhance performance by as much as 186 per cent. By any standards most managers would be ecstatic if they could achieve anywhere close to a performance improvement of 186 per cent and this study provides compelling evidence that learning transfer is indeed the missing link in training. In his study Leimbach therefore suggests that managers should incorporate as many as possible of the 11 activities into their transfer of learning strategy, suggesting that they choose the individual activities they feel most comfortable with and/or prefer to use.

I have a different suggestion. Why not just learn one transfer of learning process that will automatically cover almost all of the 11 activities that the study highlighted as being so crucial to performance improvement? Don't worry about the 11 individual elements, don't stress about which ones to try first or how to manage so many different elements. Instead all we need to do is learn one transfer of learning process and we will achieve the stellar improvement in performance that we seek. That process is called Turning Learning into Action® and I will explain exactly what it is in the next chapter.

Summary of key points

- Most people in the learning and development industry are fully aware of training's dismal record in affecting behavioural change and there is a growing recognition that this missing link is transfer of learning.

- In 2011 the American Society for Training and Development for the first time dedicated an entire conference to learning transfer.

- We may already know that training doesn't work but people *are* trying to find solutions.

- CEOs, senior managers and leaders believe, when pressed, that they are addressing transfer of learning issues and I frequently hear at least one of these nine responses:
  - 'Our managers conduct training follow-up.'
  - 'We facilitate training follow-up discussion groups.'
  - 'We run half-day training refresher/follow-up sessions.'
  - 'We have executive coaching.'
  - 'We use action learning.'
  - 'We use blended learning solutions.'
  - 'We create a social media community.'
  - 'Participants must present their learning back to their workgroup.'
  - 'We ensure everyone is properly prepared for the learning.'

- There are countless tactics currently employed by business in an attempt to improve training effectiveness and this is testament to the fact that people recognize the problem and are focused on genuinely finding a solution.

- In Michael Leimbach's report 'Learning transfer model: a research-driven approach to enhancing learning effectiveness' he identified 66 individual learning transfer activities across the 32 studies he analysed. Of the 66 separate activities the author was able to classify them into just 11 different activities across three primary categories:

  - learner readiness;

  - learning transfer design;

  - organizational alignment.

- Leimbach suggested that taken alone most of the 11 learning transfer activities would improve performance by about 20 per cent over training alone. And taken together they could enhance performance by as much as 186 per cent.

- I have a different suggestion. Why not just learn one transfer of learning process that will automatically cover almost all of the 11 activities that the study highlighted as being so crucial to performance improvement? That process is called Turning Learning into Action® (TLA).

Part Two
THE LEARNING TRANSFER SOLUTION

04
Turning Learning into Action®

Transfer of learning is the missing link in effective learning and Turning Learning into Action® (TLA) is a proven learning transfer methodology that solves the problem. TLA is a series of specific, structured and accountable one-on-one conversations that occur at various intervals *after* the training event and it is the step change I referred to earlier.

I delivered the first TLA programme in a 12-person trial in April 2004. By May the results were confirmed and my client, a large premium automotive company, ordered the programme for 120 more people that year. I was onto something.

During 2005 we did an analysis of one group of 15 people who went through the TLA programme after some sales training against another group who did not. We analysed their average sales per month before the programme and analysed their average sales per month after the programme and compared the results to the norm within the business. The norm in this case was annual sales before May and average monthly sales after May. We made this split to take into account seasonal differences in automotive sales.

The average sales consultant had a 16.2 per cent uplift in their average sales per month between the five months prior to the training and the five months following the training and TLA. Everyone we analysed in the group had similar levels of experience and yet those who went through the TLA process had a sales uplift of 43.8 per cent over the same period.

These results confirmed that I *really* was onto something.

By 2007 my coaching team in Australia and I were delivering a year-long programme for another large automotive client for 400 mid-level managers across the organization for an 18-month period. There were four of us on the coaching team and as a business we were extremely busy.

We were then asked to deliver TLA to 240 people in the UK. There were four large training events of about 60 people at a time held over the period of one month. The training was outstanding and our job was to ensure that all 240 people transferred the learning into their workplace. By the end of the year the results were in from the 400-person programme in Australia and the 240-person programme in the UK (see Table 4.1). TLA had been implemented in each case by two completely different teams trained in the same methodology and yet the results were almost identical.

TABLE 4.1   Two programmes in large automotive companies in the UK and Australia

	UK – 240 people	Australia – 400 people
Sector	Automotive	Automotive
Audience	Sales managers	Sales managers, service managers, regional managers, parts managers
Timescale	Over 4 months	Over 18 months, phased
Number of coaches	10	4
Training	Soft management / leadership skills	Soft management / leadership skills
Net Promoter Score (NPS) for the programme Based on your recent telephone coaching experience how likely would you be to recommend this to a colleague?	78%	73%
To what degree were expectations of coaching as a transfer of training tool met? (Score scale of 1 low and 5 high – scored either 4 or 5)	86%	83%

TABLE 4.1   Continued

	UK – 240 people	Australia – 400 people
To what degree have the objectives you set at the end of the training programme been met? (Score 1 to 5, 1 not met, 5 fully met – score of either 4 or 5)	88%	87%
Did you see change in particular aspects of your behaviour in response to coaching? If yes, to what extent have these been achieved? (Score 4 or 5 out of a scale of 1–5)	78%	83%
To what degree do you believe the objectives in the action plan would have been met without coaching? (1, not met – 5 fully met)	Score 1 or 2 – 47% Score 3 – 32% Score 4 or 5 – 21%* * 70% of these respondents in the next question rated it 5 (essential) for helping them follow through on the action plan (as this is a reverse-scored question – 5 is a low score – the assumption could be made that the reversed nature might have been been missed if the respondents had, for example, not read the question properly.)	Score 1 or 2 – 49% Score 3 – 38% Score 4 or 5 – 13%
How useful was the coaching in ensuring that you followed through on your action plan (scale 1 – unnecessary; to 5 – essential)	85%	82%

Net Promoter Score (NPS), made popular by Frederick F Reichheld, is a really common and acceptable way to illustrate customer satisfaction. According to Reichheld companies whose customers award them an NPS of 75 per cent to 80 per cent plus have generated world-class loyalty. In other words, the customers of the businesses that are reporting an NPS in excess of 75 per cent are very happy customers – so happy that they will gladly recommend that business to other people. In the UK and Australian

TLA programmes that we tested we achieved an NPS of 78 per cent and 73 per cent respectively.

Today TLA is being delivered in eight languages across the United States, Europe and Asia as well as Australia and New Zealand. It is solving the transfer of learning challenge for businesses across multiple sectors including banking and finance, technology, construction and manufacturing.

There can be little doubt that transfer of learning *is* the missing link in learning and TLA is a proven methodology for solving it. And the really good news is that there is no need to worry about learning countless different strategies, learn TLA, use it and training will genuinely be the lever for change that it always promised to be.

TLA as a lever for change

Businesses buy training because they want to see some sort of improvement in performance. The individuals on the training are there because they have some challenge, or need to improve a certain skill. As such they have a series of obstacles to surmount. Learning is the potential leverage point that will allow them to surmount those challenges and improve performance over the long term.

Imagine this process as a pole vault. At the start of the run-up the athlete's pole is straight and taut. He then plants the pole into the ground; the pole bends and elevates the athlete upwards, over the bar. As the athlete clears the obstacle the pole straightens again and falls back to the ground. It has served its purpose and propelled the athlete over the bar and safely back down on the other side.

Pole vaulting was not originally a sport but a practical way to pass over natural obstacles in marshy places such as provinces of the Netherlands, along the North Sea and the Fens in parts of Britain. To cross these marshy areas without getting wet and without having to walk miles in roundabout journeys over bridges a stack of jumping poles were kept at every house and used for vaulting over the canals. Traditionally vaulting was about distance rather than height and they were used to short-cut travel time and allow people to get to where they were going faster.

TLA does the same thing by utilizing structure and flexibility. Each TLA conversation starts with a structure that acts like the pole vaulter's pole and provides strength and purpose to the conversation. It allows the learner to use the power inherent in that structure to catapult themselves up and over their particular learning challenge.

As a facilitator of TLA I know the type of questions I will ask before I start the process (structure), but I never know what the answers will be (flexibility). It is this flexibility that prompts additional questions and allows the individual to navigate the obstacle in the same way that the vaulter navigates the bar. It is the questions that really matter because they hold the context of the conversation, allowing for flexibility with the answers without being so flexible that the conversation is just a pleasant daydream.

The conversation is finalized with more structure as we then get the individual's commitment about what they are actually going to do before the next conversation. The individual is accountable for this process and is choosing what to do next. As such he or she is taking responsibility and ownership of the change. This is when the pole vaulter's pole straightens and falls to the ground while the vaulter lands safely on new ground. He or she has used the structure and flexibility to get to where *they* want to go faster.

Without this lever for change the behaviour change or application of learning sought by the training is rarely realized in the business.

As outlined earlier, the ADDIE model on which the vast majority of training is developed brilliantly facilitates the delivery of learning to the participant but misses the transfer of learning from the participant back into the workplace. Archimedes said, 'Give me a lever long enough and a fulcrum on which to place it, and I shall move the world.' Turning Learning into Action® provides that lever to ADDIE's fulcrum and together they can transform training effectiveness.

The power of reflection

Turning Learning into Action® is a practical methodology that puts reflection at the heart of the learning transfer process. The idea that reflection is central to learning is not new. It goes back to Greek philosophers such as Socrates and Plato. The Socratic Method is often referred to as a teaching method that focuses on asking rather than telling. Socrates challenged everyone around him, including Plato, to question their beliefs and reflect on learning to establish how it did or did not make sense to them as individuals. Sophocles also proposed that we learn by observing what we do time and time again.

More recently the English Enlightenment thinker, philosopher and physician John Locke believed that knowing was simply the product of reflection on experience and sensations.

As mentioned in Chapter 1, the importance of reflection in the adult learning process was also acknowledged by David A Kolb in his adult learning model (Figure 1.2, page 10).

The word 'experience' derives from the Latin word *experientia*, which means trial, proof or experimentation. In other words, the way someone gets experience and learns effectively is by using information or knowledge in the real world and using the results to fine tune future results. With enough trial and error anyone can learn anything and it is actually this trial and error process that is at the very heart of high performance.

The process of gathering experience therefore follows the Kolb adult learning model. First someone does something or engages in a particular activity or approach and the results of that action are noted. Sometimes the activity will be successful and sometimes it will not be successful but it is the experience and the outcome that drive learning. Ironically people learn the most when the outcome is not as the individual had anticipated. Under those conditions he or she is much more likely to engage in the crucial ingredient for learning and change – reflection. In life we rarely stop and reflect why we've been successful or why something worked out. Instead we just take the win and move on. When something doesn't work, however, we are much more likely to stop and think about why that activity didn't pan out as we had expected. It is because of that reflection that we are then able to fine tune our approach, see the failings and try again. This trial and error process develops expertise and it is only possible with reflection. Imagine how much progress we could make if we got into the habit of reflecting on our successes as well as our failures?

The problem with reflection is that it can look like we're not doing anything – and that's not ideal for employees. In modern business it is action that is king. Assessing the training needs of an organization can easily be classed as action, so everyone is happy with that activity. Designing, developing or sourcing training is also classed as action so everyone is happy with that. The implementation stage is also action-focused so everyone is happy with that. Even the evaluation stage can be suitably complex and interesting so that people can assure themselves that they are *doing* something to solve the issue. In modern business it is *doing* that gets us promoted not necessarily thinking and reflecting. Management guru Henry Mintzberg wrote in the

Harvard Business Review 20 years ago: 'Study after study has shown that managers work at an unrelenting pace, that their activities are characterized by brevity, variety, and discontinuity and that they are strongly orientated to action and dislike reflective activities.' This pace has only quickened – the drive for short-term results and maximizing shareholder value has hampered reflection and exacerbated the transfer of learning shortfall.

For reflection to really deliver the results that it is capable of delivering it must, however, be specific, structured and accountable (Figure 4.1). The word reflection has a very ethereal feel to it. It conjures up images of resting by a babbling brook, lying on the grass and gazing up at the clear blue sky. That, however, is daydreaming and whilst pleasant it is a world away from the type of reflection that can transform learning and facilitate change.

FIGURE 4.1   The principles of effective reflection

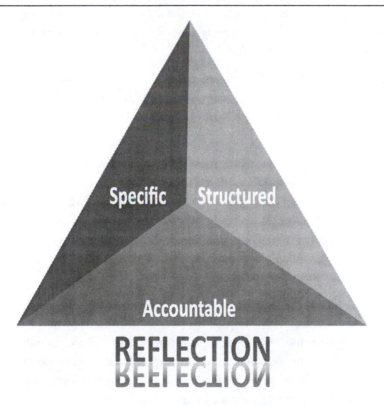

Turning Learning into Action® facilitates specific, structured and accountable reflection through a series of one-on-one conversations after the training event. When people take a training programme they will have time during the training, if it has been well executed, to reflect on how the new information or skill may help them in their daily life. If the trainer has not run over time they will have completed some sort of action plan that is supposed to help participants follow through on the commitments they make as a result of the training. Typically, without structured follow-up, nothing actually happens with that plan and it ends up stuffed in the back of the training folder and dumped in the office on Monday morning never to be opened again.

If on the other hand there is specialized follow-up after the training event and participants are made aware of this from the start of the programme then the action plan becomes a living document. The follow-up conversation becomes specific and deals with the first issue on that plan, the structure of the conversation means that it is focused on moving the individual along and creating a framework where he or she must keep their agreements with *themselves*, or explain why they have not done so. When the individual has made commitments and reflects on how he or she is progressing, and is held accountable, then real change is not only possible but almost inevitable. And that is the power of TLA.

TLA is not complicated. It is an enhanced coaching process that facilitates transfer of learning through a series of specific, structured and accountable one-on-one conversations that occur at various intervals *after* the training event.

When we consider that one of the most influential transfer of learning models (Broad and Newstrom) tells us that the critical time for transfer of learning is *before* the training then it is easy to see why learning transfer has so far been so ineffective. It certainly helps if the people on the training are enthusiastic and prepared but it is not indicative of success. In my view, what determines success or failure is whether or not there is a strategy for transfer of learning *after* the event.

We already know the statistics regarding failed training. We already know that we are wasting huge sums of money on training that never transfers back to the working environment. We know that people attend training and within weeks of the training event they are back at work doing exactly what they used to do prior to the training. It makes sense, therefore, to consider reallocating our training budget slightly to invest in training *and* learning transfer.

This shift will not alter the budget but it will radically alter results. One of the initial concerns I hear about TLA is the fear that one-on-one coaching will blow the training budget, but that's not the case and I hope the results at the start of this chapter will provide reassurance that rolling out this methodology is extremely doable – even with large numbers of training participants. By combining training *and* TLA at the same time we may end up doing less training, but if we get the results we seek in the first place then we won't need to keep buying training in the hope that the next programme will be different. TLA transforms training success and drives behaviour change into business. It is a cost-effective enhanced coaching methodology that when executed well will transform transfer of learning effectiveness.

Knowles and TLA

Knowles identified four principles for effective adult learning, which have become as good as law in the world of learning and development. As discussed in Chapter 2 the principles are:

- Adults need to be involved in the planning and evaluation of their instruction.
- Experience (including mistakes) provides the basis for learning activities.
- Adults are most interested in learning subjects that have immediate relevance to their job or personal life.
- Adult learning is problem-centred rather than content-oriented.

Like Kolb, Knowles too points to the importance of reflection – helping the individual to reflect on their own experiences and how they can make the learning relevant to them. In TLA, the TLA Plan puts the individual in charge of the learning transfer process and allows them to plan what they want to action following the training programme.

In the TLA conversations the specialist is always encouraging the individual to use their own experience, whether it is a success or a failure, to make the training relevant. Because they are in charge of the process and the learning they can choose what is the most immediately relevant to their job or personal life. It is *their* choice. And finally they are free and indeed encouraged to focus on how to rectify problems rather than get lost in the content.

It is important to realize that transfer of learning is not fully assisted or explained by the various learning theories but that effective transfer is also pulling the very best from change theory. Learning is just one part, once the learning is on board it is then important that we support individuals to change their behaviour over the long term. Learning has only really been effective when the person is using that learning on a regular basis and their behaviour has changed. Anything else is irrelevant.

At some point we have to accept that successful training and learning is actually less about the learning and more about change. The most effective change methodology is one-on-one personal coaching. When conducted over a period of time coaching allows the individual to identify what it is they want to change and then helps them to hold *themselves* accountable to follow through on what they want to do. Self-administered individual accountability is critical for change and I believe the very best way to achieve that is through enhanced coaching.

Coaching versus enhanced coaching

When I first explain TLA to people they often say something like, 'Oh so it's just one-on-one coaching then.' Everyone in L&D knows about coaching; managers are commonly trained in coaching methodologies so they can coach their staff. I have met hundreds, possibly even thousands of managers who have been taught a basic coaching model or methodology for that exact purpose. But as we already know, learning something and effectively using it are two very different things.

One of the biggest challenges facing coaching in business today is the versatility of the process. While it can be used in many ways it is often a proverbial 'jack of all trades' and master of none and is too broadly offered as a solution to all sorts of management problems. Ironically it is this broad application that is often touted as the reason that managers should learn it. So the manager attends a half-day coaching course or a module that is part of a broader management skills programme. But back in the workplace, as soon as the individual being coached reacts or answers the manager's questions in a way that is not familiar to the manager, perhaps in a way that was not adequately covered on their short training programme, they don't know how to get the coaching session back on track. Coaching is a conversation and as such it is very easy to assume 'everyone can do it'. Everyone *can* coach but it is not an automatic or easy skill to learn and it is certainly not something that can be perfected in a few hours.

Coaching, as most people recognize the term, is too fluid and flexible. As a result it works sometimes, for some people and not for others, and the people involved don't really understand why. The basic coaching that is so often taught to managers therefore becomes too generic to be useful, especially for a time-poor manager. It is very difficult to work out the actual skills we need to be a good coach when those skills are applicable to so many different scenarios, and it is much easier to learn a skill when there are very definite parameters around what we are trying to achieve.

TLA is a very specific application of an *enhanced* coaching methodology that removes all the guesswork and creates a structure that identifies very definite parameters around effective learning transfer. The TLA specialist, by adding much needed structure, puts the individual in charge of their own transfer of learning and holds them accountable for the commitments they make at the end of the training event.

Enhanced coaching takes the flexibility of traditional coaching and adds structure to the coaching process to facilitate learning transfer effectively. With enhanced coaching there is a fine balance between flexibility and structure. It is this balance that creates the results and removes the ambiguity from the coaching process, which allows us to deliver effective results consistently regardless of the training or the participant.

I remember watching Steve Jobs's 2005 Stanford Commencement speech on YouTube. He was talking about connecting the dots of his life and how seemingly obscure and unconnected parts of his life came together in the creation of Apple. It is not often I feel justified in comparing myself to Steve Jobs but listening to his speech I looked back on my life and could see the same connection of dots and how seemingly diverse experiences and choices led me to the development of enhanced coaching and TLA.

In school in the UK I studied maths, art and English to A level. It was a combination that was frowned upon by many of my teachers because the subjects didn't really belong together. At university I studied textile design, specializing in woven structure. What this course did for me was help me to appreciate fully the juxtaposition between structure and flexibility that is central to the success of enhanced coaching and, specifically, its application in training effectiveness through the TLA process. It was these two converging ideologies working together that created beautiful designs. The textile design part tapped into my love of art and it was very creative. It was all about colour, dyes, fabrics and textures. It was fun, exciting and vibrant. The woven structure part of the course tapped into my interest in maths, logic and process. It was all about numbers, patterns and systems. It was still fun for me but it wasn't sexy or colourful. What I came to appreciate was that without the creativity and flexibility of the textile design the end result was dull and almost mechanical. And without the insights of woven structure the designs were weak and slap-dash. What created beauty was the precision and symmetry of woven structure coupled with the colourful and vibrant textile design. Each was diminished without the other and each was enhanced by the presence of the other.

It is this balance between structure and flexibility that is the crux of enhanced coaching in the context of learning transfer. Traditional coaching is often too flexible and creative. It can feel incredibly satisfying, nurturing and enjoyable to be listened to – personally I think coaching feels so good to so many people because the modern world is often frantic and we don't sit down together and really discuss things and talk about issues in the way people did perhaps 50 years ago. Now we send a text message, eat dinner in front of a screen and communicate via technology rather than a good old-fashioned con- versation. But whilst traditional coaching may feel good and people may feel nourished and energized, often just through being listened to, it doesn't necessarily lead to behaviour change. It *can* lead to behaviour change when done properly but the vast majority of coaching is not done properly because it is not done with an action focus. It should be, and the model on which most coaching is built does include action, but the execution of that model rarely focuses on action.

Instead people get too carried away with the reflective part and don't make it concrete. The coaching conversation becomes about the person's 'story' and turns into a navel-gazing session, which may be enjoyable and even insightful for the person being coached but it is never made practical and therefore doesn't necessarily lead to behaviour change. And, as we know, it is behaviour change that is currently missing and absolutely critical for successful learning transfer.

The difference between coaching and enhanced coaching – ie coaching that incorporates structure as well as flexibility – was driven home to me when I moved to Sydney. One of my first coaching clients had previously been paying $500 per hour with one of Sydney's top coaches. At the end of each session she felt energized and excited. The conversation had been fun, interest- ing and inspiring. Only nothing changed. Nothing changed because coaching alone is often not specific, structured and accountable enough and so nothing takes place other than a great conversation. My new client recognized this and decided to hire me to make some changes – and she got significantly better results. Not necessarily because I was a better coach but because I balanced the need for flexibility with the need for structure. She got results and suggested very strongly that I needed to increase my fees, which at the time were under $100 per hour. Enhanced coaching guarantees results because it combines structure and flexibility for maximum impact and accountability.

Remember, in its simplest form coaching is about helping identify where an individual is trying to get to, looking at where they are now and bridging the gap between the two. Max Landsberg, author of *The Tao of Coaching* (1996), describes coaching as, 'a powerful alliance designed to forward and enhance the life-long process of human learning, effectiveness and fulfilment'.

Coaching is not a passive process; it is not something that can be done to someone without his or her consent or involvement. Whereas teaching and training is focused on telling and sharing content, real coaching is a genuine collaboration, which creates ownership for change. And it is the quality of the questions that determine the quality of that collaboration and the effectiveness of coaching. By asking the right questions coaching helps the individual find their own answers and acknowledges the fact that in their life they *are* the expert. When a coach is helping an individual to make change in their life then the coach accepts that the individual is far better placed to decide how those changes should be made and what actually needs to happen and in what order. That individual has a huge amount of information available to them that the coach will never have and is therefore always the right person to decide what needs to happen.

It is this acknowledgement of expertise that makes coaching genuinely different from teaching or mentoring. In teaching it is the teacher or trainer who is considered the expert, and for transfer of knowledge that is as it should be. But as we have already established, learning new content does not automatically mean that an individual will use that content. Mentoring on the other hand is when an individual teams up with someone who has already successfully achieved what that person is seeking to achieve. And yet a good coach can coach on any subject regardless of personal experience. The coach's job is to follow a flexible and structured process that helps the individual to identify something they want to change, work out where they are in relation to that goal and how they can bridge that gap effectively.

Whilst mentoring can be extraordinarily beneficial it relies on a number of key variables. First, the individual being mentored must absolutely trust and respect the person who is mentoring them. If they don't have total faith then the chances are they will only implement the pieces of advice that they secretly agree with anyway. Coaching avoids all those pitfalls because it doesn't actually matter if the coach is proficient or has experience in a specific area or not. Also it is less important for the individual to trust or respect the coach as it is not the coach's point of view that matters, it is the individual's point of view that matters. If a coach follows the coaching process and encourages the individual to find their own solutions and, most importantly, holds them to account for those changes then change *will* happen. And that is what makes coaching so powerful.

What really separates enhanced coaching from standard coaching, especially in the context of learning transfer, is that it allows us to fully appreciate why traditional coaching results are so variable. If we think about having a conversation with someone to help them move from A to B we need to think about what is going to work and what is not going to work. So we all know that it doesn't work to be told, we know that we need to encourage the individual to work it out for themselves. We all know that no one takes advice unless it is what they secretly thought anyway. We all know that we have to get the individual to be crystal clear about where they currently are and where they want to be so as to help them close the gap between the two. TLA is an enhanced coaching process that takes someone from where they are to where they want to be in the context of learning.

This book is about how to use enhanced coaching to facilitate transfer of learning using the TLA methodology so that we can get the results we want faster and with less hassle. TLA is the application of enhanced coaching in a very tight niche – helping people transfer learning from training back into the workplace.

The learning transfer road map

The learning transfer road map (Figure 4.2) is a visual representation of how to combine the ADDIE process, evaluation and learning transfer. It shows how each element fits into the learning process – before, during and after training – and how everyone must work together to focus on the real training finish line.

The learning transfer road map already includes ADDIE, which is the basis of instructional design, and most people are already using that process effectively.

FIGURE 4.2   The learning transfer road map

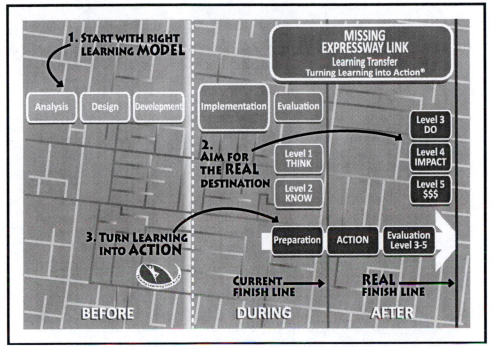

1. START WITH RIGHT LEARNING MODEL
Using ADDIE or a similar learning design process is a very important starting point for successful learning transfer.

2. AIM FOR THE REAL DESTINATION
Create objectives that help you reach your desired outcome, whether level 3 'DO', level 4 'IMPACT', or level 5 'ROI'. Having a Level 3 (or beyond) destination aim helps provide a clear focus on the best way forward.

3. TURN LEARNING INTO ACTION
Our simple 3 step Turning Learning into Action® Transfer methodology, compromising Preparation, ACTION and Evaluation, is the key to effective transfer of learning back to the workplace.

However, as I explained earlier, ADDIE alone will only take us to the current finish line. Typically the current finish line is the end of the training event and evaluation of people's reaction to the programme, what they have learnt from the training or what they can demonstrate. So we are already getting to the current finish line really well but what we want to do is push past that arbitrary and unhelpful conclusion to the real finish line. The real finish line is perhaps two or three months after the training event, where we can find out what people have actually used in the workplace and what they have implemented. To do that effectively we have to make sure that the missing link of learning transfer is added and the right people own that learning transfer process.

In its simplest form TLA can be broken down into three key parts (Figure 4.3):

FIGURE 4.3   Three component parts of TLA

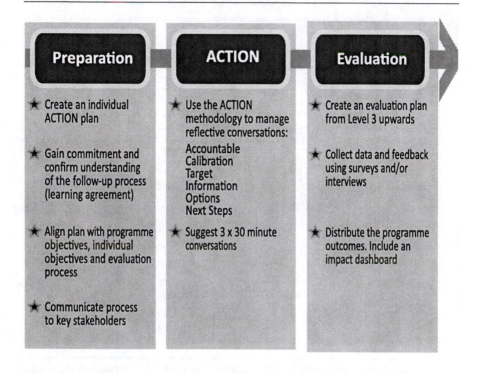

I   preparation;

2   action;

3   evaluation.

The first stage of TLA is *preparation*, which overlaps with the training event itself. Whether TLA is delivered externally or internally the preparation includes setting expectations and creating the TLA plan. It is this plan that will guide the transfer of learning back to the workplace. It is not concerned with what the participants have learnt but what they are going to do as a consequence of that learning. The TLA plan reflects the participant's commitments to change.

The second stage of TLA is *action* and is focused on what actually happens in the workplace. During the action stage we support people to reflect on their learning during scheduled action conversations that take place after the training event. The focus of these conversations is, of course, on action and what people are going to do in the workplace – the changes they are going to make between the follow-up conversations in order to progress each of their stated objectives. Regardless of whether a fully trained internal manager, L&D professional or external TLA specialist is conducting those conversations it is important to understand that they are a very different type of conversation. They are not casual discussions but focused inter-actions designed to illicit change and as such they will always require the manager or L&D professional to 'change their hat' from their normal role and communication style. Whoever is conducting the TLA conversation they must remove the 'hat' they normally wear in their normal business role and replace it with their 'transfer of learning' hat.

Finally, once participants have followed through on their TLA plan it is time for stage three – *evaluation*. Here we will be gathering information about what people have actually done since the training event and through the TLA conversations. This is why we need to be really clear from the outset about what we are going to measure.

To make the evaluation stage easier we need to aim for the real destination right from the start (Figure 4.4). This means that we need to start with our end evaluation in mind so that we can set not just learning objectives but applica-tion objectives and business objectives for what the programme is going to achieve (remember we explored learning objectives in Chapter 2).

If we embrace the idea that the current finish line is part of the reason why training is currently so ineffective and seek to push past that point to the new finish line, then we have extended the life of our training programme by getting people to actually use the learning and change behaviours. As a result, we reap the benefits we hoped to reap when we commission the training in the first place.

The TLA process, which will be explored in greater detail in the rest of the book, allows people to try out new knowledge or a skill, monitor the results and reflect on how their new behaviours or action turned out and how useful the new experience was. It is this process of trial, error and reflection that facilitates real learning and behavioural change. Knowledge and information become wisdom only once used and experienced in a real-world situation. Turning Learning into Action® empowers the individual to take control of the learning process and increase their value and productivity for individual and collective success.

And now it is time to unpack the TLA process – the remainder of Part Two will be dedicated to explaining the process and the principles that will transform learning transfer.

FIGURE 4.4 Aim for the real destination of training

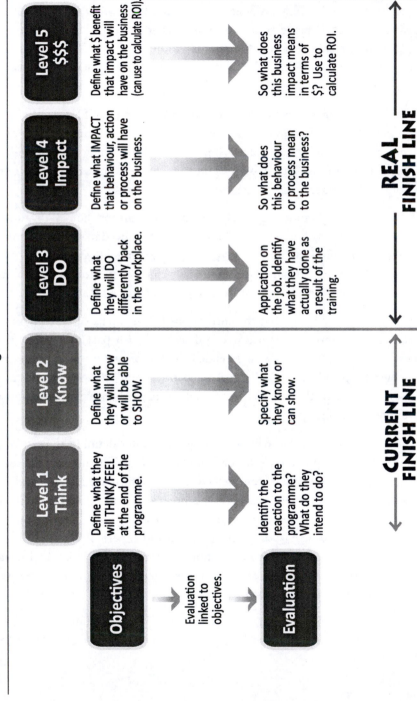

Summary of key points

- Transfer of learning is the missing link in learning and Turning Learning into Action® (TLA) is a proven learning transfer methodology that solves the problem.

- TLA is not complicated. It is an enhanced coaching methodology that facilitates transfer of learning through a series of specific, structured and accountable one-on-one conversations that occur at various intervals *after* the training event.

- In trials, TLA combined with training achieved 43.8 per cent uplift in sales. In another trial that involved 240 people in the UK and 400 people in Australia the programme achieved an NPS of 78 per cent and 73 per cent respectively. An NPS of 75 per cent to 80 per cent plus has generated world-class loyalty.

- Today TLA is being delivered in eight languages across the United States, Europe and Asia as well as in Australia and New Zealand. It is solving the transfer of learning challenge for businesses across multiple sectors including banking and finance, technology, construction and manufacturing.

- Businesses buy training because they want to see some sort of improvement in performance. As such they have a series of obstacles to surmount. Learning is the potential leverage point that will allow them to surmount those challenges and improve performance over the long term.

- Imagine this process as a pole vault. At the start of the run-up the athlete's pole is straight and taut. He then plants the pole into the ground; the pole bends and elevates the athlete upwards, over the bar. As the athlete clears the obstacle the pole straightens again and falls back to the ground. It has served its purpose and propelled the athlete over the bar and safely back down to the other side.

- Archimedes said, 'Give me a lever long enough and a fulcrum on which to place it, and I shall move the world.' Turning Learning into Action® provides that lever to ADDIE's fulcrum and together they can transform training effectiveness.

- Turning Learning into Action® is a practical methodology that puts reflection at the heart of the learning transfer process by facilitating specific, structured and accountable reflection through a series of one-on-one conversations after the training event.

- At some point we have to accept that successful training and learning is actually less about the learning and more about change. The most effective change methodology is one-on-one personal coaching. When conducted over a period of time coaching allows the individual to identify what it is they want to change and then helps them to hold *themselves* accountable to follow through on what they want to do.

- Self-administered individual accountability is critical for change and the very best way to achieve that is through enhanced coaching.

- Coaching, as most people recognize the term, is too fluid and flexible. As a result it works sometimes, for some people and not for others, and the people involved don't really understand why that is.

- With enhanced coaching there is a fine balance between flexibility and structure. It is this balance that creates the results and removes the ambiguity from the coaching process, which allows us to consistently deliver effective results regardless of the training or the participant.

- TLA is the application of enhanced coaching in a very tight niche – helping people transfer learning from training back into the workplace.

- The learning transfer road map is a visual representation of how to combine the ADDIE process, evaluation and learning transfer. It shows how each element fits into the learning process – before, during and after training – and how everyone must work together to focus on the real training finish line.

- TLA follows a three-stage process of preparation, action and evaluation.

- Knowledge and information become wisdom only once used and experienced in a real-world situation. Turning Learning into Action ® empowers the individual to take control of the learning process and increase their value and productivity for individual and collective success.

05
Preparation – setting expectations

The first stage of learning transfer is preparation and the creation of the TLA plan (Figure 5.1). However, before creating the TLA plan it is important to set the scene and set expectations so that participants know what to expect and understand what is going to happen and why. Once this is established they can begin to appreciate that training with TLA might be a little different from their experiences of training in the past.

FIGURE 5.1   Transition between the training event and TLA

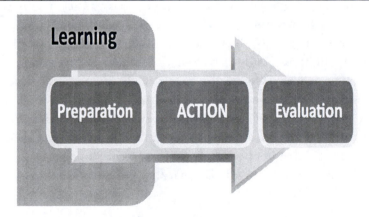

TLA can be delivered internally or externally depending on requirements. It is possible to either choose to recruit an external TLA specialist or have

key internal HR personnel and/or managers trained in the methodology. If the organization invests heavily in training then the latter option may be more cost-effective over time (we will explore the advantages and disadvantages of the delivery methods in Chapter 13).

Regardless of who is best placed to deliver TLA the process begins towards the end of the training event. The objective of preparation is to have all the participants create a TLA plan, which is covered in more detail in the next chapter. Almost everyone who has ever attended a training programme is probably already familiar with action plans and, as the saying goes, 'familiarity breeds contempt'. This is why adequate set-up is essential.

In order to ensure that participants take the creation of the TLA plan seriously they need to appreciate that what they are about to embark on is significantly different from what they have probably experienced in the past. If I were to ask 1,000 L&D professionals how to create an action plan most would know how to do it. But the *how* is not the problem. The real problem is ensuring that enough time is spent to allow participants to create a meaningful action plan at the training event and making sure that participants know how the action plan will be executed and followed-up on after the event.

When the trainer has created the course and feels pressured to pack the training with content to make sure the sponsor or client feels that they are getting good value for money, then it is only natural that they want to deliver all that content. In practice sessions the trainer may be confident that they have enough time to deliver the material over the course of two or three days. But, in reality, participants ask questions and get into discussions and if the course is content heavy it often runs over time. In this scenario the trainer must decide to cut back on content, reflection or planning. And faced with those choices the casualty is almost always reflection time or the action planning session. We have already discussed the squeeze on reflection time but that squeeze also means that 15 minutes before the course is due to end the trainer will suggest that everyone 'quickly fill out the action plan', or will tell the participants to complete the action plan themselves at home or when they are back at work. Even if the participants' intentions are good there is virtually no chance that they will complete the action plan themselves after the event.

This brings us to the second scenario – even if the trainer has managed to juggle the content delivery and still has time to go through the action plan, the plan is always viewed as the end of the course. By virtue of the fact that action plans are always completed towards the end of the programme, they become a finish point in themselves. Yet in reality the action plan is the starting point. The first part of the preparation is therefore to shift that momentum and energy around the action planning session.

Setting the scene for learning transfer

It is essential to set the scene and let participants know what to expect and why learning transfer is important. The leader or manager may recognize that the majority of training fails to deliver results and they may be troubled by it – but participants are not. Even the most committed and enthusiastic learner will rarely lose much sleep over the fact that they have forgotten most of the course within two weeks and have failed to use one single idea. Unfortunately, this is the norm.

When I run TLA programmes I always share the statistics on lost learning with the participants. When people understand that 80 per cent of all training is wasted they can at least appreciate why their employers need to address the issue. This information helps to put them at ease so that they don't feel they are being targeted or singled out in some way.

That said, change is often a daunting prospect so it is also essential that we let everyone know what they can expect from the process and from themselves. So I explain:

- the change process and what to expect;
- the need for the right attitude;
- the TLA learning agreement.

The change process and what to expect

One of the things that makes people uncomfortable about the change process is their fear or uncertainty about whether they are capable of the change required. As a result they can become resistant before the process even begins.

Part of the scene setting for learning transfer is therefore letting everyone on the training programme know about the change process. The process of successful change is well documented going back hundreds of years. Goethe stated: 'Progress has not followed a straight ascending line, but a spiral with rhythms of progress and retrogression, of evolution and dissolution.' Since then many change models have been proposed, for example from people such as Kurt Lewin and Elisabeth Kübler-Ross, who initially presented her model as the stages of grief but later expanded it to plot the process of all transition. Renowned behavioural scientists James Prochaska, John Norcross and Carlo DiClemente in their book *Changing for Good* (1998) also concur with Goethe. Having reviewed every major change methodology the authors concluded that behavioural change spirals through phases.

People can often feel as though they are making progress only to lapse or fall backwards. They will take two steps forward only to take three steps back. As a result many of the stages of change can appear remarkably like failure. When everyone understands that change is not linear and that lapses are the rule not the exception to the rule, then change becomes much less daunting.

Change can also feel uncomfortable. If I asked you to fold your arms you would do so immediately. You would fold your arms in exactly the way that you have always folded them for years. It probably feels familiar and comfortable and yet if I ask you to fold them the other way you may struggle. If you naturally tuck your right hand under the top of your left arm, with your left hand clutching the top of your right arm then asking you to reverse that will feel weird! So weird in fact that it may take you several moments to work out how to do it.

That is what change is like. It does feel weird at first, but if we persevere and don't expect perfection on the first day then it soon starts to feel more normal until the *new* behaviour becomes normal. Letting participants know what to expect from the change process can help to alleviate many of the feelings of uncertainly that push people back to old habits.

Recall Deci and Ryan's self-determination theory (STD) from Chapter 2, which gives us a more complete picture of human motivation. Intrinsic motivation is critical for lasting change because it means that the motivation to change comes from the individual making the change. This type of intrinsic motivation is always more effective than external reward or punishment and yet it relies on autonomy, competence and relatedness – all of which are challenged in the learning process. Understanding that feelings of uncertainty and discomfort are a normal and universally experienced part of the change process can alleviate the pressure from training participants to find their own pace and rhythm towards change. The fact is that everyone experiences the same or similar things when trying to change behaviour – and just knowing that fact can make a massive difference to our willingness and ability to persevere.

The need for the right attitude

On a very basic, fundamental level the distinction between how a child learns and how an adult learns goes to the very heart of why so much training is ineffective in the workplace.

When a child is learning to walk he or she will take two or three tentative steps before falling over and yet the parents are clapping and cheering as though it was the most amazing and exciting event in history. This can go on for weeks, sometimes months and the encouragement never wanes. The child is never made to feel foolish or that somehow their progress (or lack of it) is anything other than brilliant.

By the time we reach adulthood, however, things are very different. As adults we are so conditioned to be competent and so used to doing things well that we hate failure. As such we will do almost anything to avoid situations where failure is an option and, sadly, learning new information and skills is just such a situation.

We don't want to try, fall over and look stupid so often we won't even try. The child mentality understands the phrase, 'If at first you don't succeed, try, try and try again.' Whereas the adult mentality resonates more accurately with, 'If at first you don't succeed destroy all the evidence that you ever tried in the first place.'

It is this mindset difference that world renowned Stanford University psychologist Carol Dweck discusses in her book *Mindset: The new psychology of success – how we can learn to fulfill our potential* (2006). Dweck was 'obsessed with understanding how people cope with failures'. Her early research involved giving children a series of puzzles to solve. Immediately she was struck by the profound difference between how children view failure and how adults view failure. Dweck had expected to find some children who coped well with failure and some who didn't but what she found was that they simply didn't view failure in the same way as adults. They didn't consider that not being able to solve to puzzle *was* a failure, it was a challenge. They loved it. It was exciting and fun.

In her book Dweck proposes that it is our mindset that determines our ability to handle failure and learn. Everything in life comes down to mindset and from her research she proposes that there are only two – fixed and growth.

Those with a fixed mindset believe that their abilities, skills and talents are carved in stone at birth. These are the people who believe that 'you've either got it or you haven't'. For those individuals, people are either born with brains or musicality or sporting ability or they are not. Those with a fixed mindset believe therefore that IQ, skill or ability is down to the cards we are dealt at birth through environment or genetics. And if those cards end up being a pair of threes there is nothing much we can do about it. This mindset is extremely toxic because it sets up competition and forces the individual to constantly prove themselves worthy. As Dweck says: 'If you have only a certain amount of intelligence, a certain personality, and a certain moral character – well, then you'd better prove that you have a healthy dose of them. It simply wouldn't do to look or feel deficient in these most basic characteristics.'

The growth mindset on the other hand does not believe that our relative attributes are carved in stone. Instead those with a growth mindset believe that what we are born with is the starting point not the finish point and as such we can improve and enhance those attributes with effort, perseverance and practice. An individual with a growth mindset believes that their potential is unknown and the development of that potential is up to them.

All things being equal, we are all born with a growth mindset. Children don't have adult opinions, prejudgements or expectations. They instinctively know that learning is a natural part of life. They are not scared of it or threatened by it – especially in the really early years before adult cynicism has polluted the learning environment. Sadly we are trained in the fixed mindset from a very early age. We are praised for being smart (therefore not being smart is a sin), we are congratulated for winning and rarely for effort. Parents scream instructions and 'encouragement' from the sidelines of sports pitches the world over. We are encouraged not to make mistakes and we might get gold stars and smiley faces when we get things perfect first time. All of these messages slowly teach us that failure is unacceptable, until finally we wake up one day and we are an adult and we would rather risk mediocrity than try and fail. So we stop trying. We are paralysed by the need to maintain a facade of perfection, competence and expertise and as such we actively stop the learning process dead in its tracks.

Understanding the process of change and getting comfortable with the idea that training is not the end point but the start point can help participants to let go of the fixed mindset that guarantees poor transfer and instead foster a growth mindset. People need to appreciate that they will feel vulnerable but that the training will support them and provide a safe environment for them to test out their new skills – and learning transfer will help them to make the transition. Just knowing that no one is expecting instant perfection can allow people to relax and get the most from the training.

The TLA learning agreement

In the learning transfer preparation process all training participants are given a TLA learning agreement to sign, which further differentiates the TLA process from anything they may have previously experienced. I have included a sample TLA agreement in Appendix 1 and a blank version is available to download from the website **www.leverlearning.com/resources**.

Basically the agreement sets up the expectations of the coach–participant relationship. The agreement covers things such as:

- how the conversations will take place;
- confidentiality;
- how many conversations the participant can expect;
- how long each conversation will last;
- the optimum environment for that conversation;
- how the session will be documented;
- what the participant can expect from the coach and vice versa;
- signatures of the participant and the TLA specialist.

The learning agreement serves several purposes. It clarifies what the individual is signing up for and, therefore, further demonstrates that there may be something different about TLA. The participants, knowing that the action plan they will soon be asked to create will actually mean something and will be followed-up on in a very specific, structured and accountable way, are much more engaged in the creation of the TLA plan.

The learning agreement is a moral agreement regarding conduct, confidentiality and expectations for the sessions. When a participant knows that the TLA process will be confidential they begin to relax. The level of confidentiality varies depending on the programme, but even if the session actions are shared internally the detail of the sessions never are. When participants read how the sessions will take place, when they will take place and how long they will take, they get a better understanding of exactly what they are agreeing to. Usually the first TLA conversation will be scheduled to occur within two weeks of the training event so as to maintain momentum. The second conversation will take place three to four weeks after the first and the third three to four weeks after the second. Normally each TLA conversation will last 30 minutes.

Once the individual is told the details they can see that they will have ownership and control over the conversation because *they* will initiate the conversation to the TLA facilitator or coach. This is important so that the participant doesn't feel that the process is something that is *done to* them but rather something they control. The learning agreement also lays out the required environment for the conversation. Both the participant and the TLA specialist must be focused on the conversation, so that means no mobile phones, no e-mail and no multitasking. The participant must find a quiet place where he or she will not be disturbed for the duration of the conversation. When the individual also appreciates that it is their responsibility to document their own action points they are again reminded that they will own this process. And finally the expectations simply set some ground rules for the process so that the participant and the coach are on the same page.

There is considerable evidence that when someone consciously commits to a process and signs up to a code of conduct they are much more likely to follow through on that personal commitment.

Social scientists Delia Cioffi and Randy Garner conducted a very interesting social experiment when they solicited college students to volunteer for an education project to be carried out in local schools. Students were encouraged either actively to volunteer by filling out an 'opt-in' form or passively volunteer by not filling in an 'opt-out' form. Those who completed a form and actively volunteered kept their commitment 49 per cent of the time versus those who passively volunteered who only kept their commitment 17 per cent of the time. Of all the people who turned up as scheduled to help with the education programme 74 per cent had actively volunteered.

Reading the learning agreement and then committing to that agreement with a signature helps to hold everyone involved to a higher standard and emphasizes the seriousness of the process they are about to embark on.

At this early stage the TLA facilitator shouldn't worry too much about whether that commitment is genuine or not. People will only really buy-in to the process and the conversations when they start to see the benefits. Quite often people don't get the relevance or impact of learning transfer until they start to make changes and see the results.

Summary of key points

- The first stage of learning transfer is preparation and the creation of the TLA plan. However, before creating the TLA plan it is important to set the scene and set expectations so that participants know what to expect, and understand what is going to happen and why.

- TLA can be delivered internally or externally depending on requirements. It is possible to either recruit an external TLA specialist or have key internal HR personnel and/or managers trained in the methodology.

- Regardless of who delivers TLA the process begins towards the end of the training event. All training participants must understand why TLA is important.

- Participants need to appreciate that what they are about to embark on is significantly different from what they have probably experienced in the past so that they take the creation of the TLA plan seriously.

- It is important to shift the participant's perspective so they see that the action plan is the beginning of the next phase in learning transfer and behaviour change rather than seeing it as the end of the training.

- Change is often a daunting prospect so it is also essential to let everyone know what they can expect from the process and from themselves. The TLA facilitator needs to explain the change process and what to expect, the need for the right attitude and the TLA learning agreement.

- Understanding the process of change and getting comfortable with the idea that training is not the end point but the start point can help participants to let go of the unreasonable expectations and the fixed mindset that guarantees poor transfer and instead foster a growth mindset. People need to appreciate that they will feel vulnerable but that the training will support them and provide a safe environment for them to test out their new skills – and learning transfer will help them to make the transition.

- The learning agreement serves several purposes. It clarifies what the individual is signing up to and therefore further demonstrates that there may be something different about TLA. The participants, knowing that the action plan they will soon be asked to create will actually mean something and will be followed-up on in a very specific, structured and accountable way, are much more engaged in the creation of the TLA plan.

- At this early stage the TLA facilitator should not worry too much about whether that commitment is genuine or not. People will only really buy-in to the process and the conversations when they start to see the benefits. Quite often people don't get the relevance or impact of learning transfer until they start to make changes and see the results.

06
Preparation – creating the TLA plan

Everyone who has ever experienced corporate training will have come across the idea of an action plan at the end of a training programme. For most training participants the action plan is an afterthought and a sure indication that the training is almost over.

People are often cynical about action plans and perhaps for good reason. But they *are* an essential part of effective learning transfer. So we need to ensure that everyone in the training realizes that the TLA plan is different from anything they may have come across before. And the reason it is different is because their TLA plan will come to fruition through a series of specific, structured and accountable follow-up one-on-one conversations. The TLA plan is therefore the source document that will start the change process for each individual participant.

It is important to allow 45–60 minutes for the TLA planning session. Everyone in the room must have enough time to really engage with the process, this means that the creation of the TLA plan needs to happen towards the end of the training programme but not at the very end of it. There needs to be a clear distinction between the training event and the creation of the TLA plan so that participants can fully appreciate that it does not signify the end of the training but the beginning of the next stage of the training process – learning transfer. This is why TLA is often more effective when it is delivered by someone other than the original trainer. That other person can be an HR manager or L&D professional from within the business or equally it can be a trained TLA facilitator from outside the business. When the TLA facilitator is someone other than the original trainer then participants are better able to make a clear division between the training event and the follow-up transfer of learning process.

Each participant must complete a TLA plan, which includes:

- their target(s);
- what success looks like for them;
- calibration – where they consider themselves right now in relation to the target;
- why the target is important for them;
- their chosen next steps to achieve the target.

Target

The target is fairly straightforward and asks the participant to specify what they will implement from the programme and by when.

At the risk of stating the obvious, taking action from learning is not possible unless the participant pinpoints a target or outcome that they intend to achieve. Ideally the TLA plan should include three goals or targets.

The targets need to be realistic and achievable but also represent a bit of a stretch for the individual. If the target is too easy then there will be no impetus behind achieving it. If it's too hard then the individual will assume it is impossible from the start and won't even try.

The target is really about what the individual thinks will give them benefit back in the workplace. And sometimes that may have nothing to do with the training. It may well be that an individual who has been on a three-day sales training is sitting at lunch chatting with the other participants when the penny really drops. In a flash of inspiration he or she realizes that one of their main challenges at work is that people are always interrupting to ask questions and he or she can never get into a working rhythm. The target for this individual, therefore, may be to secure the use of the spare office every morning. Minimizing distractions becomes one of this person's targets and it doesn't matter if minimizing distractions was part of the training or not. Until the individual gets this distraction issue handled they won't be able to make any progress on the skills learnt in the training course anyway.

In this way the TLA plan is a personal and individual document and partici-pants need to be encouraged to view it as *their* personal success map. More often than not the targets will relate to the training but it is not essential. Often other issues are taking up an individual's head space and actively stopping them from making progress in any area, so dealing effectively with those issues first is just common sense. The participant already knows what is important to them and what is causing them problems and they know it far better than the TLA facilitator does – so acknowledge that and allow them to take ownership of the targets. Solving issues – even issues that have no obvious bearing on the training – will help individuals to do a better job and will ensure that they are then freed up to do other things on their TLA plan that may be more relevant to the training.

The other point regarding setting targets is that some people get really hung up on creating SMART goals – in other words they require that the individual makes their targets Specific, Measureable, Attainable, Realistic and Time bound. This might sound controversial but personally I would rather capture the essence and the calibration (more on that in a moment) of the goal at the training event and then probe more deeply in the follow-up conversa-tion. If an individual wants to create SMART targets and enjoys adding SMART detail to their targets they can but it's not necessary. If they don't enjoy it, making them adhere to SMART will simply drain all the energy and motivation from the process.

Success

In the success section participants are required to think about what their ideal future would be when they have implemented that target. How will they know when they have been successful in implementing this target? What will they see happening around them? What will people be saying about their new ability, skill or performance? How will they feel?

In success the participant is encouraged to use the various modalities to describe success. In other words get them to imagine what they would see, hear and feel so that they could get a full and rich impression of what success for them would be like. This acknowledges different learning styles and ensures that the participant taps into the most motivational modality for them.

Calibration

Calibration may not be as familiar as the other elements of the TLA plan. Calibration asks the participant to rate where they consider themselves against the target on a scale of 1 (low) to 10 (high) on each target they are implementing.

Calibration is particularly useful in the TLA plan when the training is focused on improving soft skills. For example, say there is a group of people who have just completed a leadership training programme. In order to work out if any progress is made over time we first have to establish a baseline for all the individual skills that make up a good leader. Without a tool such as calibration this can so easily get overly complicated.

Calibration is the perfect solution. When we ask a participant to rank their listening skills on a scale 1–10 they will invariably give an almost immediate response. They will automatically reflect on that question, think about their current experience, the outcome of events and situations that have already called on their listening skills and arrive at a number between 1 and 10. Their mind knows in that moment why they assigned a certain number. They may not always be able to articulate why they chose the number but on some level the individual was giving a measured, albeit unconscious or instinctive, response. It doesn't really matter how they arrived at that number or even if the coach thinks it is an accurate reflection of their current skill level. What matters is that the participant has graded themselves on that skill at the point of creating the TLA plan. This is now the benchmark on which to measure progress throughout the follow-up conversations.

Some people may argue that the measurement of the baseline needs to be much more scientific than calibration but I strongly disagree. If we spend too long trying to establish the baseline and getting too hung up on a formula or identifying some mystical metric all the excitement and impetus for change can drain away. If, on the other hand, we ask for the participant's gut instinct on where they are right now they will be able to answer in a matter of seconds. If they assign their current skill level at six – that's the baseline. They may tell the coach that they believe they can get that to a nine and will also probably be able to state how they envisage doing that. It doesn't matter what the metric was. And it doesn't even matter if they call it a six and the coach thinks they are probably more a three or an eight. What matters is that the individual assigned a starting place from which they and the TLA coach can measure subsequent progress.

In Malcolm Gladwell's book *Blink: The power of thinking without thinking* (2005) he presents a compelling case for paying more attention to this type of gut response or instinct. It is so often ignored in business because we cannot always explain it – and business demands explanations. There is a great story in *Blink* about billionaire investor George Soros. Apparently his son has said: 'My father will sit down and give you theories to explain why he does this and that but I remember seeing it as a kid. At least half of it is bull... the reason he changes his position is because his back starts killing him. He literally goes into spasm, and it's this early warning sign.'

There can be no doubt that George Soros is a smart guy who knows the markets, but imagine if he told his investors that the reason he changes position was because his back hurt! In the modern world those sorts of explanations are usually kept quiet because they seem too random and illogical. Instead we demand logic and numbers and solid plausibility, or at least understandable and logical explanations. And yet Gladwell presents case after case for why we should pay more attention to our initial response.

This instinctive insight is known as 'thin-slicing' and refers to the ability of our unconscious mind to find patterns in situations and behaviour based on a very narrow slice of experience. When I ask clients to calibrate their current skill level on a score of 1–10 they will instinctively thin-slice their knowledge and experience and arrive at a number. And this inner knowledge and intuition is hugely undervalued and underutilized in the modern world – even though there is a solid argument that we need to use it more not less. American author and futurist John Naisbitt reminded us of this when he said: 'Intuition becomes increasingly valuable in the new information society precisely because there is so much data. Unless we learn to trust our first response we are in danger of suffering from increasingly bad cases of analysis paralysis' (Naisbitt *et al*, 2001).

Calibration is about trusting that first response so we can get into action and not get bogged down with analysis paralysis. It is a really easy and powerful way to establish a baseline for the objective. If someone identifies their current leadership skills at a score of six and feels that it is possible to achieve a nine, then that is the objective and they have identified the gap between where they are now and where they want to be. Closing this gap will therefore be the focus of the follow-up conversations.

Why

The 'why' of the TLA plan encourages the individual to really engage with the target and their vision of success so that they connect to the motivation behind that target. This part of the TLA plan asks: 1) Why do you want to achieve this? 2) What does it mean to you personally? 3) Why is that important to you?

German philosopher Friedrich Nietzsche once said: 'He who has a "why" to live for can bear with almost any how.' Austrian neurologist and psychiatrist Victor Frankl, a Nazi concentration camp survivor, agreed in his classic book *Man's Search for Meaning*, stating: 'A man who becomes conscious of the responsibility he bears toward a human being who affectionately waits for him, or to an unfinished work, will never be able to throw away his life. He knows the "why" for his existence, and will be able to bear almost any "how"' (1959).

This idea of tapping into the 'why' behind goals and targets is a familiar one in modern personal development but its poignancy and power is best expressed by Frankl who endured unspeakable horror during the Holocaust and not only survived, but went on to create a form of existential analysis called logotherapy. He believed, and was living proof of his belief, that when people can tap into a deeper and more powerful meaning and purpose behind their existence and their aspirations they also tap into strength of character that will help them get over the inevitable bumps in the road towards that destination. Nothing is achieved without effort and, regardless of the target, everyone experiences setbacks and challenges. Without a big enough 'why' and an appreciation of that why it becomes too easy to give up and move on to a new target.

Identifying the 'why' in the TLA plan is a very personal issue. The TLA plan is a very personal document and it details why something is important to the individual creating the plan, not necessarily why something is important to the business or the boss or department. It is the individual's own 'why' that is critical and it is this motivation that will keep the person on track.

One of the simplest ways to uncover the 'why' is to drive the target to a higher meaning. Whatever target or goal the individual has chosen, simply get them to ask themselves one question over and over again – 'And why is that important to you?' Often when we are setting a goal it is not the goal itself that will keep us moving forward it is the 'why' behind the goal. It is important to be consciously aware of this 'why' so that the individual is able to reconnect to that reason when motivation starts to wane. Asking the 'why' question can be very powerful and can help the individual create meaning in anything they do. In fact, some suggest that if we ask the question layer upon layer we will eventually come to a life purpose.

As an example, imagine a person has attended a sales training programme and their goal is to build better rapport with customers. When completing an action plan the facilitator would get the participant to answer the question:

Q: Why is that important to you?

A: Building better rapport will help me make more sales.

Q: Why is that important to you?

A: If I make more sales I will make more money.

Q: Why is that important to you?

A: I will be able to take my family on a holiday overseas.

Q: Why is that important to you?

A: Because I really want to spend quality time with my family in a great location that they will remember.

Q: Why is that important to you?

A: I want to connect with and inspire my family.

Q: Why is that important to you?

A: I want to positively influence my children and leave a legacy.

By repeatedly asking the 'why' question the purpose transforms from making more money to connecting and influencing the participant's family. There is no right or wrong answer; it is just a simple method to help the individual to connect to what is genuinely and uniquely important to them. This process usually also highlights a person's beliefs and values, which can be very helpful during the coaching process.

I'm not suggesting that TLA plans should become some esoteric pursuit of life purpose, simply that if the participants are encouraged to really engage with the plan they are creating and personalize it to their own hopes and dreams, not the company's hopes and dreams, then there is a far better chance of keeping that person engaged in the change process once they are back in the workplace.

Change is a personal journey; for someone to want to take that journey and stay focused on the destination they have to have a personal reward. Only when a training participant can genuinely see the personal advantages of embracing the training and making changes will they engage with the process. And, by the way, the 'why' doesn't have to have anything to do with the training!

We stress during the action planning process that it is important that the participant creates a TLA plan that is important to them and not merely what they think the trainer or their manager would want them to write. The higher the level of ownership of the goal the greater the likelihood of change and forward momentum. This also presupposes that the participant really is the expert in their own business, job and life and they *will* know best what they want to achieve from the programme. Even if they are wrong they will discover that themselves and, as a result, be much more involved and engaged in the process. No one likes to be told what to do so it is far more beneficial to assume that each participant is best suited to identify the biggest win or the best outcomes for their own situation. Sometimes a goal that is not directly related to the programme will give the participant the biggest benefit. Frequently these goals might be around time management, getting organized, being more efficient, being less stressed, or sometimes they are around work–life balance. Typically it is only one of the three goals that might be of a 'training' topic and I encourage everyone to be supportive of any goals even if they don't appear directly relevant to the training. If someone wants work–life balance and the TLA coach helps them to achieve that then their productivity will often go up in all areas, likewise with time management. Follow-up around time management is particularly effective as it is such an ingrained behaviour. I often say there is no such thing as time management, as no one to date has managed to change the speed at which the world spins round the sun, but we can all improve our self-management – how we manage ourselves during the time we have available. Often working on time management will assist in the achievement of all other goals.

In one TLA plan the participant highlighted that he wanted to reduce his stress levels. By helping him to manage that, even though it had nothing to do with the training, he increased his sales because he began to enjoy making the follow-up calls rather than feeling the pressure of it as something that must be done. A simple shift in mindset and behaviour made all the difference.

Next steps

Again, most people who have ever completed an action plan in the past will be familiar with the 'next steps' section. This part of the TLA plan seeks to establish what action the person can take within the next 48 hours towards their target.

It is important for the momentum of the training that individuals take their first next step soon after the end of the training event, otherwise the chances of them acting on the training diminishes with the passage of time. Engaging the participants in what they plan to do next and what they will do before the first follow-up conversation ensures that they stay in motion towards the target. Without identifying next steps, inertia will set in and nothing will ever get done.

Author and psychologist Professor Richard Wiseman conducted two large-scale studies into the psychology of motivation involving 5,000 participants from around the world. Participants were tracked for between six months and a year as they attempted to achieve a wide range of goals varying from a career change to weight loss. By the end of the experiment only 10 per cent had achieved what they set out to achieve. Of those 10 per cent all broke down their aspiration or goal into a series of sub-goals and next steps so as to create a step-by-step process. This acted as a road map for the journey towards change, whilst also helping to remove the fear and hesitation often felt when making change. Next steps are about making that initial often tentative step towards change. Getting into action is the key; even if that action is small it starts the process of change and gathers momentum. Wiseman also found that the successful people in the study stayed focused on the benefits that they would gain from making the change; they told other people about their aspirations and their goals were concrete, specific, and time-bound and documented in writing.

A sample TLA plan can be found in Appendix 2 and a blank form can be downloaded from our website: **www.leverlearning.com/resources**. Creating the TLA plan is the first part of the transfer of learning process. As such it must be treated with respect and individuals must be allowed enough time to complete the plan properly, while they still have enough energy and enthusiasm to do it justice. The participants must realize that this document will form the template for the coming weeks – and the targets they identify will come to fruition.

As we mentioned in the section about learning agreements, don't worry about commitment. In most cases when individuals first come across TLA they are often cynical about training and the use of action plans. It doesn't matter. Just focus on making sure everyone leaves the programme with a detailed TLA plan. Commitment level only really shifts when they experience firsthand how useful the process is and how it does actually help *them* to achieve *their* goals.

At the end of a long training programme the participants might be mentally tired and have had the neural pathways so stretched that they can no longer think straight. Once I attended a four-day training programme and I was so frazzled by the end of it that on the way home I drove the wrong way around a roundabout. Often participants will want to use weariness as a reason *not* to complete an action plan – but don't allow it.

If participants leave the training venue without completing their TLA plan it will usually turn into a struggle to get it completed. We once had a participant join a TLA programme who had not been at the set-up at the end of the course as he'd had to be in a client meeting. The communication trail illustrated that it took nine e-mails and three telephone calls to chase down his TLA plan. This is not practical with one person – never mind a dozen or more.

As a result it is essential to get the TLA plan before participants leave. And it is not only for logistical reasons to secure the plan while people are still at the programme. When participants are told that their TLA plan will be photocopied at the end of the session they immediately know that it's not something that can be fudged or put off until another day. For those who are struggling or looking blankly at their paper I always go and talk to them one-on-one about what they think should go on the plan. Some people find it easier to verbalize things than to write, so talking it through can help to get them started. For people who feel they need more time to complete it or need to go away and think about it I explain to them that once they get back to their desk it won't be as powerful because they will be back in the day-to-day activity of work. With the new outlook from the training programme it is better to see what needs to be done from that new perspective rather than get bogged down by the old perspective back at work. Training gives us a sense of change and a sense of what is possible without the constraints of what is easy to implement. It is important to capture this optimistic possibility and work towards that before the participants physically leave the learning environment.

If participants are still hesitant I let them know that they can change their TLA plan after the course. Once they know they have some flexibility, and that what they write today is not set in concrete, the last remaining resistance usually evaporates. Knowing that they are not 100 per cent committed to what they write on the action plan is often enough to get the creative juices flowing and for them to complete the plan. Ironically I don't think that anyone who has resisted the action planning process has ever come back to me to change it at a later date – they just needed to know that they could if they wanted to.

If there is resistance to the follow-up process rather than resistance to completing the action plan I will sometimes get the participant to agree to a first session, with the proviso that if by the end of the conversation they don't feel the session has been a good use of their time then they don't have to carry on with the process. If people don't want to have the follow-up conversation the level of change is lower than someone who does – often giving them the choice can help to break down resistance.

Once everyone has completed their TLA plan, the plans need to be recorded and distributed. How this is done and who receives the TLA plans will depend on each situation and the confidentiality that has been agreed within the process. As a minimum I photocopy them on the spot, giving the originals back to the participant and keeping the copy. If a photocopier isn't close by the facilitator can take a smartphone photograph, or a scan on a tablet will do the job too.

At the end of the training programme all participants must also have confirmed a definite time and date for their first follow-up conversation. Where possible, it is always best if the participant chooses their preferred time and date as this improves buy-in and ownership. This can be achieved through one-on-one discussion between the facilitator and the participant, or the facilitator could make a variety of dates and times available and each participant chooses their preferred slot. Flip charts on the wall with various available timeslots can also work well for this.

By the time that the training participants leave the training programme they should have a copy of their signed learning agreement, their completed TLA plan and a confirmed time for their first follow-up conversation.

Summary of key points

- Everyone who has ever experienced corporate training will have come across the idea of an action plan at the end of a training programme. For most training participants the action plan is an afterthought and a sure indication that the training is almost over.

- People are often cynical about action plans and perhaps for good reason. But they *are* an essential part of effective learning transfer. The TLA plan is therefore the source document that will start the change process for each individual participant.

- It is important to allow 45–60 minutes for the TLA planning session. Everyone in the room must have enough time to really engage with the process, this means that the creation of the TLA plan needs to happen towards the end of the training programme but not at the very end of it.

- There needs to be a clear distinction between the training event and the creation of the TLA plan so that participants can fully appreciate that it does not signify the end of the training but the beginning of the next stage of the training process – learning transfer.

- Each participant must complete a TLA plan, which includes their target(s), what success looks like for them, calibration or where they consider themselves to be in relation to the target, why the target is important to them and their chosen next steps to achieve the target.

- Don't worry about commitment. It doesn't matter. Just focus on making sure everyone leaves the programme with a detailed TLA plan. Commitment level only really shifts when they experience firsthand how useful the process is and how it does actually help *them* to achieve *their* goals.

- By the time the training participants leave the training programme they should have a copy of their signed learning agreement, their completed TLA plan and a confirmed time for their first follow-up conversation.

07
Action – the ACTION Conversation model and how to use it

The next stage of the TLA process is action. This is where the follow-up conversations actually take place over a period of several weeks following the training event. This is the actual process that will move a participant from A to B; it is about questioning and getting the individual to take ownership for the changes they are going to make.

Before I explain more about the conversations and how to keep individuals on track and engaged in the achievement of their targets it is important to cover the TLA ACTION Conversation model (Figure 7.1), which is the theory and the framework behind what occurs in those conversations.

The ACTION Conversation model expresses the interplay between structure and flexibility that I first introduced at the start of Part Two. It is this balance between structure and flexibility that creates enhanced coaching and differentiates TLA from traditional coaching. If we think of any accomplishment in life there is always interplay between balance and flexibility. We may go to the theatre and be awestruck at the fluidity and elegance of a dance company, at their flexibility and creativity, which to us seems so effortless and majestic.

FIGURE 7.1   The TLA ACTION Conversation model

ACCOUNTABILITY

CALIBRATION

TARGET

INFORMATION

OPTIONS

NEXT STEPS

But that beauty and elegance took structure and discipline to create. Hours of structured practice created the framework for that flexible creativity to flourish. The same can be seen in art, sport – you name it: everything of worth is created through a delicate balance between structure and flexibility. And behavioural change is no different.

The ACTION Conversation model is an acronym for the various stages that the conversation must pass through in order successfully to facilitate transfer of learning and behaviour change back in the workplace:

A   Accountability: setting up the context of the process and the coach/participant relationship.

C   Calibration: calibrating a score for where the individual is now, and the score for where they want to get to.

T   Target: where is the individual trying to get to? What is the target for the session?

I   Information: gather information about what is happening in the workplace.

O   Option: what options does the individual have in this situation? What could they do?

N   Next steps: how is the individual going to commit to action and move towards the target? How do the coach and individual follow this up?

The TLA conversation travels through a process of structure – flexibility – structure (Figure 7.2).

FIGURE 7.2   The interplay of structure and flexibility within the ACTION model

Structure – start

Structure is made up of accountability and calibration and it is these elements that give the conversation a structure and context. Without this formality the conversation will be too flexible and easily disappear into a pleasant daydream of what might be rather than a committed conversation about action, accountability and outcome.

Enhanced coaching avoids these pitfalls. The reason TLA is so effective is because every conversation opens *and* closes with structure in the form of accountability and calibration.

Accountability

Accountability is set up from the start and begins in the scene-setting part of preparation. Participants will be reminded of their responsibilities to the process and how they are ultimately accountable for their own success. This accountability will then be reiterated at the start of the first conversation and every conversation after that.

Accountability is, however, a two-way process. The facilitator of TLA is also accountable to the individual. It is imperative that the facilitator manages the conversation from the start and manages the individual's expectations about what is about to occur. This exchange of information is really important for several reasons. First, it sets the individual's mind at ease about what is to come; second, it affirms to the individual that there is a process that is being followed to maximize results.

Imagine for a moment that you were going for a routine eye operation. You arrive at the clinic and no one tells you anything about what to expect – would you feel more nervous or less nervous? The chances are that this lack of information would add to your discomfort about the procedure, especially if you had never undergone the procedure before. If, on the other hand, a friendly nurse met you on arrival, sat you down and said: 'The procedure will take about 10 minutes to complete. It will not be painful although some clients feel a tingling sensation. Once it's complete we will give you a cup of tea and after 10 minutes of resting we'll check that everything is OK and you will be free to leave' – then your nervousness should lessen. Knowing what to expect always reduces uncertainty. People feel more in control and are therefore much more receptive to the process.

Plus, knowing that there *is* actually a process and that the conversation isn't just an exchange of pleasantries also serves to focus the other person's attention and ensure that the conversation covers everything necessary in the allocated time.

At the start of the conversation the TLA facilitator needs to cover the following set points:

1 Provide positive reinforcement if the conversation started on time.
2 Check in with the individual. The coach might ask: 'How was your morning/afternoon so far?'
3 Use the phrase 'You'll remember...' to remind the individual what was covered at the end of the training or previous conversation.
4 Tell the individual how long the conversation will last.
5 Reiterate that the conversation is confidential.
6 Remind the individual that they are encouraged to give feedback.
7 Remind the individual about the best use of time for both parties.
8 Ask their permission to manage the conversation.
9 Ask for ownership from them.
10 Remind them that they need to take their own notes and have their TLA plan handy.

11 Ask questions of the participant to establish the context for the conversation.

12 Ask: 'Are there any questions before we start?'

13 Close out this opening section by adding: 'Great! Let's start with your action plan. Which goal would you like us to begin with today?'

We will cover who is best suited to roll out TLA in Chapter 12, but the level of confidentiality in the conversation will depend on whether the TLA is being facilitated by an internal specialist within the business or an external coach.

EXAMPLE OF THE STRUCTURED START OF THE CONVERSATION

'Hi John – thanks for calling through on time. Really appreciated – it makes my day run smoothly.' [1]

'So tell me – how have you been since the training course?' [2]

'Well, John, you'll remember from the briefing at the end of the training course that today's conversation is about helping you get the most from the training experience and to use your TLA plan as a base for our work.' [3]

'The conversation will last around 30 minutes and I want you to be comfortable that everything we cover is confidential and the only feedback that goes to your company is what you choose to relay at the end of the coaching process in your feedback form.' [4, 5, 6]

'So we can make the best use of your time during our conversation – if I feel we either need to go into a little bit more detail or take a bigger picture view if I could have your permission to give you a heads up on this that would be great. Equally, if as we are going through the conversation you think this isn't something that is relevant or useful to you then you can let me know and between us we will make sure that we make the best use of our time.' [7, 8]

'Just to be clear on the process, coaching is a discussion-based process where we have a conversation – we get clear on where you are now, where you want to get to and then we work together to assist you in moving forward to bridge the gap between the two. It's not about me telling you what to do because you are the expert in your life and your position at work, but we may brainstorm ideas and share experiences to help you come up with next steps that work for you.' [9]

'One final bit of admin John – we'll be using your TLA plan as a base but you might want to take some notes during the conversation. Have you got a pen, paper and your TLA plan handy? If you need me to slow down or recap so you can jot down the things that are important to you then just let me know.' [10]

'Okay – one of the things that helps me get my head into your space is to have a bit of understanding about you. If you could tell me a little bit about your role, how long you've been with your company and how many people you have on your team that would be great. So do you want to tell me a little bit about yourself...' [11]

'Excellent – that helps put your TLA plan in the context of you. Thank you. Now the admin is all done. Before we start do you have any questions about me or the follow-up?' [12]

'Let's begin...

'I've got your TLA plan in front of me here and you've highlighted three areas that you want to work on. We'll take these one at a time. So which one would you like us to start on today?' [13]

The outline above is for the first TLA conversation after the training event. The subsequent calls have a similar level of structure at the start of the conversation, with more emphasis on accountability for the agreed actions from the previous conversation. This level of accountability is essential to the success of the process.

At the start of the second and third TLA conversations the facilitator needs to:

1 Welcome the participant.

2 Set the scene for today's conversation.

3 Check on progress.

4 Identify what 'gap' or performance improvement area the participant wants to address in today's conversation.

This reminds the participant of the process, how it works, and allows him or her to get excited about what they have achieved so far – or to show their disappointment if they haven't gained any traction. Either way, the emotion will spur them forward.

EXAMPLE OF WHAT THE COACH MIGHT SAY

'How has your day been so far?' / 'Are you having a good start to the day?' [1]

'So today what would be great is if we talk through the specific actions that you and I generated last time and get a recap on the progress of those, then we will go back to the original action plan and review where that leaves us and then we will decide what we want to use our time for today. Is that OK with you?' [2]

'So, the actions from last time were... Do you want to give me an update?' [3]

If achieved: 'Great – well done – it sounds like you've made some good progress' If not achieved: 'Is that something that is still important to you?' (It is important that the TLA coach verifies what they are being told, but we will cover more on how to handle what happens if people haven't followed through on their commitments in Chapter 11.)

'OK great, so what would you like to focus on today?' [4]

Calibration

Remember, calibration is about measuring progress in a meaningful way to the participant and it is a crucial part of the TLA process that acts as the intersection between the structured part of the conversation and the flexible part of the conversation. A skilled coach will use calibration repeatedly during the TLA process.

At the end of the course the participant will have scored their current ability against their chosen targets. At the start of each subsequent TLA conversation the participant will be asked to calibrate their new score. Once a goal for the conversation or sessions is established the coach will use calibration to ascertain a start point so that progress or otherwise can be assessed. This might include asking the participant questions such as:

- 'You were at a score of two at the end of the course. Where do you think you are now?'
- 'What are you doing differently to achieve this change?'
- 'What is the maximum score you think you can get to on this within three months?'
- 'Let's focus our conversation today on closing that gap. Do you agree?'

Before starting to work on a particular goal, as a minimum the TLA coach needs to check in with the individual to calibrate their own position so as to establish where they consider they have moved to since the course or previous conversation.

Imagine someone has been on a time management programme in an effort to prioritize their workload more efficiently. At the end of the training event they identified their current time management skills as a '2' on a scale of 1 (low) to 10 (high). The TLA coach has no way of knowing if that number is accurate or not, but it doesn't matter. What matters is that the participant has assigned a starting point or their position 'A' and identified a target point or position 'B' that they are going to use the TLA conversations to achieve. At the start of the first conversation, which is typically two to three weeks after the training event, the participant will then be asked to calibrate their time management skills. At this stage they may indicate an improvement from '2' to '4'. The coach can then ask the participant what number they want to get their time management skills up to in a three-month period.

The coach's job on that initial TLA conversation and all subsequent conversations is to work out the difference between their current calibrated score and their destination score and help that individual to identify how they can move forward. In effect, the coach is helping to close an arbitrary but very real gap that the person has assigned in their head. The uniquely powerful thing about calibration is that there is no right or wrong answer. The human brain, when asked to calibrate a score for anything, will automatically provide a number even if the person assigning the number doesn't really know why they have chosen that particular number (we talked about some of the reasons for this earlier in the action planning section). In the international best-seller *Thinking, Fast and Slow* (2011) the Nobel prize-winning author Daniel Kahneman discussed the two systems of the brain that he called System 1 and System 2. According to Kahneman, 'System 1 operates automatically and quickly, with little or no effort and no sense of voluntary control' whereas 'System 2 allocates attention to the effortful mental activities that demand it, including complex computations.'

It is System 1 that is providing the number when asked to calibrate a current skill level. Or, as Kahneman writes: 'Whether you state them or not, you often have answers to questions that you do not completely understand, relying on evidence that you can neither explain nor defend.'

The job of the TLA specialist is to help the person being coached to use the TLA process to work out why they assigned that number and what needs to happen to move from 'A' to 'B'. Just think about this for a moment: if you were to ask your friend to calibrate the current health of their marriage on a scale of 1–10 they would give you a number in a few moments. That single digit will tell you and your friend more about the health of his or her relationship than three hours of talking. And that is the beauty of calibration. It allows an individual to immediately put a stake in the ground and get a remarkably clear indication of where they are and how far away they are from their own ideal.

Calibration is also a lot more accurate and a lot quicker than trying to establish some definitive logical benchmark. Plus it naturally removes or limits emotional justifications and excuses so that the coach can get on with the job of assisting change.

This structured opening to the conversation using accountability and calibration allows the TLA facilitator to set the scene and take control. It makes the client feel safe because they know what to expect and it reiterates that they are in a 'proper' process not just a casual conversation. It also puts a stake in the ground regarding what is to be focused on in the conversation and calibration allows both parties easily to measure progress towards that goal.

Flexibility – middle

The middle of the ACTION Conversation model is the flexibility of the traditional coaching conversation (Figure 7.3 and Figure 7.4).

In the model I refer to these parts as:

T – Target

I – Information

O – Options

N – Next steps

When it comes to coaching, it is extremely important to navigate the participant through this four-part process so as to get them to take action on their agreed next steps and move them through their action plan. Take time to work through the detail mentioned in Figure 7.4 to understand the flow of the conversation. Whilst useful, I believe the effectiveness of this four-part

FIGURE 7.3   The flexiblity within the TLA conversation

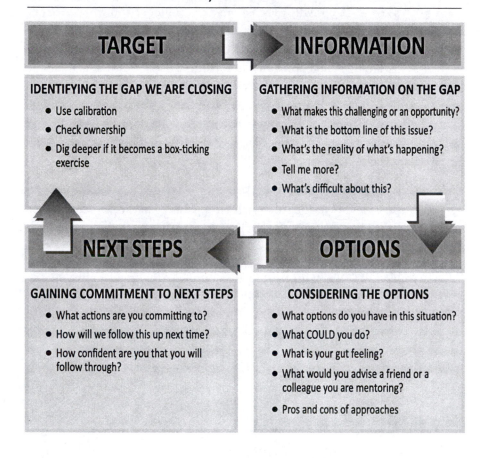

process can be transformed if we wrap up the flexibility in structure so as to create enhanced coaching. Enhanced coaching is the only way to deliver TLA effectively. Everyone is busy and neither the coach nor the person being coached has time to explore every esoteric notion that floats past their consciousness. Time is money and TLA acknowledges that. That is why the conversations are delivered in 30-minute blocks. There is no time or space for meandering and navel-gazing in a TLA conversation; instead it is a very deliberate and action-focused discussion. And that can be very different from a traditional coaching conversation.

For a worked example of the flexible process that the TLA facilitator goes through with the participant see Appendix 3. This illustrates the flow through the different stages of the process and how important it is for the coach to find out which action point(s) the participant considers most difficult so that the coach can really add value. Spending all the time during the conversation

FIGURE 7.4   Detailed breakdown of the flexibility within the TLA conversation

TARGET → INFORMATION

Identify the gap we are closing?

- Where would you like to start the action plan?
- Where are you now with the calibration?
- Where do you want to get to on a scale of 1 to 10?
- If we were taking it up to the next level – for example to a 7 – what would the difference be?
- Imagine you are a world leader in this field – what would best practice and a 10 look like?
- What do you think they would be doing differently to what you are doing now?
- If one of the trainers from the course were work shadowing you for the last two weeks specifically looking at that point – what would be the three things they would say you have been doing well? What would they say you could have been doing differently?

Gather information and get details of the gap and ownership?

- What did you learn on the course that is relevant to you in this situation?
- Which parts of this are working well?
- What parts of this have worked well in the past?
- How have you checked out if that's true?
- What other factors are relevant?
- In the past, was it the idea that was wrong or the implementation?
- What's the bottom line of the situation?
- What's not easy about the situation?
- What's the most challenging part of what you're trying to do?
- Tell me more about that?

NEXT STEPS ← OPTIONS

What are you going to commit to doing? How will we follow this up?

- Given all the ideas we have discussed which one feels best to you?
- What will you do and by when?
- What are you taking away from our conversation today?
- What are you going to do differently before we next speak?
- What is/are the next step or steps?
- Precisely when will you do them?
- How are you going to know if you are successful?
- What might get in the way?
- Can you foresee any challenges?
- How are you going to ensure you follow through?
- What support do you need?
- How will we know if you have been successful?
- How can you measure it?

What options do you have in this situation? What COULD you do?

- What are the alternatives?
- What are the first three ideas that come to mind for you?
- What are the possible ways to move forward, not what you will do, but what you could do?
- How could you move forward on this?
- What could you do differently to get a better result?
- Who might be able to help?
- What are the benefits and pitfalls of doing this?
- Which of these do you like the most?
- Of these, which are of interest to you?
- What other angles can you think of?
- What is just one more possibility?
- If you were advising a friend in your situation, what would you say to them?
- What other options are there?

talking through what he or she already knows is not going to add value. The coach should, of course, congratulate the participant for having grasped the content of the course so well and for having hit the ground running after the course, but the facilitator needs to encourage the participant to focus on the most challenging aspect of the TLA plan so they are supported through that change and experience the biggest win possible.

Due to the inherent flexibility in this part of the conversation it is impractical to provide several transcripts of possible conversations in the book, but audio samples of TLA conversations are also available at **www.leverlearning.com/ resources**.

Structure – end

All TLA conversations must close with structure, again to reiterate accountability, set the target for the next session and recalibrate skill level. The individual must leave the conversation knowing when the next conversation will take place and what they have agreed to work on before that next conversation.

Accountability

Part of the coach's role regarding their accountability to the process is how they effectively bring the conversation to a close so as to always honour the allocated time frame. This also builds credibility and helps the person being coached to relax into the process knowing that the process will never run over time and that the participant will never be asked for more than their allocated time. This means the coach must honour the structure, move the conversation along when necessary and avoid navel-gazing. Although this is a process of supported reflection it is a very structured type of reflection. Part of the skill of TLA is to ask a lot of open questions to encourage the person to talk, but when it is within five minutes of the end of the conversation the TLA coach should switch to closed questions to bring the conversation to a natural end.

So rather than asking, 'What else do we need to go through today so you can go away and be successful?' the coach might ask, 'Is there anything else we need to go through today that will enable you to go away and be successful?' I can almost guarantee that people will say 'No', which gives them ownership of the process and lets them feel as though *they* are winding up rather than feeling they have run out of time or been cut short.

If the person is a real talker, the coach can inform the person when there is 10 minutes to go. So the coach might say, 'John, we're two-thirds through the conversation today and I just want to make sure we make good use of our time. What do we need to cover in the remaining minutes?'

What that does is signal to the individual that there is only a set time left. The TLA coach cannot shy away from imposing the necessary structure. It is their job to make sure that the conversation stays on track and finishes on time.

It is also wise for the coach to get into the habit of using calibration to gauge commitment to what has been discussed in the conversation. Asking the person to rate their confidence level regarding what has been discussed allows the coach to establish how confident the individual feels about their ability to follow through on the action steps they identified. The coach might ask, for example: 'On a scale of 1–10, 1 being not confident at all and 10 being completely confident, how confident are you that you will follow through in the actions you've committed to today?' If the participant says '7' then the coach can ask them what needs to happen to get that confidence level up to an '8' or a '9' – which they will invariably know. If they answer '2' then obviously there is a problem and it needs to be addressed before the end of the conversation.

At the end of the conversation the coach needs to:

1 Recap on what has been covered.

2 Ensure that both the TLA coach and the individual being coached are clear on what the next steps and actions are.

3 Get commitment to those actions (usually before the conversation has finished).

4 Assess their likelihood of follow-through by asking the individual to calibrate their confidence level in achieving those next steps.

5 Set the time for the next conversation (for some programmes this will be prearranged).

6 Leave the client feeling clear and excited about the next steps.

7 Have clear notes that can be used to guide the next session.

EXAMPLE OF THE STRUCTURED END OF THE CONVERSATION

So, John, tell me – what are you taking away from our conversation today? [1]

And what are the actions you are going to take? What specifically are you going to do differently as a result of our conversation today? [2, 3]

When we next speak we will review how you've got on with your actions and then start moving forward with your next goal. Is that okay?

All that is left now is to arrange when we are next going to speak. Let's look at diaries. [4]

Good stuff – so you will call me on [insert telephone number] at [time] on [date] – is that locked away in your diary? [5]

Excellent. You've made great progress and have a clear plan for your next steps – congratulations! Have a good couple of weeks, John, and good luck with your new action. Enjoy it. [6]

Bye.

As always, the TLA facilitator must take control of the process and finish in a professional way. Plus it is very important to leave the individual feeling inspired and positive about the changes they have made and what is possible in their future.

Documentation and distribution

Although the coach will always take notes during the conversation it is important that they encourage the individual to take their own notes as this helps the individual to take more ownership of the process.

When I am having a TLA conversation I take around eight pages of A4 notes as it helps me to summarize and manage the conversation. I simply put an asterisk against the actions as they arise in the conversation so that I can easily find them again when the client is recapping on what they have agreed to do. One of my most senior coaches, Maree, makes very different notes. She tends to take down main points and themes as she goes along as well as any specific information such as figures, dates or names so that she doesn't forget them. She also notes down actions as they are stated so that she captures the wording as the participant says it – her notes are generally one page in total. Once the conversation has finished Maree takes a moment to go back over the discussion in her own mind and add notes on any observations and thoughts that come up for her. For example, she may note that the individual talked frequently about lacking confidence, or that there was a very brief reference to wanting to be more focused, or there was a reluctance to discuss a certain topic etc. She also flags any ideas, themes, trends and questions that she considers may be worth exploring in the next conversation.

Each coach is different and needs to find a documentation process or system that works for them and allows them to give their client their full attention whilst also being able to clearly recap on the session. When the individual tells the coach the three or four things that he or she will be focusing on before the next conversation it is important that the coach already has those things highlighted in their notes too. If a client misses out an action, either accidentally or deliberately, the coach is then able to remind them about that missed item, which also affirms that both parties are fully engaged in the process. The coach might want to check in during the conversation to make sure their client is jotting down notes as the conversation progresses as this is really important for their ownership of the process. So if the individual states a task or action he or she is going to progress before the next conversation the coach might say, 'That's a great idea, have you jotted that down? Because we'll be checking in against that point next time and I need you to be ready with your feedback.'

The coach must always finish the notes with a bullet-point list of the three or four points that the individual has committed to action. Ideally these should be recorded in the client's own words, as this will be more meaningful to the individual.

Due to the expansion of the TLA methodology we now have an online system where the coach inputs the three or four action points for each conversation, which is then e-mailed to the individual as a record of the agreed actions. Where appropriate or requested these actions can also be sent to the individual's manager, or the HR manager. Involving the manager and keeping him or her in the loop on actions and progress can enhance accountability and act as additional incentive for the individual to follow through. It is also extremely important to keep the manager of the participants engaged in the process in order to create a healthy transfer climate. If the manager is able to see that they are being kept informed of progress without taking responsibility for that progress they are much more likely to support the TLA process and create the right environment for the participant to flourish. As explained in Chapter 3, managers who feel sidelined or ignored can negatively impact the transfer climate, making learning transfer almost impossible.

Whether the coach uses the online system or not, they must make a note of the three of four action points arising from each conversation, have the client confirm them and e-mail those agreements to the client immediately after the conversation. It is these action points that form the basis of the second and subsequent conversations and it is impossible to encourage accountability without them.

Summary of key points

- The next stage of the TLA process is action. This is where the conversations actually take place over a period of several weeks following the training event.

- The TLA ACTION Conversation model is the theory and the framework behind what occurs in those conversations.

- The ACTION Conversation model expresses the interplay between structure and flexibility that creates enhanced coaching and differentiates TLA from traditional coaching.

- ACTION is an acronym for the various stages that the conversation must pass through in order to facilitate transfer of learning and behaviour change back in the workplace successfully. ACTION stands for:

  - Accountability: setting up the context of the process and the coach/coachee relationship (structure).

  - Calibration: calibrating a score for where the individual is now, and the score for where they want to get to (structure).

  - Target: where is the individual trying to get to? What is the target for the session (flexibility)?

  - Information: gather information about what is happening in the workplace (flexibility).

  - Option: what options does the individual have in this situation? What could they do (flexibility)?

- Next steps: how is the individual going to commit to action and move towards the target? How do the coach and individual follow this up (flexibility)?

- The TLA conversation travels through a process of structure – flexibility – structure.

- It is important that the TLA coach encourages the individual to take their own notes so that they take ownership of the process, even though the coach also takes their own notes. The coach must make sure they finish their notes with a bullet-point list of the three of four points that the individual has committed to action – ideally recorded in *their* own words.

- Depending on the level of confidentiality and system used to manage it, these notes may then be e-mailed to the participant for their approval and copied on to their manager.

08
Action – the 'must have' skills for successful TLA delivery

In the last chapter we explored the ACTION Conversation model that forms the basis of the TLA process. This chapter is dedicated to the TLA principles. These principles are crucial to executing the TLA process well. The 'ACTION' model can be followed like a tick-box exercise or it can be used elegantly to get great results. These principles are therefore the 'must have' skills for successful learning transfer and TLA delivery.

There are three critical qualities or skills that the TLA facilitator needs to practise and perfect in order to deliver TLA or any enhanced coaching methodology effectively. Those skills come with time and experience and successful coaches uses them all the time. The three critical skills are:

- asking power questions;
- being listening;
- using intuition effectively.

Asking power questions

Even when the challenge facing an individual is obvious or a coach can see their problem clearly and knows how it can be solved, simply telling this to the individual doesn't work. Even when the client is receptive to the advice they will forget it in everyday practice if it is not something they came up with themselves. Asking questions is therefore much more effective because it allows the individual to come to the same, or better, conclusion themselves while also taking ownership of the solution. An individual is always much more likely to implement and maintain their own solution than one handed to them on a plate by a coach.

Questions are at the heart of great coaching. The challenge, however, is that not all questions are equal. For a start there is a huge difference between what can be accomplished from a closed question versus an open question. Closed questions are questions that can be answered by either 'Yes' or 'No' and as such they tend to shut down the conversation. The most common closed questions begin with 'Is it...?', 'Are they...?' 'Do you...?' 'Have you...?' All of which will probably lead to either a 'yes' or 'no' response.

In addition to the limiting interaction of closed questions they also allow the facilitator to manipulate the agenda through 'queggestion'. Originally coined by US coach Michael Stratford the 'queggestion' is a suggestion masked as a question with the intention of manipulating the individual into a conclusion already drawn by the coach. If the coach asks the TLA participant, 'Have you considered consolidating your operations' or 'Is it useful to consider who should attend the training?', the coach is jumping to conclusions about how to solve certain issues without genuinely engaging the individual in the challenges they face. Instead of helping that investigation process to allow the individual to find out what they think will solve their problems the coach is putting solutions into the other person's head. Plus the coach is driving *their* agenda rather than holding a neutral agenda, which is essential for great coaching.

Closed questions also allow a coach to tread softly around the issue. Closed questions often feel gentler and are easier to ask – and to answer, which is probably why so many coaches fall into the bad habit of relying on them. If the coach asks 'Is it this...?' or 'Is it that...?' the question allows the person to dismiss it without a great deal of thought. It is much easier for a client to answer a closed question as it doesn't really require them to think. If on the other hand the coach says, 'What are the top three things...?' – there is no convenient escape hatch in that question, the individual's brain is directed to search for and deliver three answers. Plus *they* select the answers and are not in any way prompted or polluted by the coach's opinions or assumptions. This is an example of an open question and it is significantly more powerful.

Good open questions usually start with 'what' and 'why' and will usually illicit a longer response. Open questions direct the individual to truly engage with the question and think about a response in relation to their own situation. It is important to note, however, that asking 'why' questions can be quite confrontational as they are often associated to why we did something wrong. So when using the 'why' approach it is important to frame it in advance to take the sting out of the question. The coach may, for example, ask: 'I'd love to understand where you are coming from... can you explain more about why you chose that approach?' This question is far less threatening than 'Why did you do that?' – and is therefore far more likely to get a useful response.

'How', 'when' and 'where' are also technically precursors to open questions but they will often illicit a place, a time or a process and therefore aren't as open as a 'what' – to which the client can answer anything.

The whole point of coaching is to allow the individual to arrive at their own solution. Open questions illicit the individual's thoughts, feelings and opinions and will best facilitate that process. The person being coached knows their situation far better than the coach so they are absolutely the best person to source their best way forward. Open questions allow an individual to access in a useful way what they already know.

Enhanced coaching focuses on power questions. Power questions are a form of open question that ensures the coach does not arrive with an agenda or pollute the discussion with assumption. Power questions also prevent the coach from asking 'queggestions' or wasting too much time exploring issues that are not relevant.

The best power questions are the ones where the coach has no idea how the individual will answer – because a power question explores the participant's way of thinking, not the coach's. When a coach has asked a power question the individual will often pause for a moment and say, 'that's a good question' as they are forced genuinely to search for the answer.

Why use power questions?

- Power questions open up the conversation and allow the individual to express themselves and take ownership of the conversation.
- Power questions work to the individual's agenda not what the coach thinks the agenda should be.

- Power questions probe the individual so they can experience insights that allow them to make progress quicker.

- Power questions show the individual that the coach is interested in their situation and wants to listen.

- Power questions build the individual's confidence that they are the expert. If the coach allows the individual to engage with what they already know they will always be far more receptive to addressing what they don't know.

Examples of power questions are shown in Table 8.1.

Being listening

Anyone who has ever been involved in negotiation, conflict resolution or communication skills training or any form of coaching training will be familiar with the term 'active listening'.

Often when we talk to each other we don't actively listen to what is being said. We may hear the words but we don't engage with the conversation because we may be distracted or thinking about something else. In many conversations we can often be so distracted by what we need to say to get our point across that we are not even listening to what the other person is saying. Active listening seeks to address these issues by making sure that we are fully focused on the speaker. In a coaching situation the coach must take care to listen to what is being said and it is always useful to repeat what the person has said, in their own words, so that the person being coached feels listened to and validated. This, in turn, helps the speaker to relax and offer up more information and insight.

There is little doubt that if someone were to use the active listening approach in the way it was originally devised and taught then their listening skills would genuinely improve. However, it has now become almost clichéd. People assume they know what active listening is, when really they don't and, as a result, its impact has been diluted. It is easy to fudge active listening with a few well-timed and well-worn phrases. Coaches may nod at appropriate moments and occasionally add a sincere 'I understand', but that is not active listening and it will certainly not deliver the results necessary for TLA. When done correctly active listening has several benefits. It forces the coach to engage with the conversation genuinely and it also helps to prevent

TABLE 8.1   Examples of power questions and their possible outcomes

Power Questions	Result
Tell me more about that...?	Opens up the conversation, allows the individual to feel confident and comfortable and it gets them talking.
What do you think/feel when you say that?	Encourages them to reflect on what they think and feel about that statement, event or situation.
What does that mean to you?	Allows the individual to go into greater detail, which may offer up personal insights.
What's the bottom line of the situation?	Encourages the individual to cut to the chase and think about the outcome and all its ramifications.
What's your intuition telling you here?	Encourages the individual to view the situation from a different angle, which could spark off additional insights.
What's important about that?	Gets the individual to hone in on key issues.
What makes you say that?	This allows for elaboration, which can help both parties get a clearer picture of the situation.
What specifically...	When someone is asked for specifics they must go to a different place in the brain to retrieve a memory or experience. This journey can help to illuminate the issue.
What are three things...	Asking for a number of things stops the individual from worrying about what they do or don't know and instead focusing on the three things they do definitely know. It's a tangible goal that gives the question a context, which in turn makes it much easier to answer and always delivers a more insightful and useful answer.
What could you do differently to get a better result?	This question encourages the individual to consider different solutions without negating the previous solutions. It asks them what they could do differently, not what you could do better to improve the result.
What's important about that to you?	Encourages the individual to articulate his or her priorities.
Irrespective of whether you will do it or not what could you do right now?	This helps open the mind to possible solutions that the individual may never have considered. The pressure is taken off the answer by reassuring the individual that they will not necessarily have to implement any of the suggestions.
What if X was your biggest strength?	If someone describes something as their 'Achilles heel' or biggest weakness, flip the issue and encourage the individual to imagine for a moment what life would be like if their 'Achilles heel' was actually their 'crowning glory' or biggest strength. Getting the person to describe what life would be like can be really illuminating and inspiring for them.

misunderstandings. But it is not enough. Enhanced coaching requires a more applied approach to listening that I call 'being listening'.

Whereas active listening implies a conversation with one person on either 'side' and a level of activity, 'being listening is about *being in* the conversation with the individual, being completely still and doing nothing apart from being present and listening. The coach must be present in the moment with the person and 'hold the space' for them to open up and really communicate.

Why being listening?

- Being listening goes way beyond active listening.
- Being listening creates a non-verbal, non-visual connection with the client.
- Being listening is a practical way of ensuring that the coach delivers no opinion and no judgement.
- Being listening is a practical way for the coach to get out of *their* head and *their* ideas and into their body where they can just be a listener with no agenda.
- Being listening creates a distinction between *doing* listening as an activity and being listening as a state of mind.

EXERCISE TO GET INTO THE 'BEING LISTENING' STATE

During the TLA training programmes I get experienced coaches to have a brief coaching conversation as they would normally. Then I ask everyone to do the following breathing exercise, which was developed by HeartMath, and then to have a new coaching conversation. The level of sound in the room after the breathing exercise is massively reduced. There are hushed, gentle tones and the 'being listening' process creates a level of coherence and closeness that was not present in the first coaching conversations. The coaching is no longer about talking to each other but rather being with each other. Everyone who has ever done this exercise agrees that 'being listening' has a completely different feel. The steps of the exercise are as follows:

1   Take a couple of deep breaths and sit comfortably.
2   Imagine that you are now going to breathe through your heart (some people like to place their hand on their chest so that they can feel the rise and fall of the chest rather than the diaphragm).

3 Take five breaths, breathing in and out for five counts, with each breath focusing more on your heart.

4 As you breathe through your heart feel your heart expanding and contracting and imagine it growing in size each time it expands.

5 Now you are breathing through your heart take your mind to a time where you felt real appreciation or gratitude for someone or something. It could be when you were observing a wonderful view from nature, when you were with loved ones or when you felt very peaceful and grateful for your life.

6 Sit and relive these feelings of appreciation and gratitude as you breathe through your heart.

This simple technique allows the coach to manage their state and the environment. This means that the TLA facilitator does not look at their mobile phone or coach at their desk or in a place with too many distractions. The TLA facilitator must place themselves into the TLA cocoon where there is only the coach, their clipboard, a clock and the person being coached. Being listening is about finding coherence with the individual being coached and being in the flow of the coaching conversation. And this is only possible if the facilitator manages their environment and headspace. As such I never have follow-up conversations at my desk. I am always in a comfortable chair away from any technology or distractions. I set myself up to be in an environment where I can easily be present with the client.

Using intuition effectively

Everyone has intuition although not everyone knows how to use it effectively – especially in one-on-one coaching.

Intuition is the thought or idea that springs to mind from what seems like nowhere when an individual says something during the conversation. Trusting this intuition is a key skill in coaching, but working out what is intuition and what is simply a personal reaction to what has been said can be very tricky. Often in traditional coaching the coach is encouraged to go with their instincts and raise issues that they feel the person is avoiding. It is always easier to see other people's shortcomings or blind spots than it is to see our own, and traditional coaching sometimes encourages the coach to confront the stuff that the individual may not always see, or want to see. I believe that this can be a huge mistake.

For a start, if the coach barges into the conversation with their intuitive insights into what they consider to be the individual 'issues' they may very well be wrong. Often what we think is intuition is actually us having our own buttons pressed. Say a coach gets an insight that the individual they are coaching is a bit of a control freak but that intuition is actually a reaction to the fact that the coach has just been reminded that they are actually a bit of a control freak – not the individual!

Plus, even if the person is a control freak, pointing this out to them and suggesting ways to fix it will almost certainly alienate them. How the coach shares the insights that come to them is often more important than the insight – the last thing the coach wants is to be wrong and put the other person off side. To avoid this scenario the facilitator can reframe the insight by saying, 'I may be really off base here but are you uncomfortable in this situation because you feel a lack of control over the situation?' That way the individual has the opportunity to consider that intuition and elaborate on it or dismiss it.

No one likes being told what is wrong with them or where they could improve. Consulting requires that the consultant solves people's problems; coaching requires that the coach helps people to solve their own problems and often the coach's solution will not be the individual's solution. The very best coaching asks the individual power questions so that when answered the individual will arrive at their own solutions and have their own personal 'a-ha moment'.

There are times, however, when the coach's intuition will alert them to something that may need to be addressed for maximum benefit to the individual. Using intuition effectively is a skill that an effective TLA facilitator needs to master. It is about the coach sharing with the individual something that the coach has observed and that could be really useful and helpful, but doing so in such a way that it is safe and respectful. This therefore allows the person to consider the observation in a safe space so that they can either acknowledge it and move forward or dismiss it as irrelevant to them. Learning how to use intuition effectively requires the coach to follow the individual whilst using the ABC intuition rules.

Follow the individual

The coach needs to follow the individual and *their* agenda not the coach's agenda. Once the TLA participant starts the conversation they can often appear to wander off topic or focus their attention on something other than what the individual and the facilitator had planned. It doesn't matter whether the coach thinks it is relevant or not, the simple fact is that if the individual's attention is on something then the coach needs to have the courage to honour that and support them in where they want to go. If the coach insists on pushing the individual to a different topic, or forcing the previously agreed agenda, the individual will more often than not resist and withdraw. If on the other hand the coach follows the individual – wherever they go – and supports them to find a resolution to whatever is coming up for them in that moment then they will be much more engaged in the process.

That said, following the individual can result in the conversation going round in circles. This is not helpful to the process. It could be that the individual is just being chaotic, raising too many different themes and implications in one 30-minute TLA conversation. This is common and for some individuals it is just how their mind works, jumping quickly from one issue to another. The problem is that it raises too many issues to cover in a single session.

The coach's top priority in this type of situation is to help the participant think in a constructive way and 'split' the issues and challenges. By helping the individual to separate the issues it gives them an opportunity to choose what issue to explore so that they can drive the conversation rather than the coach making the decision or running the session to their agenda. This allows the coach to follow the client down a path of their choosing, whilst ensuring it is a worthwhile path.

How to combat a circular conversation

- The coach needs to summarize and repeat back to the individual the different issues or solutions they have raised.

- Having listed the issues the coach then gives the individual the choice as to which issue or avenue he or she would like to explore to 'make the best use of your time'.

- Once the issues have been separated out and listed the coach can then refer back to the list later on in the session to help keep the individual focused on important issues for that session.

- Often when the individual is able to separate the issues from each other they become less daunting and the individual can see a path through. Often there may only end up being two or three issues.

- Often with this kind of session the coach will need to split the issues or avenues of discussion more than once in the session.

The coach might hear the participant say something like, 'I want to work on my time management but really I just don't have time to do anything properly. I'm under such pressure and I'm worried about the implications that this has on my team. It's such a big challenge.'

The coach might say: 'I understand. There is obviously a lot going on. So where shall we focus our attention: 1) your time management; 2) not having time to do anything properly; 3) being under pressure; or 4) the implications on your team? Which is most important for us to make some headway on today?'

More often than not the participant will tell the coach that all the issues are connected, to which the coach might say: 'Absolutely, that seems clear. Let's put a stake in the ground against one of those four areas though, as an indication of where we might start. Which are you most concerned about?'

Once the participant has identified the priority from the list then the coach can continue with the TLA conversation and keep the participant on track. If the coach then needs to separate the issues again later on in the session they can use a summary of the path they have taken as a guide. So the coach might say: 'So we started looking at your first action from your TLA plan but decided that the real challenge underneath this was time management, not having time to do anything properly, being under pressure and the implications on your team. We then decided that the best path to take was to consider the pressure you are under and this has resulted in us consider-ing the implications for your health and the implications for your work. If we wanted to make some additional progress on one of these areas, which is most important to you – the implications for your health or the implications for your work...?'

Sometimes when an individual gets caught in circular conversations all the issues converge and become overwhelming so it is important for the coach to encourage the participant that sometimes even little shifts can make a huge difference. The coach might say: 'Often, John, when we make a small move in one area it can have an impact across the board so don't worry that we only have time to look at one area today.'

Learning how to follow the individual ensures that the person being coached feels acknowledged and listened to. Plus, if they can deal with whatever is on their immediate radar they will be much more willing to get back on topic once this is handled.

Ironically, the balance between structure and flexibility that is the hallmark of enhanced coaching means that individuals feel very liberated by the process, even though there is a strict structure that lies beneath it.

The ABC intuition rules

Intuition is by definition really subtle and hard to pin down. It can also be really hard to differentiate, especially for a novice coach, between intuition and when the coach is having their own buttons pressed.

The best way to effectively manage this curly challenge is to incorporate some rules of engagement when it comes to using intuition wisely and effectively. The rules I advocate are the ABC rules, which stand for:

Aware

Brave

Call it as it is

Aware

The TLA coach needs to be able to differentiate between genuine intuition and when they are making assumptions based on their own life and experiences. The individual may just be pressing the coach's buttons or straying into topics that the coach has strong opinions about. Staying engaged and consciously aware helps the coach to differentiate so that they can genuinely tap into their intuition. Remember:

- The coach's intuition could be spot on or it could be completely off the mark, but if the facilitator raises their insights respectfully it won't matter if they are wrong.

- It is always up to the individual to choose whether they want to explore what the coach has raised or not. The coach's job is to challenge the person respectfully when appropriate and not get attached to whether they take it on board or not.

- Whilst the individual being coached may be frustrating at times, they are always doing the best they can with the resources they have and the coach needs to respect that.

Brave

It is part of the facilitator's role as an enhanced coach to challenge the individual and challenge the status quo. Sometimes that means the coach has to:

- Be brave enough to go 'off piste' or follow a path outside what is expected, or on the TLA plan or coaching agenda, to give the individual the best results. Be brave enough to sit in silence having no idea where the session is going or whether the individual will come to a resolution in the session – the coach needs to be brave enough to trust the process.

- Be brave enough to throw the agenda over completely to the individual regardless of whether the coach feels they can handle what emerges or not.

Call it like it is

Putting issues on the table has a way of dissolving them. Think about a time when someone asked you if they had offended you – just by asking the question much of the simmering emotion is dissolved. Remember:

- If the TLA participant is sounding bored, resentful or disengaged it is always better for the coach to raise it with them immediately. It may not always change anything but calling the situation as it is gives the coach the very best opportunity to address the issues and get back into a positive conversation.

- The coach must call the individual to account when they are saying one thing and meaning or doing another. Without this intervention by the coach the conversation will quickly descend into a meaningless loop and waste everyone's time.

- The coach needs to call it like it is when the individual clearly doesn't want to be having the conversation or when they are openly or covertly hostile. Raising the issue will almost always defuse the situation and may help to get the conversation back on track. Unless the coach calls the individual on their behaviour or attitude nothing is going to shift.

Examples of using intuition effectively are show in Table 8.2.

TABLE 8.2   Examples of when and how to use intuition effectively

Situation in Coaching Conversation	Questions to Ask to Use Intuition Effectively
Individual is saying one thing but intuition is telling the coach that there is more to it	'Reading between the lines I get the sense that something else is on your mind – is this what you want to work on this session?'
Individual is telling the coach about lots of concerns but not highlighting one above another	'What is the biggest concern or challenge you are facing right now?'
The individual sounds bored and disengaged	'I'm hearing that you're not really inspired by this...'
The individual sounds fed-up and resistant	'You're sounding really fed up and not interested... what's going on for you at the moment?'
Towards the beginning of a session, if the coach senses that the participant is not yet engaged in the session	'What would you like to get out of our time today?'
The individual is telling the coach something but the coach has a sense there is something else going on and potentially already has an idea of what that might be	'I'm getting a sense that X might be an underlying issue here – would you agree at all?'
Intuition is telling the coach there is more to the issue than the individual is telling them about	'I think we're only looking at the surface – do you mind if I ask a couple of questions to take us below the surface?'
Intuition is telling the coach to ask a question that could potentially be difficult or challenging to the client	'I know this sounds strange but I've got a question that's niggling in my mind – do you mind if I ask you...'
The coach has something that they want to say to the individual that could be perceived as being direct	'I'm not going to beat around the bush – I know you would rather I am straightforward...'
The TLA participant is completely disengaged with the action plan	'Let's rip up the action plan...'
The individual says something that initiates the coach's intuition	'I have no idea whether this is relevant but...'
The individual doesn't seem engaged in what the coach is working on	'What would you really like to work on right now?'
The TLA participant needs more help than the coach can offer, they might be suggesting signs of depression or hopelessness or the coach may feel out of their depth	Hold the space for the individual whilst directing them to counselling

Summary of key points

- There are three critical qualities or skills that a TLA facilitator needs to practise and perfect in order to deliver TLA or any enhanced coaching methodology effectively. Those skills come with time and experience and successful coaches uses them all the time. The three critical skills are:
  - asking power questions;
  - being listening;
  - using intuition effectively.

- Questions are at the heart of great coaching. The challenge, however, is that not all questions are equal. There is a huge difference between what can be accomplished from a closed question versus an open question.

- In addition to the limiting interaction of closed questions they also allow the coach to manipulate the agenda through 'queggestions'. The 'queggestion' is a suggestion masked as a question with the intention of manipulating the individual.

- The whole point of coaching is to allow the individual to arrive at their own solution – open questions elicit the individual's thoughts, feelings and opinions that will best facilitate that process. The individual being coached knows their situation far better than the coach so they are absolutely the best person to source their best way forward. Open questions allow the TLA participant to access in a useful way what they already know.

- Enhanced coaching focuses on power questions. Power questions are a form of open question that ensures the coach does not arrive with an agenda or pollute the discussion with assumption. Power questions also prevent the coach from asking 'queggestions' or wasting too much time exploring issues that are not relevant.

- The best power questions are the ones where the coach has no idea how the individual will answer – this is because a power question explores the participant's way of thinking, not the coach's.

- Anyone who has ever been involved in negotiation, conflict resolution or communication skills training or any form of coaching training will be familiar with the term 'active listening', only it has now become clichéd. People assume they know what active listening is when really they do not and, as a result, its impact has been diluted. It is therefore easy to fudge active listening with a few well-timed and well-worn phrases.

- Whereas active listening implies a conversation with one person on either 'side' and a level of activity, 'being listening' is about *being in* the conversation with the individual, being completely still and doing nothing apart from being present and listening. The coach must be present in the moment with the person and 'hold the space' for them to open up and really communicate.

- Everyone has intuition although not everyone knows how to use it effectively – especially in one-on-one coaching. Intuition is the thought or idea that springs to mind from what seems like nowhere when an individual says something during the conversation.

- Trusting this intuition is a key skill in coaching but working out what is intuition and what is a personal reaction to what has been said can be very tricky.

- There are times when the coach's intuition will alert them to something that may need to be addressed for maximum benefit to the individual. Using intuition effectively is a skill that every TLA facilitator needs to master. It is about sharing something that the coach has observed with the individual that could be really useful and helpful, but doing so in such a way that it is safe and respectful. This therefore allows the person to consider the observation in a safe space so that they can either acknowledge it and move forward or dismiss it as irrelevant to them.

- Learning how to use intuition effectively requires the coach to follow the individual, whilst using the ABC intuition rules: Aware – Brave – Call it as it is.

09
Action –
helping others to
'get in the gap'

Although the facilitator will now have the TLA process through the ACTION Conversation model and understand the crucial interplay between structure and flexibility and the TLA principles that will guide every TLA conversation, it can sometimes be hard to find the groove in the process. If the conversation isn't really working then the chances are that the individual isn't genuinely 'in the gap'. Unless the TLA facilitator can identify something that the individual wants to change, get them to acknowledge that their calibration on that skill is currently lower then they wish it to be and encourage them to commit to bridging the gap between where they are now and where they want to be, then change is unlikely and both parties are just wasting their time.

Most managers in a modern business, even small businesses, know about coaching and the chances are that they have had some training in how to coach and how to use a core coaching model. The problem is that people are unpredictable and they come to work with a range of 'stuff' that makes it very difficult to squash them into any sort of theoretical model. The core coaching model probably worked a treat in the training event when the role playing was straightforward – either positive or negative. But then the manager goes back to work, perhaps even confident that they have the tools to effectively coach their people, and as soon as one of their people answers a question in an unexpected way or throws a curve ball into the conversation the manager has no tools or experience about how to navigate that person back on track. Often they will then assume that the model doesn't work.

This chapter is about realizing that people are not straightforward and more often than not they will say something completely left-field, which will throw even the best theoretical model into disarray. So, the TLA facilitator needs to know how to deal with that effectively and nudge them gently, or not so gently, into the gap. Coaching – even enhanced TLA coaching – almost never goes to plan.

So this chapter is about what the coach needs to do as soon as they hear participants say things like:

- 'That training programme was a waste of time.'
- 'I didn't really get anything from the training.'
- 'It was great but it doesn't really apply to me.'
- 'It's not going to work here/in my team.'
- 'Oh don't waste your time on me with this learning transfer stuff.'
- 'I've done something like this before and it just doesn't make a difference in this team.'

One of the biggest reasons that traditional coaching produces such hit-and-miss results is because the coach does not take the time to identify the issue that the individual is seeking to resolve at the start of the conversation. The coach doesn't get in the gap so the conversation meanders without the necessary focus on outcome and action. Enhanced coaching ensures the TLA facilitator always starts the conversation by getting the participant into the gap they are seeking to close. Without this initial identification and ownership of the issue then no real progress can be made.

In the TLA plan the individual will have identified approximately three things they want to address. At the start of every TLA ACTION conversation the coach needs to have that person choose which issue they want to focus on and reaffirm their calibration regarding that issue. In other words, they must state where they think they are in that moment against that issue on a score of 1–10. As I said earlier, calibration is often used throughout the enhanced coaching TLA process and acts as the bridge or transition from structure into flexibility. It allows the individual to put a stake in the ground about what they want to address and their current ability against that target.

In traditional coaching the coach may help the individual identify the goal but unless the coach also helps the individual identify the gap between where the person currently is and where they want to be – and get the individual aware of that gap and willing to acknowledge the shortfall and commit to handling it – then the conversation will be futile.

Getting in the gap is absolutely critical for success because it encourages the individual to take ownership of the challenge ahead. Otherwise they will simply have a nice conversation about what it might be like to be better at sales or how it would feel to be a better leader but there is no distinct outcomes or altered behaviour, which is what TLA is designed to illicit.

This is one of the reasons why I feel it is unfair to expect managers with minimal training to be overnight coaching superstars just because they were sent on a half-day coaching workshop. Often when I'm working with a manager, the manager already knows how to coach people. Chances are they have even completed a coaching training programme and are familiar with a coaching framework so that they can and do coach their people. But the truth is that the manager is only really effective as a coach when the person being coached reacts in a familiar way or answers the questions in the way that the manager is familiar with from their training. As soon as someone reacts outside that framework and fobs off the coach by being unable to identify the gap, or refusing to take ownership, the coaching process falls over and the coach has no idea how to get that process back on track. There are a thousand ways to avoid ownership and responsibility in the coaching process.

The American baseball player and manager Yogi Berra once said: 'In theory there is no difference between theory and practice. In practice there is.' This is absolutely true of coaching. Knowing a coaching model is one thing but being able to apply that model in the real world, regardless of what the person being coached says or what excuse or curve ball they throw, is quite another. Enhanced coaching allows the TLA facilitator to use the ACTION Conversation model as a framework whilst also using various tools and techniques that I have perfected over the years to ensure that the coach keeps the individual on the trajectory towards behaviour change and brings that person back to account – regardless of how they try to dodge or evade the coaching.

One of the first tools is the use of calibration throughout the coaching process as a quick and effective way to establish where the individual currently is in relation to the target and where they want to be. The individual already knows what their key issues are and they also know instinctively how good or otherwise they are against those issues, so it is very easy for them to assign a personal score to that issue. They also will have a fairly accurate idea of how much they can improve and how they could go about making those improvements. If, for example, the individual wants to learn how to handle objections more effectively in a sales situation then that is the goal. Identifying the gap comes when that person acknowledges that they are currently at score six for that skill and want to reach score eight. The gap is the skill level between six and eight and the individual has ownership of that because they identified the goal and the gap regarding their own skill level. The process would then move on to identify what specifically needs to be done to close that gap.

Getting the individual into the gap is a straightforward process if the actions they put on their TLA plan are real and relevant. If the coach finds that the person is not taking ownership of the gap then they need to uncover why before they progress with the conversation, otherwise nothing will change.

If the individual is reluctant to identify a gap that they want to reduce for a particular action then it may be that they put something in the action plan that they thought was expected of them but don't really believe in. It could be that they feel they have already completed their TLA plan; it could be that they feel they don't want to go through the coaching process and there-fore will deny that any gaps exist in an effort to get out of the TLA process. Whatever the reason for not taking ownership of the gap, the coach must get the individual to do so before they can move forward in the session.

Typically there are three things that the individual will say when they are not in the gap. The individual being coached will either:

- Identify a gap and explain in detail why they can't fix it.
- Identify a gap but won't be able to decide whether it is something they want to address or not.
- Say they can't identify a gap

Each of these responses requires a different approach and a different solution to get the individual to take ownership and move into an effective coaching conversation.

Solution 1: OARBED

The most common problem in coaching conversations is when the individual can identify a gap but spends all their time and energy telling the coach why

FIGURE 9.1   The OARBED process

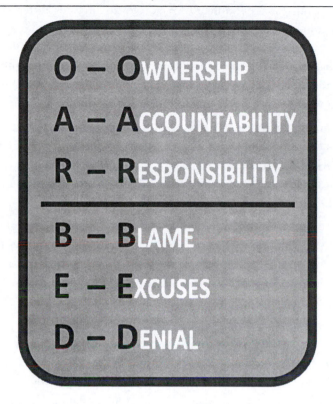

they can't fix it. This person will enthusiastically recount all the reasons why they have not been able to action any of their targets between the training programme and this conversation or between TLA conversations.

The best solution I've ever come across to rectify this is the OARBED process (Figure 9.1). I first heard of this brilliant little technique at a coaching conference in 2002 when John Matthews from the Institute of Executive Coaching explained this exact issue and what he did to help individuals really take ownership of the gap.

The OARBED process is perfect when the TLA facilitator hears the individual blaming external circumstances or other people for not being able to move forward.

How to use the OARBED process

I The TLA coach starts by briefly summarizing the conversation and repeats back to the individual what they have heard so far.

The coach might say for example, 'I'm hearing that there are several reasons that made it difficult for you to do anything differently. I'm going to take you through a little process that often helps in this situation so I can best support you to get the best result. Is that okay?' This introduction to the process acts as a signpost for the individual and lets them know that the coach is going to change approach and is seeking their permission to do so.

2 Assuming the coach gets the individual's permission, the coach then asks the individual to get a clean sheet of paper and write the word OARBED vertically down the left-hand side of the page, starting with O at the top and D at the bottom and drawing a line through the middle below the R and above the B.

3 The coach will remind the individual that this step is crucial so that they can move forward. The TLA facilitator might say, 'I often use this process to help people who feel they are stuck in a particular area and can't move forward. What usually happens is that the individual gets a new awareness that they are stuck below the line and that insight can create new opportunities for progress.'

4 The coach then tells the individual that he or she is going to run through the situation using the OARBED process to see if most of their reasoning is either 'above the line' or 'below the line'.

5 It is important that the coach reassures the individual that there is nothing wrong with being below the line – it's the awareness that is really important. The coach may say, 'Before I explain the model I want to remind you that there is nothing wrong with being "below the line". This process simply allows us to be really clear about where we are right now so we can decide whether or not we want to do anything about it.'

6 The coach then explains the model and might say, 'So, looking at your sheet of paper, O stands for Ownership, A for Accountability and R for Responsibility. These are all "above the line" characteristics because they empower you to take control and take action. The characteristics "below the line" are B for Blame, E for Excuses and D for Denial. It is very hard to effect change when we are "below the line" because these are disempowering characteristics and leave us feeling helpless.'

7 The TLA facilitator then reassures the individual again that although the below the line elements can sound harsh they are

intended to crystallize thought and help people move into a more empowering position. The coach may say, 'I know these sound quite harsh but that's not their intention. This process is about encouraging you to think a little differently about your situation so that you can stop feeling helpless, take back control and make any changes you genuinely want to make. Would it be fair to say that... [insert statement] could be described as an excuse? And remember this isn't about right or wrong. You may decide that you are actually quite angry and want to blame [insert person's name] for a day or so, just as long as you also understand that you won't take control and change much from that position.'

8   The coach must then encourage the individual to think of even a small part of the situation that they could move above the line. The TLA facilitator might ask, 'Looking at where you are now what percentage of this situation is below the line for you and what percentage of the situation is above the line?' This question uses calibration again but is particularly useful in this situation to help the individual to take ownership. Even if the coach can get the individual to take a tiny percentage of ownership of the situation that is a start and can open the door to progress the part that they do feel they have control over. So if the individual says, 'I'm 80 per cent below the line and 20 per cent above the line', then the coach can focus on the 20 per cent. This helps the individual to relax as it is not so confrontational. By taking the heat out of the situation the coach can really help to open up the discussion.

9   Again the coach needs to reassure the individual that if they genuinely cannot think of anything that they could influence, however small, then it's okay. If the individual suggests something, even if it is small then use that as the gap and progress the conversation on that basis. If they can't think of anything or don't propose anything they could influence then the coach needs to move on. The facilitator may say, 'If you can't think of anything, even something that may feel really minor that you could influence in this situation then it's okay, it just means that this topic or situation is probably not the best use of our time so we'll need to move on to something else from your TLA plan.'

10 If the coach needs to move on, he or she must remind the individual to give the issue more thought so that it can be revisited in the next conversation. Ideally the coach should encourage the individual to

think about one small thing they could influence in that situation. Once someone moves above the line for a minor issue they are much more capable of moving above the line for larger issues and to retake the power to change their situation and behaviour.

Other questions to help shift the individual above the line are:

- 'What part of this situation do you think you could influence?'
- 'What part of this can you control?'
- 'What will the benefit be if you manage to influence it?'
- 'What's the truth in the situation here?'
- 'Who can help you to resolve this?'
- 'What resources do you have that could be useful right now?'
- 'What have you learnt in the past that can help shift the situation now?'

EXAMPLE OF THE OARBED PROCESS IN ACTION

Say, for example, that a team was put through sales training and because behaviour change was sought back in the workplace it was also being followed up with TLA to ensure that the training was effective and participants were using in the workplace what they had learnt. The TLA coach's first conversation is with Roger, a key member of the sales team but someone who seems to suffer from inconsistent performance. During the conversation Roger admits that he has had a few poor sales calls since the course. The coach asks him what he could have done differently during those calls to make them more effective and duly hears a list of reasons such as: 'The prospect wasn't prepared for the conversation. He didn't really have time to talk to me', or 'He wasn't really in the right mood for a sales meeting', or 'The prospect was just too busy to make time for me.'

All the coach hears are reasons outside of Roger's control. Unless the coach has a tool or technique to get past this bluster then it will be tempting to let Roger off the hook. Only the coach knows that if he or she does let Roger off the hook then he is never going to own the issue and change his behaviour and he probably won't improve his results. But if the coach suggests to him, 'Roger, perhaps you could have done X, Y or Z', then Roger has zero ownership of the situation and will not make any changes and it is highly unlikely that he will action any of the coach's suggestions.

The coach needs to find a way to get Roger to take ownership and see that there is a way forward and that he does have control over the situation. And the OARBED model is a great technique for that. So instead of letting Roger off the hook the coach works through the process above, all the time assuring Roger that there is no right or wrong in this process – it is simply a way of seeing the situation more clearly so as to give him more options about what to do in the future.

When Roger writes OARBED on his sheet of paper and understands what each letter stands for he can more easily see whether his 'reasons' are above the line or below the line.

We have been taught that blame, excuses and denial are bad traits – but they are not. Change requires that we are honest about where we are right now and if we recognize that we are wasting time and resources in blame, excuses and denial then at least that is an honest appraisal of the situation. It may be that the individual acknowledges that and still decides that their excuses are valid or they stubbornly hold on to them for the time being, but at least the conversation isn't wasted discussing something that is not going to change.

In most cases the individual will acknowledge the futility of 'below the line' behaviour and move 'above the line', take ownership of the situation and move towards a different result. Unless the coach can move the individual above the line then the individual will always be looking at other people to change, which doesn't work. The only thing that we can effectively change is our own behaviour. Trying to change other people or the environment is a waste of energy. And that's why getting the individual into the gap in the first place is so important. Unless they take ownership, accountability and responsibility for the change the change will not happen, or if it does it will not stick.

The TLA facilitator absolutely needs to frame this process properly from the start because blame, excuses and denial are quite challenging words. If the coach just springs them on the individual without explaining the purpose of the model and how it is designed to support them to get the results they want then the individual may very easily get defensive. An enhanced coach, however, will not flinch from that potentially challenging scenario because they know they cannot coach that person effectively until they get them 'above the line'.

When someone is 'below the line' they are not coachable on that issue. Getting that individual to a point where they acknowledge that fact is essential. If the coach can't get someone 'above the line' then they need to change to an action that the individual is willing to make changes on or take them out of the TLA process. Unless the coach can identify a gap and get the individual to own that gap nothing will change and the process is a waste of time for both parties.

If you would like to listen to an audio recording of the OARBED process in action please visit **www.leverlearning.com/resources**.

Solution 2: off the fence

The next most common problem in coaching conversations is when the individual can identify a gap but is undecided about their desire to change it. They may, for example, be able to identify the gap, assign a current score and an ideal score but they may also be unsure if they want to reach the new score.

Every change carries with it advantages and disadvantages. Even if a person can see what needs to be changed and agrees that it is their responsibility there may still be strong advantages in the status quo. As a result the person is sitting on the fence regarding the gap or perceived gap and the coach's job is to get them off that fence. Ideally the coach is seeking to get them off the fence onto the side for change where they identify the gap and want to make improvements. If that isn't possible then get them off the fence to the side where they accept that they don't want to change. That way the coach can shelve that action for the time being and move on to another item from the TLA plan where the individual is willing to close the gap. It is always possible to come back to the first issue later when the individual has had experience of the TLA process working and feels more enthusiastic and confident about their ability to change.

Use the 'off the fence' process to help an indecisive individual to identify a gap and agree to take action on that issue, or shelve the issue and move on to something they will take action on.

How to use off the fence

1 The TLA coach starts by briefly summarizing the conversation and repeats back to the individual what they have heard so far. The coach might say: 'So what I'm hearing from you is that in some ways you want to... but at the same time you can see the

benefits of the current situation. As such you are unsure if tackling this particular issue is the best use of your time today.'

2 The coach needs to remind the individual how important it is to be clear about the advantages and disadvantages of each course of action so that they can decide if it really is something they want to pursue.

3 The coach can then explain to the individual that they are effectively running two arguments and that change won't be possible while they are running these two arguments.

4 The facilitator must then get the individual to look at and explore the two different arguments and articulate them to the coach. By getting the individual to explain their thinking and the pros and cons of each one they can get really clear on their own thought process around the alternatives.

5 Once unpacked in this way most participants will be able to see which alternative is the best.

6 The coach then reassures the individual that there is nothing wrong with where they are right now but together they need to make a decision and move forward or they need to decide not to change and choose something else to tackle. The coach may say: 'There is no pressure here, there is no right or wrong answer. I'm not trying to make you change or going to try to convince you to change – it's none of my business! If after we have been through the pros and cons of the situation you decide there is more benefit not changing then we simple move on to a different issue. My job is to make sure you get the most out of these sessions and discussing a change that you're not 100 per cent committed to is not a good use of our time. It may be you need more time in contemplation and that's absolutely fine.'

7 If the individual needs a little more coaxing then the coach can go through the respective pros and cons of the situation further. Focus on the upside if they decide to change and the upside if they don't, while encouraging the individual to make a decision – either to make the change or maintain the status quo. If the individual decides to change then the coach should calibrate their commitment to following through with the outcome and move forward with the conversation. If they are unsure then the coach needs to encourage them to think about the issue for the next conversation and move on to a different issue identified on the TLA plan.

It is not the coach's job to move the individual from contemplation to action. The coach's job is to help the individual become aware of where they stand in relation to the pros and cons of change and let them decide what to do about it.

EXAMPLE OF THE 'OFF THE FENCE' IN ACTION

One of the companies I work with regularly to transfer learning into the workplace has an objection-handling training programme for sales that the sales executives are often reluctant to use. They often put the process on their TLA plan and then once the TLA coaching begins they are happier to stay with the traditional process for handling objections.

It is almost as though they add it to their TLA plan because they feel they ought to, but when it comes to implementation of the objection-handling process there is huge resistance to even trying it.

In these situations I have to draw their attention to the fact they have either decided not to change or are in the middle of the change process. To keep them engaged in the conversation we have to be very clear that if they opt not to change that is absolutely fine and that they can have that option.

I then explore why they think the process was included in the training in the first place. I will ask: 'Tell me, why do you think this objection-handling process is included in the training as your company's recommended way of handling sales objections?' I will also try to ascertain why they liked it at the course and why they are resistant to it now. I may also ask them:

- 'What's difficult about the process?'
- 'What could make it easier to use?'
- 'What might the benefits be of using this approach?'
- 'What's the benefit of maintaining the status quo?'
- 'What could the risks of using it be?'
- 'How could we minimize the risks?'
- 'What could it cost you not to change?'
- 'What are the pros and cons of the change?'
- 'How would you feel if you made the decision one way or another?'
- 'Can you think of a time when you have been in a similar position and not known whether to make a change or not? How did you handle that?'

Having this kind of neutral exploratory discussion really helps the individual to gain clarity about what they feel about the new approach and can help to shift their perspective enough to allow them to identify the gap and commit to closing it.

If you would like to listen to an audio recording of the 'off the fence' process in action please visit **www.leverlearning.com/resources**.

Solution 3: the management consultant process

The last common problem that arises in coaching conversations is when the individual has either done everything they think they can on their action plan, they can't find something they want to work on or improve in the follow-up TLA coaching conversations or they appear to just want to tick the TLA follow-up box without adding a great deal of value. In short, this process is useful for when the TLA participant either doesn't know where they can improve or seems reluctant to improve anything.

This can be really frustrating for the coach and the individual. Sometimes the individual will say they don't know where they can improve because they are disengaged and, as we covered earlier, the best way to handle that situation is to call them on it and try to work past it. There is no point pretending that they are engaged or that there is no hostility when there is – call it like it is.

Sometimes the individual will resort to, 'I don't know what to work on' because they genuinely don't know how they can improve. This can be extremely difficult for TLA participants to deal with, especially seasoned and experienced individuals who are paid to 'know'. It can be extremely confrontational to realize that they don't know how to improve further or what is expected of them. They could be a top performer who receives little feedback on how they can go to the next level or they could be very self-assured and not see any opportunity or way they *could* be better. Often I hear, 'Well obviously I'm not perfect but I don't know what I could do differently to get an even better result.' It is the TLA coach's job to help them find out.

The coach must always let the participant know that it is okay not to know, and reassure them that getting better may not be a radical departure from what they are already doing and perhaps a little tweak is all that is needed.

The idea behind the management consultant process is for the coach to help the participant take a 'helicopter view' so that they are looking at the situation from a different perspective. This altered perspective can help the individual to bypass their rational mind and see things in a new light.

How to use the management consultant process

1   The TLA coach starts by summarizing the conversation and repeats back to the participant what they have heard so far. The coach might say: 'I'm hearing that you really feel that you've got everything covered or that you are unsure what else you could discuss in this conversation. Is that right?'

2   The facilitator would then ask for the participant's permission to work through a process that could help unearth something that might be useful to work on. It can be helpful for the coach in this situation to play to the individual's ego a little by suggesting deviation from a TLA conversation into an executive coaching conversation. If appropriate, the coach should remind the individual that highly paid executives use coaching or that athletes who have won two or three Olympic Gold medals still work with a coach. The facilitator might say: 'If it's okay with you I'd really like to shift away from TLA for a moment to executive coaching and use a little technique to see how we can add value and perhaps help us to get a different perspective on the situation. Is that okay with you?'

3   Assuming permission is given the coach might say: 'Imagine you no longer work for your current employer because you've gone out on your own as a management consultant. In a twist of fate your old company hires you back, for a large fee, to review your role and work shadow the person who is now doing your job (a bit of brain flexibility is needed here as you, the management consultant, are actually observing yourself in your job as you do it now). For a week you watch how that person works. From the perspective of an accomplished and insightful management consultant can you see any areas for improvement in the role?'

4   The TLA coach then asks the questions: 'What three things would the consultant feed back to the company as being the three key things that they see the manager under observation doing well?' 'What makes them really successful in their role?' As this is focused on the

positive, most individuals can identify three things that are done well in the role. From this altered perspective, once the individual has created the list the coach would then repeat the three things back to the participant. (In this case the manager is the participant, or they could be a sales executive – use whatever their role title is.)

5 Once the coach has repeated the strengths and the individual has acknowledged them the coach might say: 'Now obviously you need to create a detailed analysis and feedback in your management consultant role and it's important for you to get the best possible results, so what three things might you mention that could possibly be done differently to get an even better result? I stress here that it could be things that are already done well but could be done even better, or it could be the smallest tweak that if changed a fraction would help the business get an even better result. What are the three things you as a management consultant would suggest?' (Note here that the coach doesn't use the words doing badly or doing wrong it's just 'done differently to get an even better result'.)

6 Buoyed by the previous strengths the individual is much more likely to find a few things in response and move past 'I don't know'. Once the individual has identified the three things that could be done differently for better results the coach plays them back and asks the TLA participant to pick one item from the list of things that could add the most value and progress at that point in the TLA conversation.

7 If the individual is undecided the coach simply gets them to rank the three items they identified in terms of easiest to hardest or what will add the most value and least value. The coach should always encourage the individual to work on the hardest issue or the one that will deliver most value. That way they are supported through those issues during the TLA process, gain the win and are then much more confident about handling the other less difficult issues on their own.

If the coach gets the sense that the participant isn't responding to the idea of being a management consultant then you could try having them imagine they are someone else they admire, or have access to other people they admire.

Say, for example, that the training was in leadership or sales, then instead of asking the participant to imagine themselves as a management consultant to help identify potential improvements the coach could ask them to name a leader or salesperson they really admire. These can be famous people or people from their own experience – past or present. Once they have chosen someone the coach simply goes through the same process but has them imagine that person is work shadowing them.

Alternatively the other version of this technique involves asking the individual to pretend they have the option to create a panel of people – alive, dead, famous, known or unknown – whom they admire and whose advice they would respect. This can also be a useful option if the management consultant process does not yield avenues for discussion. The 'panel' version takes the individual even further away from their own perspective and can help to break the deadlock:

1   If the coach decides to use this altered version, he or she must still get the participant's permission and might say, 'Let's try a bit of a different technique to see if we can unearth another angle on what it would be useful for us to work on. It will take about 10 minutes to go through and if it is useful we'll continue with it – if it's not we'll park it... is that okay with you?'

2   Assuming permission is given the coach would add, 'Okay, take a moment to think of three people who you really admire in business – they can be from inside or outside your industry, they could be people you have worked with in the past who you admire or they could be people who you don't really know but respect nonetheless. The individuals you choose can be famous or not, alive, or not – it's totally up to you. They just need to be three people you admire and whose opinion you would value.'

3   As the participant is thinking, the coach could add, 'It might not be that you admire everything about that person (no one is perfect, after all) but you appreciate certain positive traits that you feel could help you and steer you in the right direction.'

4   The coach then asks the TLA participant who they would choose to have on their panel of three (it doesn't matter if the coach knows who the people are or not).

5   Once the individual has identified his or her three panel members, the coach might say: 'Imagine that for whatever reason all three of your panel members have cleared their diary for the last three weeks and have had the time to work shadow you. They have been able to observe every meeting you have attended, every conversation you've had with your team and every twist and turn of your role. Imagine

that they really want to support you in your career and share with you their top insight into what they observed you do well and that contributes to your success in your role. Imagine each panel member provides one insight...'

6 Once the individual has identified these issues the coach would play them back to reiterate these positive traits. Again, because they are positive traits the TLA participant is likely to be less defensive and deliver the three requested insights.

7 The coach might then say: 'Your panel also want to help you get even better results so [state panel members names, ie Sir Richard Branson, your old mentor Bob Smith and Kerry Packer] have got their heads together and agreed about what three things you could do slightly differently that would help you get even better results. What might those three things be?'

8 Positioned in such a way the participant is often able to distance himself or herself from these areas and see their identification as an opportunity not a threat, so as to move past 'I don't know'. Once the individual has identified the three things that could be done differently for better results the coach plays them back and asks the TLA participant to pick one item from the list of things that could add the most value and progress at that point in the TLA conversation.

9 As with the management consultant version, if the individual is undecided the coach simply gets them to rank the three items they identified in terms of easiest to hardest or what will add the most value and least value. And the coach should always encourage the individual to work on the hardest issue or the one that will deliver most value. That way they are supported through those issues during the TLA process, gain the win and are then much more confident about handling the other less difficult issues on their own.

These techniques can be particularly useful for depersonalizing the feedback. If the individual is defensive or reluctant to identify possible issues then this approach massages their ego a little while providing them with a less confronting way to get the issues on the table so that the coach can move forward and help the individual make behaviour change.

If the participant is unable to find the gap that they want to work on then any version of the management consultant process can help to create a new perspective and highlight a potential gap.

EXAMPLE OF THE MANAGEMENT CONSULTANT PROCESS IN ACTION

I remember one conversation where the individual was very resistant to coaching and was playing the 'I don't know' card over and over again. So I quietly moved into the management consultant process to see if I could move him forward.

I asked the participant who they respected in the industry, someone they had worked with or knew of, or maybe someone from elsewhere in another industry. Every time I asked for a name the individual told me he didn't know anyone he respected.

Eventually after a little probing he admitted that he respected Nelson Mandela. So I used the technique above and said, 'So if Nelson Mandela had been work shadowing you in your workplace for the last three weeks what would be the three things he would say you've done really well and what would he suggest you could have done differently to get a better result?'

Just by shifting his perspective and standing in the imaginary shoes of Nelson Mandela this person was able to rattle off suggestions, which then led to the identification of a gap and we were able to move forward with the TLA conversations. Just taking a new perspective, even an imaginary one, made a huge difference to his ability to access his own innate intelligence and move forward constructively.

When the coach encourages the individual to stand in someone else's shoes and look at their own situation from a different perspective, although this might seem a little odd it can be incredibly powerful. No one really understands why this type of guided imagery works but it is a recognized way to help people to connect with their innate wisdom and cognitive resources.

Science has already demonstrated that the brain processes about 400 billion bits of information per second and yet we are aware of about 2,000 of those bits. The vast majority of the information is therefore shunted to the subconscious mind. What is fascinating about the subconscious mind is that not only does it know things our conscious mind has forgotten but it knows things our conscious mind never even knew. It may be, therefore, that shifting someone's perspective or viewpoint through guided imagery allows that individual to access different information that can provide innovative solutions. This type of process is a simple way to increase creativity and imagination, which in turn helps to solve problems more effectively through visualizing situations from different angles and sourcing possible outcomes to different alternatives.

If you would like to listen to an audio recording of the management consulting process in action please visit **www.leverlearning.com/resources**.

All the techniques in this chapter are designed to get the person into the gap. The ACTION Conversation model will not yield results unless the individual in the process has been assisted to first identify an issue they want to improve, and calibrated a starting score for that issue and a target score so they appreciate the gap between where they are now and where they want to be. Without acknowledgement of that gap, and a willingness to own the gap and do something constructive to close it, nothing will change.

That said, even when someone engages with the gap there are many additional ways for someone to derail their own change process even once they have identified something *they* wish to change. Since I started delivering TLA I have personally delivered more than 2,500 individual one-on-one coaching sessions and the business has delivered over 10,200 sessions. That means that collectively I've heard or come across every excuse, reason and procrastination tactic that individuals will commonly use in an attempt to derail change. Once a coach gains experience in TLA they will begin to realize that there are patterns and similarities in the responses and excuses that they hear time and time again. Obviously there is much more to learn than simply how the coach must get the individual into the gap. I have identified, for example, five internal and five external progress blockers that appear and reappear during the TLA process and formulated proven coaching solutions, which are detailed in the TLA training, that allows the coach to get the individual back on track and keep them there.

Summary of key points

- One of the biggest reasons that traditional coaching produces such hit-and-miss results is because the coach doesn't take the time at the start of the conversation to identify the issue that the individual is seeking to resolve. They don't 'get in the gap', so the conversation meanders without the necessary focus on outcome and action.

- Enhanced coaching ensures the coach always starts the conversation by getting in the gap. Without this initial identification and ownership of the issue then no real progress can be made.

- Typically there are three things that the individual will say when they are not in the gap. The individual being coached will either:

    - Identify a gap and explain in detail why they can't fix it.

    - Identify a gap but won't be able to decide whether it's something they want to address or not.

    - Say they can't identify a gap.

- The most common problem in coaching conversations is when the individual can identify a gap but spends all their time and energy telling the coach why they can't fix it. This person will enthusiastically recount all the reasons why they have not been able to action any of their targets between the training programme and this conversation or between TLA conversations. The best solution I've ever come across to rectify this is the OARBED process.

- The next most common problem in coaching conversations is when the individual can identify a gap but is undecided about their desire to change it. The coach can use the 'off the fence' process to help an indecisive individual to identify a gap and agree to take action on that issue, or shelve the issue and move on to something they will take action on.

- The last common problem that arises in coaching conversations is when the individual has either done everything they think they can on their action plan, they can't see what they can improve or haven't been able to identify what to work on in the follow-up TLA coaching conversations. In short, they don't know where they can improve. The solution to this challenge is any version of the management consultant technique.

10
Action – managing the TLA conversations

At its heart the TLA process is about the facilitator supporting the participant in their working environment to reflect on the learning they received in the training programme and help them to apply that learning so it becomes habit or so that they have completed their TLA action plan. The objective is to help the individual to identify a gap that he or she wants to address and support them while they close that gap and make the behaviour transition in the workplace.

This chapter is therefore focused on what happens between the first conversation and the second and subsequent conversations and how the TLA facilitator can maintain forward momentum or get the individual back on track.

The opening of the TLA conversation is slightly different depending on whether it is the first session or a subsequent session. In the first conversation it is important for the coach to set the scene and reiterate how the coaching will work and what the individual can expect so as to set the participant's mind at ease about the whole process, whilst at the same time reiterating the joint commitments. In the second conversation there is no need to repeat the set-up information, although the coach may remind the individual of the length of the conversation and how it is important to stay focused in order to get the most from the session.

TLA is a series of deliberate and focused conversations that take place after the training event over the course of two or three months, but it is what happens *between* the conversations that determines whether the individual is going to genuinely benefit from those conversations or not. Everything about the way TLA is structured and delivered is aimed at getting real-world behaviour change *in between* the conversations. It is only when the coach and participant come to the beginning of conversation two and the beginning of conversation three that they find out if any change has actually occurred.

In order to achieve this real-world change it is essential for the coach to get the participant to identify what action point they wish to focus on first. If left to their own devices most participants, especially at the start of the process, will want to work on the easiest action point or the one that they have secretly already achieved! This allows the individual to showcase expertise and tell the coach exactly what they are going to do. Choosing an action that is already accomplished or partially completed will also allow the individual to demonstrate 'progress' when there really hasn't been any. To avoid this the coach might say: 'Often people choose to work on the most difficult action from the action plan or the one that is likely to deliver most value to you or your business. This makes sense because when you can get a significant win during the TLA process then you are more likely to be able to bring about change for yourself once we've finished.'

If the coach feels that the individual is avoiding the more difficult action points then he or she might say: 'John – I know as we were working through we said [action X] was the most important thing for us to work on today, but as we talk it through my sense is that you pretty much know what needs to be done there. I'm happy for us to keep on this track but to be able to add real value today it may be more useful to work on what is challenging about the other goal. What is the trickiest/hardest part of your action plan?'

More often than not the individual already knows what is the hardest part of the plan and will usually say so straight away. The coach can then add: 'So as we look at it is it more useful for us to keep exploring [action X] (which is the easier task) or [action Y] which you've already identified could have a huge impact on your results?'

If the individual has an action point or goal that they have been avoiding, or which has not been getting much traction, then the coach can allow them to work on the easier action in the first conversation and then, five to 10 minutes before the end of the conversation, the coach might choose one of the following:

- 'So, John – great that we've managed to work out today some more information on how you are going to progress action X but before we close off I want to swing back to action Y. What is one thing you could commit to doing before our next conversation that would ensure you get some momentum on this goal?'

- 'I know you've got valid reasons for focusing on action X not action Y but I am a bit concerned that we aren't making any traction on action Y – what's one thing you could do before the next conversation that would help move this forward?'

- 'I'm really glad that we've spent some time on action X – next time we will make sure we get up to date with action Y – for now, though, so that we don't get behind on that goal, what's one thing you could do to move the goal forward before we next speak?'

At the start of the second and subsequent conversations the facilitator needs to check in with the person against the agreed actions from the training course or previous conversation. When conducting TLA conversations the coach should have a clipboard, clean sheet of white paper, pen and glass of water to hand. Five minutes before the conversation is due to start the facilitator needs to review the TLA participant's notes from their TLA plan, or from the first or second conversation, and put those agreed action points on the fresh sheet of white paper as bullet points. That way the coach is clear on what the individual is supposed to have followed through on or what tasks he or she committed to at the end of the previous exchange. Remember, these are action points that the individual chose in their TLA plan or subsequent follow-up conversation so these are *their* commitment not the coach's.

In order to facilitate real behaviour change the coach needs to check in with each action one at a time. When the coach asks the individual what they have done since the course or previous conversation they will typically respond in one of four ways:

1 The individual will be excited and enthusiastic because they have followed through on their action and will want to share, often in detail, what they have done.

2 The individual will be upfront and tell the coach they haven't done it.

3 The individual will be really vague and proceed to provide a list of excuses about why they haven't done the action but how it's not their fault.

4 The individual will lie, although this is rare and can usually be spotted due to the lack of detail.

Whatever feedback the TLA facilitator receives from the individual it is important not to take what they say at face value. The coach needs to allow for personality, hyperbole and politics and dig underneath those potential distractions to uncover what has actually happened since the last conversation. To do this the coach needs to ask questions to check the validity of the participant's responses but to do so in a way that doesn't questions their integrity, honesty or judgement regarding whether they have done what they said they would or not. The individual is not on trial; the coach's role is purely to help the person get results.

'Yes, I've done it and I'm excited to share what happened'

When the individual tells the coach that they have completed the task or followed through on a particular action point from the previous conversation the coach might respond in one of the following ways:

- 'Wow, that's exciting tell me more about what actually happened.'
- 'That's great news, so tell me... what benefits do you think this change in behaviour or action has given you?'
- 'That's terrific progress, so tell me how that is different to how you would have handled that in the past.'

These types of responses help the coach to gauge validity and if the individual really did do what they said they would do. Plus it helps the participant to gain contrast so they can really appreciate where they were and where they have progressed to. This can further foster commitment, ownership of the process and the individual gets to appreciate how the process is genuinely helping them to be more effective in the workplace and how they are creating change.

If their explanation feels valid to the coach and they are genuinely making progress against an action point then the facilitator needs to reinforce that positive momentum and encourage the individual to continue to build on what they have already achieved. The coach might say: 'That sounds fantastic, well done. So what needs to happen now on this point to help you move even further?' Or, 'What is going to be your continued action between now and when we next speak to maintain forward momentum on this?'

All this need only take a few moments but it is important for the coach and participant to acknowledge the win and encourage forward momentum.

The coach needs to make sure the individual knows what they have to do for next time and remind them that the facilitator will check in with them at the next conversation. Beyond that, simply move on to the next action point on their TLA plan and repeat the process.

'No, I didn't do it (vague no) – but it wasn't my fault'

If the individual tells the coach upfront that they have not done what they said they would do, or they become vague and offer up excuses about why they haven't done anything against the commitments, then the coach needs to dig deeper to uncover why.

The coach needs to work out whether the lack of action is because the participant didn't have ownership of the action in the first place or they didn't think it was going to work. It may be that the individual is fearful or confronted by the task. It is the TLA coach's job to uncover whatever it was that stopped the individual from following through. This must be done, however, in a way that does not make them feel as though the coach is chastising or judging them.

As a result, the TLA facilitator can't just ask the individual why they didn't follow through because the person will almost always get defensive and the conversation will break down. Once someone feels challenged the coach will never get to the bottom of the situation so will probably not get the opportunity to get them back on track. It could be that the individual thought they would get away with not doing it and didn't think the TLA coach would actually follow up. This can be especially true when there has been a legacy of failure in training and follow-up programmes. It could be that the action point was rushed during the training event, or that they thought their chosen action was going to work but when they got back to the workplace it was obvious that it wouldn't work, or it could be that they were simply overwhelmed by the size of the task. It is always wise for the coach to preface their comments in a non-threatening and non-judgemental way so that they can open dialogue and rectify the situation. The coach may say: 'I really want to support you in getting the best results possible but ultimately it's up to you whether to follow through or not. This is not about me it's about you and you getting the best result, and if you don't want to put anything into place then that's your call. But tell me...':

- 'What are you thinking now about the actions you set last time and how important they are to you?'

- 'If you had your time over would you still stick with the action we agreed last time?'

- 'Do you still think that action would bring you any benefit? Seek to understand why/why not. What's changed?'

The coach must remind the TLA participant that the conversations are confidential and give them permission to be really honest about why they haven't followed through.

Often, when an individual hasn't followed through, their inaction or apathy is masking fear. For example, I once conducted TLA for consulting training. My client wanted all their consultants to take a particular approach when engaging with their clients and the action from the training was basically to try it! What I found with a few individuals was that there was deep resistance to the training because they felt their own approach did just fine. So I acknowledged their point and asked, 'Why do you think your company has chosen this process and rolled out the programme internationally?' Invariably the resistant individuals would eventually acknowledge that the company must have chosen the process because of evidence that it works. We then probed to search why it works and how it is similar to and differs from their current approach. With that altered viewpoint they were less resistant and we could formulate a plan for moving forward.

It is also important for the coach to reiterate that some new skills, especially soft skills, are not going to work first time. This gives the individual permission to fail and takes some of the pressure out of the situation. Although few people will admit that they are scared of trying, most adults are! If there is hesitancy about trying out the new skills then the coach needs to find out what result the individual was expecting. In the consultancy training TLA for example it turned out that some people thought they should be able to master the process almost immediately. That is unrealistic for most processes. It is much more likely that the person will 'fail' when they first start to use a new skill but if they know that's normal then they are often more willing to give the process and themselves a chance.

The quicker the potential win from the training the easier it is to change behaviour, but with some training that win isn't going to be immediate and behaviour change is therefore harder – but part of the coach's role is to help the participant to appreciate that.

This is something that ideally should be covered in the training set-up so that participants have a realistic expectation about how long it is going to take to master the skill, and how their company is not expecting immediate results but they are expecting effort and practise towards mastery.

Another reason why people don't follow through on their agreements is because they don't believe they need to. The assumption is that training is for people who are poor at a particular skill rather than training being for people who may already be good at that skill but who could achieve even more with a little fine tuning or tweaking. This faulty assumption can then create resistance in participants who are irritated at having to attend the programme in the first place and who by default assume it doesn't apply to them so think they can ignore the follow-up process. It is important in this situation for the coach to reframe the training so that the participant realizes that they are not being asked to reinvent the wheel but instead are being asked to try making a few small tweaks to the way they work.

In this situation the coach might offer an analogy to take the sting out of the process by saying: 'Think of these changes like the difference in approach between the gold medal winner and the silver medal winner. Sometimes the difference that makes the difference can be almost imperceptible and doesn't require Herculean effort.'

Once someone realizes that the training already acknowledges their ability and is seeking to fine tune rather than re-create they will relax into the process and are more likely to embrace the changes.

'Yes, I did it but the dog ate it!'

Remember at school there was always a pupil who tried to convince the teacher that he had done his homework but the dog ate it just as he was leaving for school? Everyone knows the kid didn't do the homework and the teacher is left questioning if he even has a dog! The same happens in TLA follow-up but it is rare.

If the coach really senses that the individual is being less than truthful or is embellishing their progress in the hope that the coach will take the responses at face value and let the participant 'off the hook' then this needs to be illuminated gently through the use of some artful questions. Even if the coach is sure the participant is lying, to say so would almost always end badly so instead the coach needs to probe a little further. The coach might say:

- 'That's great; tell me more about what exactly happened.'
- 'When was it that you tried that?'
- 'So what feedback have you got for me from your experiment?'

When someone is unable to furnish real-life detail it is a reasonable sign that a little white lie may be in progress. So if the answers that the individual provides don't ring true and remain vague then the coach must call them on it. Again, the coach would preface their comments in a non-threatening and non-judgemental way. The coach might say:

- 'I really want to support you in getting the best results possible but ultimately it's your business whether or not you follow through. I'm just going to be really honest here and tell you that you're sounding vague. I don't mean to challenge you but if I'm going to be able to really help you get the best results I have to understand if you are sharing with me what actually happened, or if you're just telling me what you think I want to hear.'

- 'Please remember this is a completely confidential environment and regardless of what you've done or not done I'm not going to be angry, disappointed or judgemental – this is your process not mine. Would I be right in thinking that perhaps you haven't yet quite got to where we need to with this goal?'

- 'Let me first ask: is this still something that is important to you?' If the response is that it is not then park it and move on to another action point from their TLA plan or have them decide on something that they *are* committed to.

- To help with this process the coach might add: 'Let's take a moment to review all three goals you highlighted on your TLA plan to see if this is something you still want to progress further or if you would prefer to use our time today on a different outcome.'

- Assuming the individual does want to progress the issue, the coach might ask: 'So what do you think has been the real barrier to getting traction on this?' – and then move forward from that point.

When the TLA coach can get the individual to be really honest about what they are going through it will make a massive difference to their results. And part of this process is for the coach to get them to recalibrate, on a scale of 1–10, where they are now in relation to their action point so that they can appreciate their own progress.

The TLA process belongs to the participant not the coach. The coach's job, therefore, is to manage the process not the content of the process. It is not about the coach trying to get the participant to do something, it's about the coach holding the participant to account for the things they said they wanted to do. The individual being coached is the one who drives TLA, not the coach, and the less attached the coach is to the outcome the easier it is to help that person get the results.

The TLA coach must support the individual in a process of reflection so as to help them to hold themselves to account, and that is impossible without a really clear system for documenting what has been agreed. Towards the end of the conversation, therefore, the coach needs to recap on what has been agreed for next time. The coach might say:

- 'Before we wrap up today, play back to me the three things that you are taking away from the session.'
- 'So to get really clear tell me what three things you are taking away from today that you will report back on next time.'
- 'And how are we going to measure that, so we can gauge the impact of your follow through against those actions?'

The individual's answers to these three questions then form the basis of the follow-up in the subsequent conversations. And, depending on what the individual has done towards those objectives, the coach then needs to manage the conversation to either get them to recommit to an existing action or move them on to a new action from their TLA plan. It is important that the coach always celebrates the wins that have been made between conversations and that this process then continues until the final conversation.

Once the TLA follow-up process has finished – usually following three or four conversations – the TLA participant has successfully worked through several action points and made behaviour change. It is important for the coach to end the process on a high so that the individual is able to celebrate and feel confident by the wins they have made during the process and acknowledge them, even if there are still some outstanding actions to complete.

It is also important that the individual doesn't feel that the process is over and that they can now coast or go back to old behaviour or ways of working. The coach needs to congratulate the person for the progress they've made and ask them to articulate their next steps after the final conversation so that they maintain the forward momentum and remain consistent with the changes they have made.

By now the individual will have an experience of behaviour change and will be reaping the benefit of setting targets and achieving them, so they will probably continue to make adjustments and there is no reason why this positive momentum should stop. The facilitator should therefore close the conversation with new next steps and ensure that the individual has made commitments to those actions. The coach should probe what the participant needs to do now to stay on track and what processes they can put in place to maintain results.

When I run the TLA process I always remind people that if there is anything I can help them with then they are free to call at any time. In practice, perhaps two people in eight years have ever called after the end of a programme. The offer, however, gives participants the feeling that they remain supported and don't feel cut adrift at the end of the final conversation. Towards the end of that final conversation the coach will also need to ask for feedback on the process.

At the end of the final conversation the coach needs to:

1 Congratulate the individual on the wins they have achieved through the follow-up TLA process.

2 Ask for feedback – or explain the feedback process, generally this is different for each programme and depends on the method of evaluation.

3 Leave the client feeling clear and excited about their next steps, even though the coach will not be checking in on them.

4 Leave the individual feeling supported, knowing that they can contact the facilitator if they need to at any time in the future.

This final closure allows the coach to take control of the process to finish professionally. It ensures that the TLA participant feels good about what they have achieved so far, which in turn builds confidence and helps to maintain forward momentum. And finally it ensures that the coach gets the necessary feedback to evaluate the results.

Summary of key points

- At its heart the TLA process is about the facilitator supporting the participant in their working environment to reflect on the learning they received in the training programme and help them to apply that learning so it becomes habit or so that they have completed their TLA action plan.

- The objective is to help the individual to identify a gap that he or she wants to address and for the coach to support them while they close that gap and make the behaviour transition in the workplace.

- TLA is a series of deliberate and focused conversations that take place after the training event over the course of two or three months but it is what happens *between* the conversations that determines whether the individual is going to benefit from those conversations genuinely or not.

- Everything about the way that TLA is structured and delivered is aimed at getting real-world behaviour change *in between* the conversations. It is only when the participant and facilitator come to the beginning of conversation two and beyond that they find out if any change has actually occurred.

- In order to achieve this real-world change it is essential for the coach to get the participant to identify what action point they wish to focus on first. If left to their own devices most participants, especially at the start of the process, will want to work on the easiest action point or the one that they have secretly already achieved! The coach needs to be mindful of this and encourage the participant to focus on the hardest action or the one that will yield the most value.

- At the start of the second and subsequent conversations the coach needs to check in with the person against the agreed actions from the training course or previous conversation.

- When the coach asks the individual what they have done since the course or previous conversation they will respond in one of four ways:

  - The individual will be excited and enthusiastic because they have followed through on their action and will want to share, often in detail, what they have done.

  - The individual will be upfront and tell the coach they haven't done it.

  - The individual will be really vague and proceed to provide a list of excuses about why they haven't done the action but how it's not their fault.

- – The individual will lie, although this is rare and can usually be spotted due to the lack of detail.

- Whatever feedback the TLA facilitator receives from the individual it is important not to take what they say at face value. The coach needs to allow for personality, hyperbole and politics and dig underneath those potential distractions to uncover what has actually happened since the last conversation.

- To do this the coach needs to ask questions to check the validity of what they are being told in a way that doesn't question the individual's integrity, honesty or judgement.

- When the TLA coach can get the individual to be really honest about what they are going through it will make a massive difference to their results. The TLA coach's job is to support the individual in a process of reflection so as to help them to hold themselves to account – and that is impossible without a really clear system for documenting what has been agreed. Towards the end of the conversation the coach must therefore recap on what has been agreed for next time.

- At the end of the *final* conversation the coach needs to congratulate the individual on the wins they have achieved through the follow-up TLA process, ask for feedback, leave the participant feeling clear and excited about their next steps even though the coach will not be checking in on them, and leave the individual feeling supported.

- This final closure allows the coach to take control of the process to finish professionally. It ensures that the TLA participant feels good about what they have achieved so that they are motivated to maintain forward momentum. And finally it ensures that the coach gets the necessary feedback to evaluate the results.

11
Evaluation – how to measure and report success

You may remember from Chapter 2 that I was quite scathing about the industry-wide obsession with evaluation. Attempting to fudge, hide or ignore results by cherry picking what to evaluate is pointless. Genuinely evaluating success or failure against worthwhile objectives is not.

Evaluation of success is an important part of any endeavour. After all, if we can't establish whether we have met or exceeded our objectives then it is very hard to establish if something has been worthwhile or not. If we can't work that out then we could be throwing good money after bad.

So what type of evaluation really matters?

In an effort to answer this question definitively Jack and Patti Phillips of the ROI Institute surveyed the CEOs of Fortune 500 companies. They didn't ask L&D professionals, managers or participants what they thought was important – they went to the top and asked the people leading the biggest and most successful companies in the world what they considered important.

They asked the CEOs three questions:

1 'What do you currently measure in terms of your training?'
2 'What do you think you should measure in the future?'
3 'How do you rank each measure in terms of its importance?'

FIGURE 11.1   Results of Jack and Patti Phillips's research

Measure	We Currently Measure This	We Should Measure This in the Future	My Ranking of the Importance of This Measure	
			Average	Rank
a. Inputs	(90) 94%	(82) 86%	6.73	6
b. Efficiency	(75) 78%	(79) 82%	6.92	7
c. Reaction	(51) 53%	(21) 22%	7.15	8
d. Learning	(31) 32%	(27) 28%	4.79	5
e. Application	(11) 11%	(59) 61%	3.42	4
f. Impact	(8) 8%	(92) 96%	1.45	1
g. ROI	(4) 4%	(71) 74%	2.31	2
h. Awards	(38) 40%	(42) 44%	3.23	3

Note: The first column gives the percentage of CEOs who checked each item as a measure being reported; the second column gives the percentage indicating that it should be reported; and the third column gives the average ranking number for the group, recognizing that the lower the number, the higher the ranking. Please note too that the survey was asked of 96 CEOs, so the figures in brackets in the columns are the numbers of respondents out of those 96 CEOs.

The answers to these questions are detailed in their book *Measuring for Success: What CEOs really think about learning investments* (2009). As we can see from Figure 11.1, the top three things that the CEOs identified as currently being measured – number of people trained (inputs), cost per hour of training (efficiency) and employee opinion (reaction) – were considered the *least* important three things to measure in the future. In other words, the evaluation that is happening right now in the L&D industry is not considered important by the leaders driving the companies and signing off the training budgets.

And to make matters worse the bottom three things that the CEOs identified as not currently being measured also happen to be the top three things that they want measured. Just 8 per cent of respondents said that their business currently measures impact where, 'Our programmes are driving the top five business measures in the organization.' And yet 96 per cent said it was their number one priority in the future.

CEOs don't care how many people went through training last year, they don't really care if those people enjoyed the course or not and they don't even care that much about how much it cost on an hourly basis. What they care about is the result. What did participants do differently and how did that impact the business? That is the information they need in order to establish the worth of training.

As an L&D professional this survey has to be a real wake-up call regarding effective evaluation, because those professionals are clearly not giving the CEOs what they want – and ultimately the CEO is steering the ship and controls the budget. It would probably be a career-limiting move on behalf of all L&D managers to dismiss these findings.

Something needs to be done about evaluation so that business leaders can get useful and pertinent information about the effectiveness of training programmes, make better use of the training budget and get the results they seek.

There are five levels of evaluation as illustrated in Figure 11.2. The first four were identified by Donald Kirkpatrick and the fifth was identified by Jack and Patti Phillips. I will use the Phillips version here because it is important to appreciate that the five levels of objectives we explored in Chapter 2 correspond to the same five levels of evaluation. It is a mirror model because clearly the objectives of a training programme need to be in place at the start so that we have something concrete to measure against at the end.

What usually happens in evaluation is that the training is finished and then, after the fact, the training facilitator will think about how to evaluate the programme so as to present it in the best light! That is not real evaluation, it is manipulation.

The trends in evaluation are suggesting that people are finally waking up to the fact that anything below level three evaluation is meaningless. The key to transformation and genuine training success is application or behaviour change.

FIGURE 11.2   The objectives connection

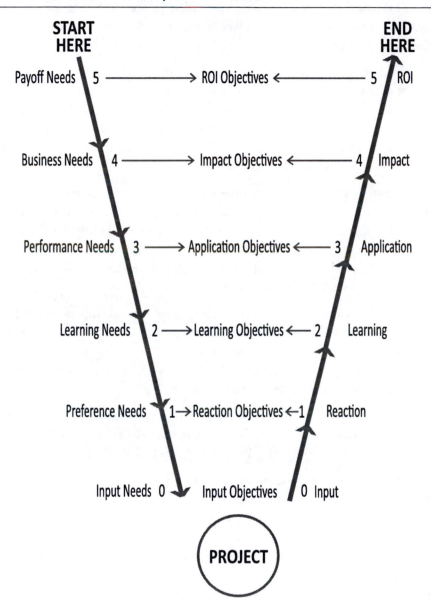

The Phillips team are the leaders in the field of evaluation, having written 50 books on the subject. The Kirkpatricks have also made their mark in the area and it was Donald Kirkpatrick who first identified the importance of behavioural measures in evaluation. Donald's son Jim and his wife Wendy are also putting renewed emphasis on level three evaluations, as discussed in Chapter 2.

What makes the Phillips model so useful is that it emphasizes the importance of tying the evaluation to the objectives. For evaluation to be truly effective we must start with the end in mind. Only when we set the objectives at the start can we effectively evaluate against those objectives at the end. And this has been part of the problem – when people think about evaluation they think about it after the programme has been run – but it's too late then! We need to decide what the course objectives are at the very start, before the programme has even been designed, and then evaluate the outcomes in relation to those objectives.

Remember in Chapter 2 we talked about wrong objectives being one of the reasons the missing link in learning has been missing for so long. If the objective of the course is to finish on time and collect some 'happy sheets' about what participants intend to do then it is very easy to fudge success. But reaction evaluation is not enough.

If the objective of the course is to ensure that the participants can effectively demonstrate their new skill at the end of the course then again it is too easy to distort success. Learning evaluation is not enough either, because the presence of learning or new skills doesn't automatically mean participants will use that new learning or skill back in the workplace. The absolute minimum objective and evaluation that needs to happen is application.

As a result, the evaluation necessary for successful learning transfer must focus on application evaluation and above, which is why we use the Impact Dashboard to document our evaluation. Using the Impact Dashboard stakeholders are able to assess reaction and learning evaluations as well as application and first-stage impact evaluation. With the dashboard as a base level of information then the client has the choice to go to a full ROI analysis if desired.

Impact Dashboard

I am totally committed to and passionate about TLA. I love to witness the magic that is possible when people realize that they can genuinely improve after training. After years in this business I still get a real buzz from seeing people make behaviour change so that they can reach their goals and objectives. It is often a genuine revelation to them as they realize that they *can* change – and the implication of that insight lights up all the other areas in their life. From believing that they couldn't change or were too old to change, everything again seems possible, and being part of that metamorphosis is really awesome. It is a great process, the TLA coaches love it and the participants love it because it really helps people to get some traction and succeed in their role. The client or person who commissioned the training and TLA on the other hand – they *love* the Impact Dashboard!

It is almost as though the dashboard gives them a tangible way to illustrate those results even though it does not actually generate the results. TLA generates the results and the dashboard allows a manager, CEO or L&D professional to showcase them. Until the Impact Dashboard, the person going through the changes knew how well it worked and sometimes the manager also but it was not reported across the TLA programme. When I introduced the dashboard it gave the CEO or manager a bird's-eye view of just how collectively effective the programme had been.

I have said before that there is an industry-wide obsession with evaluation – and the dashboard tapped into that desire to be able to prove that what companies authorized and paid for actually worked!

After each TLA programme the owner of the training and learning transfer will receive an Impact Dashboard similar to the one illustrated in Figure 11.3.

Programme details (top left)

The programme details box offers the reader an immediate overview of the programme that the results relate to. In the example in Figure 11.3, 78 participants went through the TLA programme and were asked to complete survey feedback. Of the 78 requested feedback forms 53 people completed the feedback and the results in the Impact Dashboard relate to that feedback. Where the client is familiar with Net Promoter Score (NPS) then the dashboard also includes this popular metric.

NPS is the scoring system made popular by Frederick F Reichheld, director emeritus of the consulting firm Bain & Company who wrote the article 'The one number you need to grow', which appeared in *Harvard Business Review*. Reichheld proposed that we don't need expensive surveys and complex statistical models, instead we simply ask our customers one question: 'How likely is it that you would recommend our company to a friend or colleague?' The theory is that the more 'promoters' a company has the greater the loyalty, impact and ultimately the bigger the growth.

FIGURE 11.3 The Impact Dashboard

IMPACT DASHBOARD

Turning Learning into Action

SURVEY RESULTS

Participants were asked to consider the progress that they made with coaching following up and what they thought would have been achieved without coaching.

- With coaching objectives met
- Without coaching objectives met

% of participants

INDIVIDUAL OBJECTIVES

All participants set 3 objectives each at the end of the programme. The pie chart illustrates the distribution of the objectives by area.

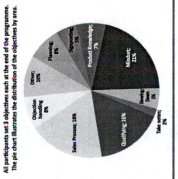

- Mindset: 21%
- Qualifying: 16%
- Sales Process: 18%
- Objection handling: 8%
- Other: 10%
- Planning: 6%
- Signposting: 5%
- Product Knowledge: 7%
- Slowing Down: 5%
- Take notes: 2%

BUSINESS BENEFITS

This wordcloud below is generated from the statements describing the benefits to the business that the programme has generated.

CHANGE

This wordcloud was generated from the statements describing the changes participants have made in the business. The comments were collected at the end of the coaching process, 3 after the training finished.

NO. PARTICIPANTS	78	
COLLATED FEEDBACK FORMS	Counter 53	Response 78
NET PROMOTER SCORE		87%

1	2	3	4	5	6	7	8	9	10
					1	6	13	33	

PROGRAMME DATES Dashboard is created for 6 programmes in total held between May 2010 and May 2011

CONSIDERATIONS 60% of participants submitted feedback with results and benefits 3 months after the programme, sales were analysed for 30% of participants who had been in the business for greater than 6 months before they attended.

LEVEL 1 EVALUATION ON TLA	1	2	3	4	5
PROGRAMME EXPECTATIONS MET	2%	7%	44%	47%	
COACHING EFFECTIVENESS	4%	25%	71%		

SALES ANALYSIS

The sales performance was analysed pre and post the programme for those that had been in the business for greater than 6 months before they attended the programme.

Programme	DATA used	Sales units 6 months prior	Sales units 6 months post	Participant Uplift	Company Uplifts same period
May 2010	5 people			+15.4%	
July 2010	3 people			+34.5%	
Sept 2010	5 people			+64.0%	
Nov 2010	6 people			+53.3%	
March 2011	4 people			+32.0%	
May 2011	6 people			+13.4%	
Average uplift for period May to March				+26.8%	

Every company's customers can be divided into three categories: promoters, passives and detractors. When asked the one question customers respond on a 0–10 point rating scale and are categorized as follows:

- Promoters (score 9–10) are loyal enthusiasts who will keep buying and refer others, fuelling growth.

- Passives (score 7–8) are satisfied but unenthusiastic customers who are vulnerable to competitive offerings.

- Detractors (score 0–6) are unhappy customers who can damage a corporate brand and impede growth through negative word-of-mouth.

A company's NPS score is therefore calculated taking the percentage of customers who are promoters and subtracting the percentage who are detractors (Figure 11.4).

FIGURE 11.4   How NPS is calculated

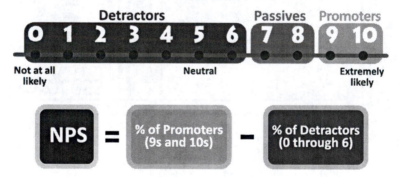

The programme details box also specifies the dates of the TLA programme and any considerations that need to be appreciated to interpret the dashboard effectively, such as people who have left the business or had extended leave.

This section also provides level one, reaction-based evaluation data. This data allows the reader of the dashboard to establish on a scale of 1–5 whether the participants' expectations of the programme were met. It also demonstrates on the same scale of 1–5 whether participants considered the coaching effective in supporting their learning transfer.

Remember, level one evaluation is just interested in the reaction of participants to the process. The only genuinely useful evaluation is level three – application – and above, but this is a good indication to a manager as to what his or her people actually thought of the programme. It is a sense check and flushes out any major problems.

Individual objectives (top middle)

At the end of a training programme everyone in the programme commits to three actions, which they detail in their TLA plan. This pie chart is a visual representation of the distribution of objectives by topic or area. Everyone's objectives are then grouped under relevant subheadings to create relevant categories.

This offers managers a quick snapshot of the key themes or types of actions that participants have focused on during the change process – and most of the time these key themes will relate to the content of the training programme. This is a quick way to see what issues were the most popular for participants to implement and work on during the TLA process.

This can be really useful information for the trainer because it tells them what parts of the training the participants think is most relevant to them. This then offers insights about how to improve the training for maximum impact. And it may even offer insights on how to create future training solutions. This information is also very useful for the head of L&D for similar reasons. If this pie chart indicates that participants are using one topic or section of the training more than others then it may influence future content.

Survey results (top left)

In the feedback process we ask all the participants from the TLA process to answer two questions: 1) On a scale of 1–5, to what level did you meet the objectives that you set at the end of the programme? and 2) On a scale of 1–5, at what level do you think you would have met those objectives without coaching?

These questions get participants to reflect on how far they have come in the TLA process and also what they think would have happened had they not had coaching support.

This box represents all actions for all participants so it offers a big-picture view of how effective the participants have considered the learning transfer process and shows the manager how relevant the participants consider the process to be. What we have found over many years is that when we ask people to self-score from 1–5 they view themselves in three ways:

- low level of objectives met (1–2);
- average level of objectives met (3);
- high level of objectives met (4–5).

If a participant gives themselves a score 3 then they are saying that they are average – and we know that average in the context of learning transfer is about 10–20 per cent implementation. If someone self-scores a 1 or a 2, we know that it means they were going to transfer nothing at all.

Interestingly, it is typically around 10 per cent of people who believe they would have met their goals without coaching, which I think instinctively is about right, with 10 per cent of learners being focused enough or ready enough to create their own change. This section in the Impact Dashboard provides the first level three application or behaviour evaluation and indicates whether or not real behavioural change has occurred, if objectives have been met, and what knowledge people have applied.

Sales analysis (bottom left)

This is the box that is most tailored to each client and the information that appears here will often depend on the type of training that was undertaken. In the example above it was sales training. This box therefore details the results of the training and TLA programme on sales uplift for each group of participants who went through the programme.

To make the comparison meaningful and fair only people who had existing results six months prior to the programme were compared. The performance of individuals was compared before the programme and then after the programme. So in the example in Figure 11.3 all the programmes had around 12 participants but if we look at the programme run on May 2010 only five of those people had been in the business six months before the programme. To make a genuine and valid comparison this box demonstrates the change in performance between those five people and their results six months prior to the programme.

For some clients this dashboard results section looks at the individual goals set on the programme and how far the participants have come in achieving those goals during the coaching. So we will ask participants to rate themselves on a score of 1–10 on their objectives when they set that objective and then again after the coaching. For example, if a participant were to set a goal of generating more leads they would be asked to rate themselves on generating leads before the coaching and again after the coaching and this results section would illustrate those improvements.

Much of the feedback displayed in this section of the Impact Dashboard is received from the TLA participants themselves. This is because we genuinely believe that it is the participants who know their roles best and therefore know what they have achieved (or not). In Phillips's terms we are using 'Expert Estimation' with the participant as the expert.

To add an additional level of validity to these results so that managers and leaders can be confident that the results reflect real-world performance improvements, and are not just wishful thinking by the participant, this section can include a manager's corroboration score. When each participant sends us the feedback on how they have done on the programme, and what changes they have made, we relay that to their manager and ask the manager to verify their score. So the manager is asked: 'On a scale of 1–10 how confident are you that you have seen this level of change?' This is then documented on the Impact Dashboard as the manager's corroboration score. The higher the score the more the manager agrees with the participant's own assessment of their performance.

This section of the Impact Dashboard provides more in-depth level three evaluation by exploring the real-world changes that have occurred in the business as a result of the training and TLA process.

Change (bottom middle)

In this section we generate a 'word cloud' around all the anecdotal information we receive in the feedback forms. Participants are asked, 'What changes have you put into place?' and their responses generate the word cloud.

Word clouds or tag clouds were developed in the mid 1990s. They are a basic visualization method for text data, originally used to depict keyword meta-data on websites. The importance of each 'word' is shown in terms of size or colour. Software developed later in 2008 is used more widely to visualize word frequency in free-form natural language sets, which is great for analysis of individual changes made due to training. We use **www.wordle.net**.

In the example shown we can see that the words 'process', 'customer', 'better', 'questions' and 'selling' are larger than 'listening' or 'positive' because the larger words appeared more often in the way that the participants described the changes they had implemented following the TLA process.

This can be really useful in order to get a sense of what participants are really taking from the experience and what is actually changing. The larger words will reflect the content of the training and the genuine real-world changes that the participants have made in the workplace.

This section of the Impact Dashboard provides an additional perspective on level three evaluation by describing the changes that have occurred as a result of the training and TLA process.

Business benefits (bottom right)

The last section of the Impact Dashboard is another word cloud. This time it is generated using all the answers we receive from participants to the question: 'What benefits have your changes created?'

Again, the larger words represent the words or descriptors most often used to describe the business benefits achieved as a result of the TLA process. This 'business benefits' word cloud provides a level four evaluation and explores the impact that the training and learning transfer process has had on the business.

The feedback process to create the Impact Dashboard is simple and effective and we have a 90 per cent success rate at collecting feedback forms – or as we call them 'progress review' forms – at the end of the TLA coaching process. These forms are important because everything that is discussed in the TLA conversations is confidential and the feedback form and subsequent evaluation is often the company's only way of definitively assessing whether or not the coaching is adding value. I am surprised when I hear people say 'I can't get participants to fill out feedback or reporting forms after a training event'. In my experience when people have changed after training they are excited to share the wins and will happily find five minutes to capture that information. This Impact Dashboard therefore gives decision makers and invested parties an accurate one-page indication of value and allows them to evaluate the programme from level one (reaction) to level three (change or application) and finally touches on level four (business impact). It can also be used as a tool for identifying where case studies and success stories can be captured.

While there are still undoubtedly opportunities to improve these measurements they are all created through information that can be collected easily and some information is better than no information. It is also a process that either L&D or the external TLA specialist can have control over without needing additional management reporting from the client.

Summary of key points

- Attempting to fudge, hide or ignore results by cherry picking what to evaluate is pointless. Genuinely evaluating success or failure against worthwhile objectives is not.

- So what type of evaluation really matters? In an effort to definitively answer this question Jack and Patti Phillips of the ROI Institute surveyed the CEOs of Fortune 500 companies and asked them what they considered to be important.

- The top three things that the CEOs identified as currently being measured were considered the least important three things to measure, and the bottom three things that the CEOs identified as not currently being measured also happen to be the top three things that they want measured in the future. Just 8 per cent of respondents said that their business currently measures impact and yet 96 per cent said it was their number one priority.

- CEOs don't care how many people went through training last year, they don't really care if those people enjoyed the course or not and they don't even care that much about how much it cost on an hourly basis. What they care about is the result. What did participants do differently and how did that impact the business? Business leaders need access to useful and pertinent information about the effectiveness of training programmes so they can make better use of the training budget and get the results they seek.

- The trends in evaluation are suggesting that people are finally waking up to the fact that anything below level three evaluation is meaningless. The key to transformation and genuine training success is application or behaviour change.

- For evaluation to be truly effective we must start with the end in mind. We need to decide what the course objectives are at the very start before the programme has even been designed and then evaluate the outcomes in relation to those objectives.

- As a result, the evaluation necessary for successful learning transfer must focus on application evaluation and above, which is why we use the Impact Dashboard to document almost all levels of evaluation.

- Using the Impact Dashboard stakeholders are able to assess reaction and learning evaluations as well as application and first stage impact evaluation with the option of going all the way to ROI.

- The Impact Dashboard gives decision makers and invested parties an accurate one-page indication of value and allows them to evaluate the programme from level one (reaction) to level three (change or application) and finally level four (business impact). It can also be used as a tool for identifying where case studies and success stories can be captured.

Part Three
MAKING LEARNING TRANSFER HAPPEN AND THE BENEFITS BY STAKEHOLDER

12
How to roll out TLA successfully

So far we have explored the reasons why corporate training has traditionally been so ineffective and identified the missing link as learning transfer. In Part Two, I introduced Turning Learning into Action® (TLA) – a transfer of learning change methodology that ensures that what is learnt in the training event is actually transferred to the workplace by way of performance improvement.

TLA is an enhanced coaching methodology that facilitates behavioural change. The success of training initiatives can no longer be measured by how many people attend a programme or even what skills they can demonstrate at the end of it. The only real measure of success is when individual participants use the learning on a regular basis, change their behaviour and improve performance as a result of the training. In Part Two we explored the three stages of TLA – preparation, action and evaluation and explained how to achieve genuine transfer of learning through TLA.

In Part Three we will look more closely at the logistics of how to make learning transfer happen in any business. We will explore how TLA can effectively be rolled out across large training programmes and cover the pros and cons of TLA according to each of the training stakeholders.

In this chapter we will explore:

- *who* rolls out TLA;
- *when* TLA needs to support training;
- *how* to roll out TLA effectively.

Who rolls out TLA

It is worth noting that for some readers the mere idea that learning transfer be someone other than the manager's responsibility will be radical. But as I've said throughout the book, teaching managers how to coach in a half-day workshop and expecting them to be able to coach learning transfer is unrealistic and unfair. Managers by definition are juggling many varied tasks and their natural drive is towards efficiency. So even if they can coach they will try to conduct the TLA coaching follow-up conversations in 10 minutes rather than 30 minutes. And whilst it is possible to have a 10-minute conversation and tick a box to say we've had the conversation it is impossible to make lasting behaviour change with 10-minute conversations. Participants simply tell the manager what they think the manager wants to hear – and it's easy to bluff in 10 minutes. That is why we advocate 30 minutes for each TLA conversation, because it is short enough to be really efficient but not too short to allow for fudging and box ticking only.

If you believe that learning transfer is part of the manager's fundamental responsibility I would ask you to suspend belief and lay your assumptions aside until you have considered the other options. I realize it is a potentially controversial idea, but if we already appreciate that the manager is rarely the right person to run the training then the manger may not always be the best person to transfer the learning. Obviously it depends on the complexity of the performance change needed, but if behaviour change is required then it simply does not happen in a 10-minute conversation tacked on to an existing agenda. I encourage you to bear with me and just consider that there may be a better person to manage learning transfer.

The size of the TLA roll-out will, of course, depend on how many people are scheduled to attend a particular training programme and how much training a business buys in any one year. Managing the TLA process for 50 people is a very different logistical consideration to managing a roll-out of 250 or 2,000 people. The volume of TLA required and the relative importance of the training will clearly impact who is best placed to roll it out.

It is important to realize, however, that even if the roll-out runs into hundreds or even thousands of people it is all manageable and feasible through the cascade process. If 25 people are trained in TLA and they each give 2 hours per week for 2 months then those 25 people can effectively roll out TLA to 250 people. The big question, of course, is whether those people should be internal personnel trained in TLA so the skill set can be used again and again and remain inside the business or outsourced to external TLA specialists as and when they are needed.

There are two internal options and two external options to choose from:

- the manager of the participant;
- the internal specialist;
- the trainer/facilitator;
- the external specialist.

The manager of the participant

The first internal option for rolling out TLA following a training programme is to have the participant's manager trained in TLA.

The advantages of the manager

- A manager trained in enhanced coaching and specifically how to use that skill for effective learning transfer through TLA will increase their internal and external value.

- Once a manager knows how to facilitate behaviour change through enhanced coaching they can use that skill after training programmes to turn learning into action or they can use it in a variety of different management roles and situations that require behaviour change, such as performance improvement. Learning TLA – fundamentally a behaviour change methodology – can make managers better managers.

- The TLA skill set stays inside the business for future use.

- The participant's manager is close to the business results so they can see the impact of the process first hand.

- It is a very good way to get the managers engaged in the learning, growth and development of their people.

- The manager learns a proven methodology to successfully hold people accountable for actions. It gives the managers greater confidence in their own skills as managers.

The disadvantages of the manager

- For TLA to be truly effective and transformational the participant needs to be very honest and this requires a certain level of vulnerability about their weaknesses or shortcomings. Often it is hard to be *that* vulnerable and honest with the person who directly influences the participant's future position or salary.

- Managers are already time poor so finding 3 × 30 minutes over a two-month period for each of their reportees who attended the course can be difficult.

- Managers can lack the focus and discipline to invest in TLA, especially if they have numerous competing priorities.

- Managers will want TLA to happen through a casual conversation or they will want to tack the learning transfer conversation on to the end of an existing agenda, but that won't work. They need to 'change hats' for the coaching conversation to be effective.

- Specialized behavioural change is a skill set that needs to be taught and practised and yet managers often assume they can automatically shepherd the transfer of learning process without specific training. They can't. TLA will only be successful if the person facilitating learning transfer is trained in TLA or some other behaviour change methodology.

When to use the participants' manager

- If there is a high level of skill within the management team and the manager is proficient in another change methodology, TLA or is willing to be trained in a specific learning transfer methodology.

- When there is a large programme roll-out.

- When there are several important training initiatives in the pipeline over the coming years – each requiring real-world behaviour change to improve performance.

- When there is a trusting and productive relationship between the manager and his or her reportees.

- When the manager is attending the same programme as his reportees he will then be close to the programme. Remember, someone will also need to hold the manager accountable for change.

- When the manager understands the importance of 'changing hats' – taking off their manager's hat for the TLA conversation and replacing it with their learning transfer hat.

The internal specialist

The next internal option is the internal specialist. The internal specialist is someone inside the business who may or may not be the manager. This may be someone in the L&D department, Human Resources (HR) or someone identified as a 'high potential' in the business. Often senior managers will seek to identify individuals with high potential who they recognize as future managers or people who will drive the business forward.

If a business is highly focused on training and development then training an internal team in TLA can be an excellent way to implement TLA over the long term. This team may be cross-functional or reside inside the HR or L&D department.

The advantages of the internal specialist

- An internal specialist trained in enhanced coaching and specifically how to use that skill for effective learning transfer through TLA will increase their internal and external value.
- The TLA skill set stays inside the business for future use.
- Creating a team of internal TLA specialists can be a brilliant way of enrolling high potentials who need more from their role but are perhaps not fully ready for a management position.
- Facilitating TLA often gives people a rewarding sense of supporting others in the organization.
- If the internal specialist is not linked to the participant in their day-to-day environment the participant is more likely to be honest and open in the conversation, which will always improve results.
- Using an internal specialist can help build cross-functional relationships and reduce silos in an organization.
- Using an internal specialist can give both parties an experience and insight into different parts of the business, which can often assist creativity, understanding and performance in their own roles.
- If the internal specialist is within L&D or HR then issues of seniority are less important. Depending on the level of seniority of the training

it would not be appropriate, for example, for a junior high-potential to be coaching a senior leader. But it could still be appropriate for an L&D internal specialist to coach that senior leader.

The disadvantages of the internal specialist

- Depending on the size of the organization, the relationship between the internal specialist and the participant there could still be an issue of trust in the conversations even with a confidentiality agreement in place. It may take a while to build a sufficient level of trust to get people to open up.

- TLA requires a high level of skill so there will still be people who are naturally better at it than others. It is important to acknowledge that, so that the internal specialists are all very proficient at learning transfer and can be picked to suit the process.

- Depending on how much training is done annually, being an internal TLA specialist could involve a big time commitment from people who already have other roles and responsibilities. Being a facilitator for TLA must become part of that person's role and responsibilities otherwise they may not prioritize it.

When to use the internal specialist

- When it is a large-scale programme roll-out.

- When the business has good internal people with the necessary time available.

- When the business has internal people who are interested and want to learn the skill, use it and help grow the organization.

- When senior management wants to give their high potentials more responsibility without promoting them too early.

- When the internal specialist understands the importance of 'changing hats' so they take off the hat they usually wear in their day-to-day role and replace it with their learning transfer hat.

The trainer/facilitator

The first external option for rolling out TLA following a training programme is the trainer/facilitator of the training event.

The advantages of the trainer/facilitator

- It is useful for the trainer or facilitator because they become closer to the business and are then in a position to advise about other training requirements.
- Increases their ownership for the real finish line.
- Where the validity of training is being increasingly questioned, incorporating a transfer of learning methodology into their training means that trainers and facilitators can massively increase real-world results.
- If they are trained specifically in a transfer of learning methodology they can partner up with other trainers and derive income from training they didn't personally deliver.

The disadvantages of the trainer/facilitator

- The trainer is so familiar with the content that it can be hard for them to ask questions rather than 'telling' the participant how it should be done. Even if the trainer is correct and the participant agrees with them, this situation makes it very hard for the participant to take ownership of the process and the necessary behavioural change. When we remove the autonomy from the process and stop the participant working things out for themselves then we remove the possibility for intrinsic motivation, which is essential for effective change.
- Even if the trainer is conscious of this challenge and deliberately holds back from telling the person the solutions, the participant is used to the trainer being the trainer and will expect them to provide solutions. As a result, the participant may not fully engage with the process because they assume if they get stuck the trainer will step in and solve their challenge. If the trainer doesn't do this the participant can feel resentful, as though the trainer is deliberately holding back.
- It is often more expensive to have the trainer conduct the TLA follow-up because they are used to calculating their costs based on a day rate where they work with, say, 15 people. TLA is a one-to-one process and the danger is that the trainer will cost the process based on high-end executive coaching, which is not comparable or necessary in the transfer of learning context.

- As I will explain shortly, TLA is most effective when the conversations are conducted over the phone rather than face-to-face and yet trainers are, by definition, more experienced and proficient in the face-to-face environment.
- The TLA skills stay outside the business.

When to use the trainer/facilitator

- When the trainer is specifically skilled in behaviour change in addition to delivering training; *and*
- When the trainer is providing TLA for a programme *they did not* personally deliver.

The external specialist

The final external option for delivering TLA is the external specialist.

The advantages of the external specialist

- The external TLA specialist is an expert in the field.
- They are highly proficient in transfer of learning because they are doing it all day every day.
- There is no relationship or politics between a participant and external specialist, which makes it easier for the participant to be open, honest and vulnerable regarding what he or she wants or needs to address. The conversations are more focused and productive as a result.
- It means that the business doesn't have to invest any additional time to get the results it seeks. This is especially valuable if the people in the business are already time poor.

The disadvantages of the external specialist

- The manager can feel as though he or she is being kept out of the loop and extra effort is necessary to make sure they are still engaged in the transfer of learning process. This is easily facilitated, however, using a propriety learning transfer system, which sends the managers the goals of each participant at the start of the process and keeps them informed all the way along.
- Bringing in external specialists to implement TLA following training programmes can be more costly in the long run than training an

internal resource. This is not always the case, however, and we will explore costs in more detail in the next chapter.

- The skills stay outside the business.

When to use the external specialist

- When senior management has a highly visible programme that is critical to the business and change needs to be guaranteed.
- When the internal people are already stretched for time and don't have the resources or capability to deliver TLA internally.
- When a business doesn't invest in a great deal of training each year and it is not worth up-skilling people internally but senior management still wants to ensure that what they do invest in delivers results.
- When a business is trialling the TLA process to see what results can be generated.

Selecting the best TLA roll-out strategy for your needs

When deciding who is going to be the best person to roll out TLA ask yourself the following questions:

1 Is this person proficient in a change methodology?

2 Is this person an effective coach?

3 Does this person have the time to effectively facilitate behaviour change? They will need 3 × 30 minutes per participant over a two-month period after the course.

4 Does this person already have the skills?

5 Could this person learn the skills?

6 Does this person have the desire to support the transfer of learning process?

7 Can they make transfer of learning a priority in their schedule?

8 Do we have the resources in the L&D department?

9 Do we have access to a system that could be used to disseminate actions and outputs after the coaching conversations so as to keep everyone on track?

10 Will we be able to evaluate the success of the programme?

If the answer to these questions is mostly 'No' then it may be best to outsource transfer of learning to an external TLA specialist or train an internal specialist in TLA – especially if the training budget is significant year on year.

I make no apologies for saying that the best behavioural change methodology for transfer of learning is TLA. If we are serious about getting results from our training then someone in the business should be trained in TLA or the process should be outsourced to an external TLA specialist – even if we only do this once to get a sense of how effective it can be and get everyone enrolled in the outcome.

But, if this is not a viable option at this point then there is enough in this book to facilitate vast improvements in transfer of learning. As an absolute minimum, however, the person assigned to manage the transfer of learning process must be an effective coach and proficient in a change methodology, because transfer of learning is not just about learning it is also about behavioural change. And that person must have enough time in their existing workload to dedicate to the process over the course of two months after the training. Typically, enough time is 3 × 30 minutes per participant. They must also have access to some sort of administrative support so that agreements and actions can be automatically e-mailed to participants to keep everyone on track. It is a well-known business adage that what gets measured gets managed. The same is true of successful transfer of learning. The process must be measured and managed, which means that someone owns it, drives it and a record is kept and distributed of all conversations, actions and outputs from the sessions.

When TLA needs to support training

Not all training is created equally. For some training programmes the fact that the learning is never used or applied in the business is not that important. For most training, however, it is disastrous.

There are different types of training and the type will determine whether a transfer of learning methodology should be used or not. In the case of compliance training, for example, there is often no need to follow up the training event to ensure transfer of learning because the objective of the training is to ensure that the participants know how to do a certain task or behave in a certain situation. The training is not seeking habitual behavioural change it is simply seeking to ensure that should a certain situation arise in the workplace everyone knows how to act or what to do. This is true of certain health and safety training where the objective of the training is to ensure participants have the necessary information and knowledge to keep them safe in the workplace and to limit liability for the employer should someone ignore the guidelines and get injured.

Learning transfer is also hard to run effectively when the training is not habitual. Say, for example, we decide to run presentation skills training. Unless the participants are making several presentations every month and they have a habitual way of presenting that we are seeking to change then learning transfer is not going to be very effective. If participants will only practice their new presentation skills once or twice a year then we are not actually seeking habitual behaviour change.

The real value of learning transfer and when it should be applied to training programmes is when the purpose of the training is to change or improve habitual ongoing behaviour. It is therefore a vital component for any soft skills training programmes such as leadership skills, communication skills, management skills, sales training – anything that alters habitual behaviour or is seeking a change to the way participants operate or show up in their working life.

If we want to genuinely improve performance back in the workplace for any form of soft skills that participants use on a regular basis then we must support those people to change after the training event through learning transfer or some other behavioural change methodology.

In an ideal world TLA should be used for every training programme that is seeking to improve soft skills back in the workplace, but I appreciate that is unrealistic and would represent a huge cultural shift from where training is right now. So this section is about helping us decide when we really need to use it and why.

When a training programme is really visible or critically important to the business then use that programme to dip a toe in the learning transfer water. If it is absolutely essential that results are achieved from the training and there is no previous experience in successful learning transfer implementation then recruit the assistance of external TLA specialists.

This is a cost-effective and logical approach that allows a business leader to experience the uplift in results and improved performance that TLA can deliver before committing time and energy to training their own internal specialists. In addition it is also smart to choose a training programme that will or could deliver fast results. Sales training is a great programme to start with because it is so easy to measure before and after results. Hire an external transfer of learning specialist to deliver the programme and compare the results for yourself.

TLA works. There is no doubt about it. I appreciate, however, that business leaders and senior managers must verify that for themselves. The best way to do that initially is to choose a suitable training programme and hire an experienced external specialist to facilitate transfer of learning. A suitable programme would be either one that will deliver fast and easily measureable results or one that is critical to the business. Once a business unit has confirmed the results then senior management can decide whether to train a dedicated internal TLA team or simply buy in the skill as and when it is needed, depending on the importance and impact of the training.

The bottom line is that if we are seeking soft-skill habitual behavioural change – where the participants on the training apply their new knowledge back in the workplace and create new, better work practices and improve performance – then we *must* source good training *and* include a transfer of learning follow-up methodology to ensure behaviour change.

If we do not then the training will be wasted on at least 90 per cent of the participants. There is always a small percentage of any training programme who will love it and actually do something with it without prompting. But sending people through loads of training in the vain hope that a few of them might pick up something useful is the shotgun approach to training. It is bad for morale, extremely expensive and time consuming.

Investing in transfer of learning as well as good training allows for a much more precise and targeted approach to training, which allows us finally to reverse the terrible statistics on learning effectiveness. Just as there are always a few people who will love the training, there are also always a few people who will hate it and never do anything with it. But if we can reverse the statistics through learning transfer, so that up to 90 per cent of participants do make the changes and improve performance, then we can make a fundamental difference to the profitability and performance of the business.

If we are serious about seeking to change behaviour and performance then training needs to be backed by a robust transfer of learning process to ensure that the learning is transferred back to the workplace and is being applied by participants on a regular basis. And let's face it, if we are not seeking behaviour change and real-world application from the participants then why are we even running the training programme in the first place?

How to roll out TLA effectively

The secret weapon to productive and cost-effective learning transfer roll-out – irrespective of the numbers of people – is the telephone.

When I was first trained as a coach in the UK I remember being told of the power of the telephone as a coaching medium but I immediately discounted it. Anyone who knows me will vouch for the fact that I'm a people person. I love people and I understand people face-to-face. I genuinely didn't think it was possible to coach effectively over the phone because I was sure I'd miss the visual cues that are so important in developing rapport and creating a trusting environment.

I moved to Australia and began coaching. And I'm a little embarrassed to admit that one of the reasons I chose to coach by phone was that at the age of 30 in the executive coaching field I knew I needed to 'look' older than I was and over the phone I was able to sound more mature than my years. What started off as a necessary evil soon ended up being my preferred method of coaching, not just for the efficiency but for the results.

Telephone coaching is infinitely more time efficient than face-to-face coaching for both the coach and the person being coached. There is no commute, no travel expenses, less time for chit-chat and it is easily scalable across geographically dispersed participants. There is less opportunity to wander off topic and, perhaps more importantly, it is more effective in the process of change.

As I have said many times throughout this book, successful training is as much about behavioural change as it is about learning. And behavioural change is only really possible when we engage the individual in the change process and get them to appreciate the need to change for their own benefit not someone else's. Change comes about through a process of self-reflection and personal contemplation. It is initiated from within and is facilitated by encouraging the individual to listen to their internal dialogue and allowing them effectively to have a conversation with themselves. This process is made far easier on the phone because the questions and the conversation go straight into the individual's ear. When we have a face-to-face conversation with someone the conversation can often bounce around the room: it is easier to ignore tough questions, people get distracted more easily and the interaction is not as intense. The telephone is like whispering in someone's ear, where the communication goes straight down the ear canal to the brain. It can't be deflected; it has nowhere else to go. As a result we get access to a greater level of truth because we talk directly to the person before they have had a moment to filter their thoughts and message.

Effective learning transfer is not about the coach it is about the individual. The TLA coach doesn't need to see visual cues – they have an effective structure instead. It is much harder to tell someone something difficult when we are face-to-face with that person, even if we don't know them personally. On the phone that discomfort is reduced because we are not in the same room. It can be really hard for someone who is very competent in their role to admit they are struggling in one particular area or have vulnerabilities. It can also be difficult to even see these possible areas for growth if someone is a high performer – even the Olympic gold medallist will work with their coach to ensure they keep improving in order to retain the gold at the next championship – this is the approach to take with the top performers. That process is made much easier if the conversation occurs over the phone and if the coach is not someone who is intimately involved in the individual's daily activity.

Many years ago I stumbled across a report from the United States (which I wish I had kept) which confirmed that people *are* more honest and open on the telephone compared to face-to-face interactions, although we don't need a report to know this is true.

Most of us have had the experience of chatting to someone on a long-haul flight or on a long train journey and telling them things we hadn't even told our friends or partner. This openness comes from the anonymity of the interaction. This anonymity is fostered when we either won't see that person again or – in the case of the telephone – when we *can't* see them. It is this 'not seeing' the other person that is so crucial in the telephone debate. Modern technology has allowed us to move away from face-to-face com-munication, which in turn has allowed us sometimes to conveniently forget that the communication we are sending out is read by other human beings. As such there has been a rise in career-limiting 'over-sharing' on social network sites or e-mails. But in a coaching situation the honesty that comes from 'not seeing' the coach with whom we are in conversation can be a real bonus, because honesty is imperative for successful change.

Using the telephone for TLA follow-up means that the individual cannot see their coach, as a result they feel less self-conscious and are more likely to open up and be honest. It can often feel as though the individual is actually having a conversation with themselves and the coach is simply shepherding the conversation and supporting the participant towards behavioural change. This idea is critical to the TLA methodology and I firmly believe that telephone coaching is not just more efficient but infinitely more effective because it allows the individual to be more honest with the coach and, perhaps more importantly, with themselves. It is the internal dialogue and internal conversations that we have with ourselves all the time that ultimately control our thoughts and feelings and it is those thoughts and feelings that then determine how we act and how we behave. So if we are looking for behaviour change we have to create a safe environment where the individual can access their own thinking and really bring that internal dialogue into awareness. The telephone is the easiest way to access this state.

As an addition to this – it may be tempting for a TLA coach to use Skype, webcams or video conferencing for coaching, because they feel that when they see the person they can have better rapport and gauge the non-verbal cues even if they are not in the same room. I firmly believe that the telephone is better than any form of video conferencing – as TLA needs to be about the participant talking to himself or herself in an accountable format. Put simply – the phone works.

But there are some rules!

First, the TLA coach and the participant must treat the meeting with the same respect and seriousness as a face-to-face meeting. That means the coach should look the part and be fully prepared. The coach must *be present* even if the individual can't see the coach, so that means no distractions. The coach must turn off their mobile phone and ask the individual being coached to do the same. The coach needs to move away from their computer screen so that they are not distracted by e-mails or other work. If the coach works with music in the background it is important to turn it off during the TLA conversations. If the coach hears the keys on a keyboard being tapped or the ping of an e-mail coming in, or noises that sound as though the TLA participant is moving around – call them on it by saying something like, 'John, are you moving around?'

Never conduct a coaching conversation when the individual is driving or doing some other activity. They must be focused. And finally the coach should always use a headset or handset; don't put the participant on speaker phone because it creates distance between the coach and the individual. Using the phone is not just convenient – it is the best way of facilitating a great process.

Summary of key points

- The size of the TLA roll-out will depend on how many people are scheduled to attend a particular training programme and how much training is bought by the business in any one year. Managing the TLA process for 50 people is a very different logistical consideration to managing a roll-out of 250 or 2,000 people. The volume of TLA required and the relative importance of the training will clearly impact who is best placed to roll it out.

- There are two internal options (manager of the participant and internal specialist) and two external options (the trainer/facilitator or external specialist) to choose from.

- Not all training is created equally. For some training programmes the fact that the learning is never used or applied in the business is not that important. For most training, however, it is disastrous.

- When the purpose of the training is to change or improve habitual ongoing behaviour then learning transfer is particularly valuable. It is therefore a vital component for any soft skills training programmes such as leadership skills, communication skills, management skills, sales training – anything that alters habitual behaviour or seeks a change in the way that participants operate or show up in their working life.

- If a training programme is really visible or critically important to the business then use that programme to dip a toe in the learning transfer water. When it is absolutely essential to guarantee the results and the business has no previous experience in successful learning transfer implementation then recruit the assistance of an external TLA specialist.

- The telephone is the secret weapon to productive and cost-effective learning transfer roll-out – irrespective of the numbers of people in the roll-out.

- Telephone coaching is infinitely more time-efficient than face-to-face coaching, for both the coach and the person being coached. There is no commute, no travel expenses and less time for chit-chat. There is less opportunity to wander off topic and, perhaps more importantly, it is more effective in the process of change.

- Change comes about through a process of self-reflection and personal contemplation. It is initiated from within and is facilitated by encouraging the individual to listen to their internal dialogue and allowing them to have a conversation with themselves effectively. This process is made far easier on the phone because the questions and conversation go straight into the individual's ear.

- Using the telephone for TLA follow-up means that the individual can't see the coach, as a result they feel less self-conscious and are more likely to open up and be honest. It can often feel as though the individual is actually having a conversation with themselves and the coach is simply shepherding the conversation and supporting them towards behavioural change.

- But there are telephone rules. Both parties must treat the meeting with the same respect and seriousness as a face-to-face meeting.

13
The benefits of TLA by stakeholder

There are many different stakeholders in the training process. As in the training design process they all have different objectives and outcomes and their perception of the finish line or ideal outcome is often quite different. This final chapter explores the benefits of TLA from the perspective of the various stakeholders; while not an exhaustive list, it covers the key players.

The stakeholders in the training process are:

- CEO;
- L&D professionals;
- commissioning head;
- participant;
- manager of the participant;
- trainer or facilitator of the training;
- TLA specialist.

CEO

As the head of the business the CEO wants learning to impact the business positively and help deliver strategic outcomes. On the whole they don't really care how that is achieved as long as it is achieved.

For years CEOs have questioned training budgets and been left wondering whether the business is really getting value for money. This is especially true during difficult economic times, when everyone from the top to the bottom must justify expenditure and demonstrate return on investment.

And whilst there may still be the occasional CEO who just wants to tick some training boxes in order to keep their people feeling valued and suitably developed, the vast majority see training as necessary but staggeringly unsuccessful – most of the time.

It is clear to everyone in the industry and every stakeholder in the training process that the finish line of training is not the end of the course – it is the demonstration of the new skills in the business. There is a growing acceptance that real-world behavioural change and application is the new finish line for training, and unless training is bought and developed with a learning transfer process as part of the package then change will not happen for the vast majority of participants. That represents a colossal waste of time and money. But it also represents a huge opportunity.

CEOs need results and increasingly they need to justify expenditure, and all their managers must do the same. So when a business needs people to improve skills, performance or apply new knowledge then TLA almost guarantees that outcome. We know that TLA supports change and it works regardless of the quality or type of training. That means that CEOs can be much more confident that the training that is proposed is going to deliver. When performance improvement training is sourced and purchased with a learning transfer process as part of the training solution then results will *always* improve.

TLA provides certainty of outcome and improved results and business benefits. And all this can be achieved without increasing the training budget. The reason why so much training fails is due to lack of learning transfer and post-training follow-up and support. That is a readily accepted industry-wide fact. Unfortunately, for too long the solution to the failure of training was more training. So more and more was spent to deliver less and less. Even if the training was fantastic, without a learning transfer strategy nothing much will come of that training. But if learning transfer is always purchased with the training or factored into the budget then the training *will* work and there will be no need to waste additional resources on more training in a desperate attempt to improve performance.

Instead of spending $100,000 on two training courses that don't work the business could spend half of that amount on one training course with a learning transfer strategy that did work. Surely that is a better outcome for everyone. The business gets the essential performance improvement it seeks. Those results are achieved without spending more money – possibly even less money – and the participants are actually using their new knowledge to improve productivity and performance. Plus they are no longer upset and irritated at being asked to attend *yet another* training programme that they know, before they even arrive, they will never use in the workplace.

TLA is therefore a smart solution to an old problem and ensures that the CEO can really get value for money from training initiatives. The Impact Dashboard also allows the CEO to get a clear one-page summary of the training and TLA results without having to wade through a 20-page report.

L&D professionals

One of the biggest issues that learning and development leaders face in almost every business is credibility, validity and how to 'get a seat at the table'. In other words, how do these professionals get a seat at the board table and become an integral part of the strategic decision-making process? More often than not it is the operations manager, the sales manager or the manufacturing manager who help to forge the strategy and decide future direction.

The more that L&D leaders and employees can be seen as effective contributors to successful business results, rather than a just a business support function, the more valued they are going to be. If the L&D professionals embrace the need for an effective learning transfer process and, where behaviour change is required, always ensure that a learning transfer process is included alongside the training solution, then their credibility and results will improve exponentially.

Learning and development professionals will no longer be regarded as the corporate third cousin, constantly taking money and people out of the business for training that delivers no discernible outcome. Instead, if they embrace TLA, or indeed any proven transfer of learning methodology, then they can quietly shift that perception so that they are seen as the providers of genuine cost-effective business solutions. And from that vantage point they would finally get the seat at the table that they clearly deserve.

Transfer of learning is instrumental in bringing change to the business. By embracing TLA as a learning transfer process the L&D professionals finally get to demonstrate how their training programmes are bringing change to the business and improving performance.

The challenge for the head of learning and development is in the transition from the old way to the new way. The old way is training that they secretly accept will probably not work; the new way is to purchase training only alongside a proven transfer of learning component. Making that transition will often require an acknowledgement of past failure – and that is never easy. It requires courage and strength of character. No one likes to admit they are wrong or that what they have done in the past was inefficient or unproductive. So much so that it is often easier to stay with the herd and stick to what doesn't work, safe in the knowledge that 'at least everyone else is doing it!' If the L&D managers maintain the status quo at least they can trot out facts and figures and talk of industry standard and how 20 per cent implementation is normal. The problem, of course, is that it doesn't matter if it is normal – achieving 'normal' results does not alter the fact that it is an unforgivably poor statistic for training effectiveness. Most L&D managers and professionals already know that training is largely ineffective. The big question is what they are going to do about it. Will they choose to maintain the status quo and accept poor results they can easily justify as being 'normal'? Or will they break free from the past and embrace a proven transfer of learning methodology, which – to them at least – is untested?

TLA works. Of that I have no doubt. However, I do recognize that taking the plunge to source and deliver training differently, especially the first time, takes courage. But if you are an L&D professional reading this I absolutely guarantee that it is worth that risk and you will be staggered at how effective good training and TLA can really be in facilitating real-world behavioural change.

This is important to remember, whether you are the head of the department or not. Often an L&D professional is charged with sourcing training and making sure it is delivered effectively. As such they are instrumental in the success of training and yet they don't own the budget; they are not delivering the training but are accountable and almost always in the firing line when it doesn't deliver. These professionals just want something that works, but without a proven learning transfer methodology their job can be a thankless task. Traditionally the best way to minimize the backlash was to take owner-ship up to the point that the training was delivered and then bump all post-training responsibilities on to the manager of the participants. On the face of it, this was a reasonable course of action because L&D professionals were then charged to source another training programme for another manager – and there are only so many hours in the day. But with TLA there is no need to do that. Everyone in the business must take ownership of training and drive it to the new finish line – application into the business – otherwise training is useless.

Without successful transfer of learning it can be a rollercoaster ride for everyone in L&D, just churning out courses that have little impact in the business. With TLA, however, the training is implemented, creates results and everyone wins.

Commissioning head

The commissioning head is the person in the business who commissions the training programme. Very often they have a particular business problem or want a business outcome and have decided that training of some description will provide the answer. It is therefore likely that any subsequent training will be paid for by his or her budget or he or she will have to convince L&D of the merits of their requested training.

It is then L&D's job to work out the best way to deliver that training result, which may or may not include learning transfer. But when a commissioning head says 'I want some training' it is not really training they want – they want an outcome or a solution to a problem and have assumed that training may be a valid way to solve that problem.

So the benefits of learning transfer for the commissioning head are very straightforward – it massively increases the likelihood that the commissioning head will get what he or she wants. If a commissioning head is really frustrated that their team leaders are not leading very well, then they don't really care *how* that is fixed they just want it fixed. But putting those individuals through a leadership programme alone will make no difference. Even if the training is phenomenal and the participants were keen to attend the programme and loved the course, leadership is a behaviour not a one-off action. To make effective changes to an individual's ability to lead they need to set targets around what they would like to achieve and be supported to meet those targets over the course of several weeks. TLA provides that support and therefore ensures that the commissioning head gets the outcome of better team leaders.

Participant

Most people want to do better in their job if they can. The problem is that years of training failure has built up a residue of cynicism and irritation around training that can be hard to penetrate. As soon as anyone even mentions the 'T-word', eyes are rolling across the department and there is a collective sigh of 'Oh no – not again'. People know from often bitter experience that training wastes their time and puts them behind so they have to work late for a fortnight – and then nothing actually changes.

What effective learning transfer does for the participant is help break down that cynicism through a respectful process of ongoing support. They come to realize that the business doesn't expect overnight miracles. They get to self-select targets and objectives that are meaningful to them and will actually help them in their role and future career. And, perhaps best of all, learning transfer does not require a huge extra commitment beyond the training event. When participants realize they can achieve results with just a few extra hours spread out over a few weeks they don't feel so resentful. Besides, they have already had so much experience of failed training they already know that unless they are held accountable they won't get the results.

For the participants of training programmes, transfer of learning almost guarantees that they will have to endure less training in the future – not more. They will be supported to make the changes over a reasonable period of time and don't have to be fearful about not being able to master the new skill or manage the change. Most people are resistant of change, or a little scared of trying new things, even if they won't admit it. TLA helps to manage that fear and often the benefits spill over into all the other areas of the participant's life.

Manager of participant

The manager of the participant usually wants the result too, but they may or may not be the commissioning head. How much they are brought into the result will usually depend on how closely they were consulted and involved in the suggestion and selection of the training.

They want things to be easy but the mere mention of training makes them sweat a little. Managers already know that they probably will be expected to shoulder the responsibility for application. They also know that they probably won't do more than the bare minimum to allow them to have an adequate conversation with *their* manager about learning transfer. They don't feel good about that and most feel a sense of guilt, similar to the guilt we all feel when we know we should do something but also know we won't. It is awkward and uncomfortable but we just cannot see how it can be done, so we shrug our shoulders and accept it. It is almost always assumed that transfer of learning is the manager's job and, considering that they are usually already under pressure, training failure is simply a matter of time – and everyone involved knows it.

When I was at the AITD conference in Melbourne in April 2011 the head of learning for a major bank in Australia told the audience that learning transfer was of the upmost importance to his company but he didn't want to be pushing it back on to the desk of his managers when the managers were already stretched to the limit. I completely agree with this sentiment – thinking that the manager of the participant is going to be the solution to the learning transfer problem is unrealistic.

For the manager, learning transfer offers a viable solution that not only gets them off an unwinnable hook but allows them to stay connected to the change process and know what is going on for each of the participants. As part of the TLA system the participant's TLA plan, including the three objectives that the person has committed to, can be automatically sent to that person's manager. That way, the manager feels connected to the changes and involved in the process without the headache of actually having to implement the change. This can be extremely liberating for the manager and help to influence the transfer climate positively. After all, if the manager no longer feels responsible for making the change but is involved in the outcome then he or she is much more likely to support the individual and encourage the change, rather than imply through lack of interest that it is a complete waste of time. Often this implication is not genuine but is instead born out of fear that the manager simply does not have the tools or time to make the transfer of learning happen.

Plus, if a manager decides to be trained in TLA and becomes proficient in the enhanced coaching methodology of TLA then they can effectively support change in a variety of situations outside the training context. The manager would then have the tools to support behaviour change, which could be implemented following everything from employee reviews to new projects or software installation – and that is incredibly valuable from a career progression perspective.

Trainer or facilitator of the training

What makes learning transfer so beneficial to the trainer of the learning solution is the growing requirement that training takes participants to the new finish line instead of the old finish line. In the past, delivering quality training and achieving level one and level two evaluation (reaction and learning) was considered good enough. That is no longer the case. The new finish line is demanding that participants be taken past reaction and learning outcomes to application or behavioural change outcomes and possibly into business impact and ROI. The new training finish line, or the place where training will be considered to be genuinely successful, is when the participants of the training are using the information and skills they learnt in the training in their everyday working lives.

That means that the trainer is no longer considered successful if they simply deliver a good programme and participants can demonstrate some new learning. This is no longer enough. For the trainer there are two alternative responses to this. They can get irritated that they will be judged on something they have no control over, or they can embrace the need for learning transfer and incorporate TLA into their training offering.

I've already said that the person delivering the training programme is not always the best person to deliver the learning transfer follow-up. Certainly it is better if there is a clear distinction between the training and the transfer of learning. This can be achieved best by having one person deliver the training and a different person delivering the TLA follow-up. That might mean that trainers choose to become trained in TLA and offer the TLA follow-up support to other trainers and vice versa. Or if they really don't feel they have the personality for one-on-one versus one-on-many then they team up with a TLA coach who then delivers the coaching component. The benefits of either approach are that the trainer who pitches the full solution, including the crucial transfer of learning component, will get the kudos for the improvement. They will then have access to case studies and success stories that can be further used to sell more training to new clients and additional training to existing clients. Plus if they don't want to learn TLA themselves or don't want to get involved with one-on-one coaching activity then they can earn additional income from bringing a TLA facilitator on board without being directly involved in the delivery of TLA. Trainers interested in these types of partnership options can find out more by visiting **www.leverlearning.com**.

The trainer of the learning solution is also given a copy of the Impact Dashboard so they can use that as evidence of the effectiveness of their training coupled with TLA. They can also use the information provided on the dashboard to fine tune the training or come up with new training offerings.

I believe that learning transfer is a huge opportunity for trainers. They can either drag their heels towards the inevitable or they can embrace that opportunity and prosper. Whether trainers like it or not there is going to be a time in the very near future when they will be expected to take responsibility for the transfer of learning process and they will not be able to abdicate responsibility once the training part is over. But that is not a threat it's an opportunity. An opportunity to either extend their product offering or to team up with a TLA specialist for better results so that everyone wins.

TLA specialist

The TLA specialist is the stakeholder responsible for supporting the participant to create the change and deliver on the outcome. But to do that they just need to follow the process rather than trying to take ownership of the change themselves. TLA coaching is not about the coach making the individual do what they said they would do. They are not therefore personally responsible for whether or not the participant follows through. They are responsible for following the process so that they foster ownership in the participant and support them to hold themselves accountable for follow-through. It is a subtle distinction but an extremely important one to understand.

The benefits of the transfer of learning process to the TLA specialist are huge. There are few things more rewarding in life than helping people get what they want – and that is essentially what a TLA specialist does all day long! They don't have to sit at home worrying if the person they are coaching is going to reach their objectives, because they know that if they just follow the process and support the TLA participant to hold themselves to account then the outcome is very likely. That is incredibly liberating, not just for the TLA specialist but also the participant. Their role is simply to keep that individual on track towards their own self-selected goals.

The TLA process is a proven methodology so the specialist does not have to reinvent the wheel every time. They don't have to worry about every conversation and what might happen; they simply learn the methodology, follow the process and bask in the reflective glory of accomplishment and achievement.

The key driver for the TLA facilitator is the achievement of a business out-come, whereas traditionally the key driver of a trainer is the achievement of a learning outcome. Put those two individuals together and training as we know it will be revolutionized.

In the end, effective learning transfer pushes everyone involved in training to the new finish line so that the value expected from the training is actually realized in the business. When people initially hear that the TLA process is a series of one-on-one follow-up conversations the immediate instinct is that it is going to be prohibitively expensive. It's not. What *is* required, however, is a shift in perspective. At the moment training is at least partly 'justified' because of the one-to-many cost structure of training. When a training cost is provided it is relatively easy to work out the cost per attendee and massage that figure so that it appears suitably acceptable. The side effect of this reality is that people are sent on training 'because it can't hurt'. Only it does hurt because sending people to training that has zero relevance to their role – just so that someone can keep the cost per person training to an acceptable and justifiable level – is crazy. For a start we have people on training who would otherwise be back at work being productive, so there is an opportunity cost involved in this approach. Also, if that person is attending a training that isn't relevant then they will never transfer the learning anyway, so what is the point of it? For too long the thinking has been, 'Okay so the training is $15,000. If we get 30 people to attend that works out at just $500 per person. That seems reasonable. Let's do it!' But when only 15 people should actu-ally be attending the training it is unproductive and wastes money and participants' time, which further intensifies training cynicism within the workforce. Even if the training works out at $50 per head, without some transfer of learning strategy in place to coach people through the process of behavioural change nothing will happen. Waste is waste regardless of how reasonable the cost per attendee may appear to be.

What is required therefore is a new perspective. If we are looking for behav-ioural, real-world change back in the workplace that involves an improve-ment of soft skills such as leadership, sales, communication skills etc, then we need to purchase training with a transfer of learning component otherwise we will not get the gains we are seeking from the training. That may mean we do less training but we get better results, it may mean that we redistribute the budget we already have for training or use alternative budgets. Learning transfer is not expensive. Yes, it will add to the overall cost of training but if it guarantees that we get the results we sought from the training in the first place then surely it's worth it. The alternative is to pay for training, even brilliant training, and watch once again how nothing actually changes in the workplace until someone suggests that we try some other training to see if *that* will work. This is unproductive, demoralizing and inefficient. And when everyone is already stretched for time it is simply adding to the legacy of failure that makes employees the world over groan in despair as soon as their manager mentions the 'T-word'.

There are a variety of ways to deliver TLA that suits any budget. As discussed in the last chapter, the cost will often come down to who implements it. In an organization that does a lot of training it may be more cost-effective over time to have an internal L&D professional trained in the TLA methodology. If senior management are seeking a particular change in behaviour and feel confident that if the business can demonstrate that change they will not need to purchase any other training for a while then outsource the TLA follow-up to a specialist TLA facilitator. There are many ways to successfully deliver learning transfer but there is no longer any debate about whether or not learning transfer is necessary.

Good training and a proven transfer of learning methodology are crucial in liberating the benefit that training has promised for so long but failed to deliver alone. Only when the two components start to work together will businesses finally experience the benefits they were seeking that prompted the training in the first place. Only then will we finally eradicate training failure.

Summary of key points

- There are many different stakeholders in the training process. As in the training design process they all have different objectives and outcomes and their perception of the finish line or ideal outcome is often quite different.
- Effective transfer of learning offers each stakeholder specific benefits. Those stakeholders are:
  - CEO;
  - L&D professionals;
  - commissioning head;
  - participant;
  - manager of the participant;
  - trainer or facilitator of the training;
  - TLA specialist.

- Instead of spending $100,000 on two training courses that don't work the business could spend half of that amount on one training course with a learning transfer strategy that did work. Surely that is a better outcome for everyone. The business gets the essential performance improvement it seeks without spending more money – possibly even by spending less money – and the participants are actually using their new knowledge to improve productivity and performance. Plus participants are no longer upset and irritated at being asked to attend *yet another* training programme that they know, before they even arrive, they will never use in the workplace.

- The more that L&D leaders and employees can be seen as effective contributors to successful business results rather than just a business support function the more valued they are going to be. If the L&D professionals embrace the need for an effective learning transfer process and, where behaviour change is required, always ensure that a learning transfer process is included alongside the training solution then their credibility and results will improve exponentially.

- The benefits of learning transfer for the commissioning head are very straightforward – it vastly increases the likelihood that the commissioning head will get the behaviour change that he or she wants.

- For the participants of training, transfer of learning almost guarantees that they will have to endure less training in the future – not more. They will be supported to make the changes over a reasonable period of time and do not have to be fearful about not being able to master the new skill or manage the change. Most people are resistant to change or a little scared of trying new things, even if they won't admit it. TLA helps to manage that fear and often the benefits spill over into all the other areas of the participant's life.

- For the manager, learning transfer offers a viable solution that not only gets them off an unwinnable hook but allows them to stay connected to the change process and know what is going on for each of the participants. As part of the TLA system the participant's TLA plan, including the three objectives that the person has committed to, can be automatically sent to that person's manager. That way, the manager feels connected to the changes and involved in the process – without the headache of actually having to implement the change.

- Learning transfer is a huge opportunity for trainers. Whether trainers like it or not there is going to be a time in the very near future where they will be expected to take responsibility for the transfer of learning process and they will not be able to abdicate responsibility once their part is over. But that is not a threat it is an opportunity. An opportunity to either extend their product offering or to team up with a TLA specialist for better results so that everyone wins.

- The TLA process is a proven methodology where the specialist doesn't have to reinvent the wheel every time. They don't have to worry about every conversation and what might happen; they simply learn the methodology, follow the process and bask in the reflective glory of accomplishment and achievement.

- The key driver for the TLA facilitator is the achievement of a business outcome, whereas traditionally the key driver of a trainer is the achievement of a learning outcome. Put those two individuals together and training as we know it will be revolutionized.

- If we are looking for behavioural, real-world change back in the workplace, which involves an improvement of soft skills such as leadership, sales, communication skills etc, then we need to purchase training with a transfer of learning component, otherwise we will not get the gains we are seeking from the training.

- The alternative is to pay for training, even brilliant training, and watch once again how nothing actually changes in the workplace until someone suggests that we try some other training to see if *that* will work.

- Good training and a proven transfer of learning methodology are crucial in liberating the benefit that training has promised for so long but failed to deliver alone. Only when the two components start to work together will the businesses finally experience the benefits they were seeking that prompted the training in the first place. Only then will we finally eradicate training failure.

Conclusion

My greatest wish for this book is that it has inspired hope about how to finally solve the problem of ineffective training. For decades everyone involved in training, from the designers to the facilitators to the participants to the managers and leaders, have been disappointed with the outcomes of training and the lack of any real-world measureable impact. There are always some people who will action training and make strides in the right direction, but when it is considered normal and acceptable that 80 per cent of participants will not, then surely something is seriously wrong with the process.

Over the course of the last 20 to 30 years people in the industry have sought to rectify that problem with limited or, at best, mixed results. We have become extremely proficient in identifying training needs and designing courses and training events that will bridge the knowledge shortfall and upload the information necessary for change. We have become extremely proficient in delivering those training programmes and getting good feedback – and yet three weeks after the training event the workbooks and training folders are filed away or dumped at the bottom of a drawer and the participants are back at work doing exactly what they were doing before they left to attend the course.

And so for years we have been faced with the mounting, almost overwhelming evidence that training for the vast majority of people doesn't work. Training is by and large commissioned to solve a problem in a business, whether that is a sales problem, operations problem, skills problem, productivity problem or time-management problem. Training is supposed to be the solution because the assumption is that there is a skill or knowledge shortfall. So training is commissioned and that shortfall is rectified. And yet the problem remains largely unchanged. Why? Because *knowing* and *doing* are very different things. Just because I know I should go to the gym and eat more vegetables does not mean I will. Just because you learn a new sales technique and really appreciate how useful and valuable it may be doesn't mean you will use it when you get back to work.

Training doesn't work because all the focus is on the wrong finish line. With so many stakeholders involved in the process, each one shunts the responsibility for success on to the next person in the chain until it falls in a heap – usually at the feet of the participant or that person's manager. And yet this isn't fair. The finish line is not the end of the training – no matter how brilliantly that training is designed and delivered. The real finish line is when the knowledge or skill taught in the training can be witnessed in action in the workplace. And this is true whether that training is formal or whether your company has embraced the 70/20/10 model and most of the corporate learning occurs on the job. Remember, new information, knowledge or skills are only really useful when the people receiving that new information, knowledge or skill use it on a regular basis. It is only successful when people change and improve their performance.

Training is not just governed by learning theory, even adult learning theory, it is governed by change theory. Successful training, therefore, must include a transfer of learning process that helps and supports participants to make those changes in the workplace after the learning or training event. And the only real way to do that is through one-on-one follow-up conversations.

TLA is a one-on-one follow-up process that takes the basic principles of coaching and adds to them in order to create an enhanced coaching methodology specifically designed to address the transfer of learning problem.

What is especially exciting about TLA is that not only does it finally address the dismal results inherent in corporate training but it also has far-reaching implications across any business.

Follow-up in the form of coaching has been around for centuries – especially when we look at the arena of sports. Over the last few decades it has moved successfully into business. I became a coach in 2000 and one of the reasons I decided to move to Australia was that Sydney University was the first university in the world to offer a degree in coaching. To me that demonstrated a commitment to coaching and that Australia was clearly a country that took its coaching seriously. As someone who also takes coaching very seriously I moved from the UK to Australia in 2002.

Sir John Whitmore, executive chairman of Performance Consultants and pre-eminent thinker in leadership and organizational change, believes that coaching has the potential to bring about real behavioural change, which has implications across all society. He believes that no matter what context – be it family, community, business or relationships – the more coaching conversations we all have the better the world will be.

If, for example, two people are discussing what must be done to protect the environment then Whitmore believes those discussions should be coaching discussions not circular discussions. Too often 'normal' conversations don't go anywhere. Of course there are some conversations that are enjoyable simply *because* they don't go anywhere, but when there is a challenge or a problem that needs to be solved these 'normal' circular conversations are useless and counterproductive.

Just think for a moment what the world would be like, what your business would be like, what your life would be like, if all the important conversations you had were coaching conversations. In other words, instead of engaging in a circular, never-ending debate about problems, everyone involved in the conversation instead sought to identify where they want to be, where they are now and how to bridge the gap. Imagine what Parliament would be like – imagine what could be achieved if politicians stopped trying to score points off each other over the other's inability to solve some problem but instead engaged in coaching conversations about what needs to change and changing it. Imagine what families would be like – if parents did not have to scream at their children to do their homework but were able to ask a series of questions that alerted the teenager about the need for homework and allowed them to take responsibility for their actions. Imagine what a business would be like – if managers didn't have to micro-manage their staff or send them on endless training programmes that delivered no result. Imagine if, instead of endlessly complaining to work colleagues in the canteen, everyone in the business was having coaching conversations – identifying the problem, working out where they were right now and forming a plan to bridge that gap. Imagine the productivity. Imagine if training really did deliver the results that were intended.

Turning Learning into Action® (TLA) is fundamentally a way of taking what we *know* and making it something that we *do*. This is achieved through follow-up conversations that focus on outcomes, solutions and action. So, the more people who really master the TLA skill and swap their circular conversations for solution-focused TLA conversations – with accountability to action – the better. Everything from families, to the environment, to businesses, to communities, to politics would be very different.

TLA is a proven methodology that works for transfer of learning, but once we learn the methodology we soon appreciate that the enhanced coaching methodology that is at the heart of TLA can be used in any aspect of life. In the end, coaching is only really powerful when we apply it to a particular context. TLA applies enhanced coaching to the context of transfer of learning so that training finally delivers the benefits to the participant and the business that it was designed to deliver. But we can use the methodology in many different contexts.

Everything in our life can be improved by the ability to have an effective coaching conversation and it is a skill that is permeating all parts of society. Coaching is a powerful skill and when mastered holds the key to changing behaviour and therefore changing the world – let's start with training.

Appendix 1: Turning Learning into Action® learning agreement

 Turning Learning into Action® (TLA) Learning Agreement

OUTLINE

This agreement covers the TLA coach/participant relationship which is being entered into between you, the participant, and your TLA coach specialist with the intended outcome of implementing into your role the new skills and knowledge learnt on the programme you are attending. The sessions will be tailored to your individual objectives. Turning Learning into Action® (TLA) follow up, which is not consulting, advice or counselling, will address the specific outcomes detailed by you in your action plan. The telephone sessions will cover any issues that directly or indirectly affect your ability to follow through or implement your action plan. You need to enter into the sessions with the full understanding that you create your own results.

CONFIDENTIALITY

Confidentiality is the cornerstone of TLA. Essentially, everything you share with your TLA coach within the session is confidential, whether it is business or personal information. Your coach undertakes not to, at any time, either directly or indirectly use or disclose any information you share with them during the sessions. In the unlikely event that you bring to your TLA coach's attention a matter that would constitute gross misconduct or a serious contractual breach, your programme sponsor will be informed. Your manager will have a copy of the action plan that you complete in the session today to support you internally through the change process.

SESSIONS

Sessions will last 30 minutes and will be conducted over the telephone. **You call your TLA coach** at the scheduled time on the office number, most local to you, below. Your company will be notified as to missed sessions. Please swap your session time with a colleague, and notify your TLA Coach if you cannot make your appointment. In the event of you calling late for a session, then the finish time will remain the same.

▶

ENVIRONMENT FOR SESSIONS

It is your responsibility to ensure the environment that you are calling from is suitable for TLA. Ideally, it is a quiet, private area away from your personal office space, on a landline phone with a phone handset. You must ensure that you can speak freely and are not interrupted or distracted during the call. Mobile/Cell phones and computers should be switched off for the session. Having the best environment will help you get the best value from the process.

DOCUMENTATION/NOTES

It is your responsibility to document your own action points from sessions. Most clients also take notes during the session. Using your own language and emphasizing what is important to you increases the level of ownership and your results.

EXPECTATIONS

You can expect your coach to:
- Maintain confidentiality
- Encourage and support you
- Be punctual
- Keep your appointment in high priority
- Put your interests first
- Work with you to ensure that the sessions are a good use of your time
- Respect your decisions, skills and knowledge

Your coach expects you to:
- Be honest with your coach and yourself
- Be punctual
- Keep your appointment in high priority
- Create a physical environment where you can focus on the call
- Be prepared to experiment and do things differently
- Offer feedback at the end of the process

A copy of your coach's bio can be found at www.leverlearning.com/about-us/our-team

Signature: _Emma Weber_ On behalf of your TLA Coach

Contact details for your session Telephone: **Europe/UK** +44 333 301 0714
Asia/Australia +61 2 8221 8833   **USA** +1 214 530 0643
Email: coach first name @leverlearning.com

Appendix 2: Sample TLA plan

Action Plan – IT Client, Account Manager's Programme

Participant Name: __John Haslow__   Course Date: __23rd May 2011__

TARGET What specifically will you implement from the programme and by when?	SEE SUCCESS How will you know you have been successful in implementing this target? What will you see happening around you? What will people be saying? How will you feel?	CALIBRATE Where are you now with this target on a scale of 1 (low) to 10 (high)?	MOTIVATION Why do you want to achieve this? What does it mean to you personally? Why is that important to you?	NEXT STEPS What action can you take within the next 48 hours? What other steps will you take before your 1st coaching call?
1. Create a stakeholder map for my top 2 clients and use this to create more business with my clients. Map by middle of June, Impact within 3 months.	Map will be completed. Business projects will increase in number and value to the business. My meetings will be more strategic.	2	Best practice, want to be a top performer in the business. Possible promotion, increased remuneration, satisfaction of a job well done.	Start the stakeholder map.
2. Win the trust of Andrew Bell. ASAP	Andrew will call me when he has problems and will be more open with me in meetings.	3	I don't know him well and he is the sort of person I need to be able to influence and work closely with. I want to be respected within the business as a key player.	I will schedule a meeting with him for next week and work on building confidence and intimacy in the meeting.
3. Be more of an active listener in meetings. Have made a change within the month.	I won't be missing information and I will be more across what is going on.	5	Get a better understanding of what is going on, will make my life easier and I will be more efficient.	Listen to resource TFT. Podcast Active Listening.

Appendix 3: Sample conversation to illustrate the flexible TION part of the ACTION model

Context: in this sample the participant wanted to tick the box and talk through how he knew how to build trust, but he had clearly identified it as being difficult. The TLA facilitator needs to find out which bit is difficult and where they can add the most value.

	The TLA Conversation	Commentary	Model
Coach	*Which target would you like us to work on today? I often suggest people choose the one that will be hardest or trickiest to implement.*	Use this question to gauge where the most value will be gained.	Target.
Participant	*Number 2.*		
Coach	*Okay, so number 2, winning the trust of Pete Simmons. And earlier you said you currently felt that was at 3.5.*	The coach will have got this usually at the very beginning of the call.	Clarifying gap/target (plus calibration).
Participant	*Yes.*		
Coach	*Great – so it's currently at 3.5 having moved up from a 3 at the end of the course, if you really put some focus on this goal in the next three months where do you think you could get it to?*	Identifying the gap.	Target.
Participant	*If I really worked at it I could get it to a 7, maybe an 8.*		

	The TLA Conversation	Commentary	Model
Coach	*What score would you be really happy with?*		Target.
Participant	*I'd be really happy at an 8.*	Confirming what number he wants to go for.	
Coach	*So let's go for an 8. What would be happening at an 8 that's not happening now at 3.5?*		Target.
Participant	*Well – I'd be invited into meetings at a more senior level. Pete and I would have open dialogue and I wouldn't be kept in the dark like I sometimes am now. I'd be across what is happening.*	Temptation here could be to get into the story of past examples – the coach doesn't need to know.	Target.
Coach	*Okay – that sounds as if you have a clear view of an 8, and if you were to get some immediate traction going in the next three weeks where could you get it up to?*		
Participant	*Well – it's going to take time but I guess I could get it to a 6.*		
Coach	*Okay. So let's get a snapshot of what would be be happening at a 6 that's not happening now.*	Narrowing the timeframe to something immediate.	Target.
Participant	*Regular meetings would be the first step. Also he would reach out on an ad hoc basis. We would have more open conversations. I've got our first meeting set for next Tuesday.*		

	The TLA Conversation	Commentary	Model
Coach	*What needs to happen at that meeting to get you on that trajectory towards a 6?*	Gap, gathering info. The coach may think they have a gap so they start to gather information.	
Participant	*Well I know what needs to happen. I need to be open with him and tell him what I am trying to achieve and why. I'm going to ask a lot of questions to understand where he is coming from and my sense that we can quite quickly get to an improved trust level.*		
Coach	*Sorry to interrupt you John – it's sounding as if you have a really clear idea and we don't need to go into too much of the detail just yet – I want to make sure we make best use of your time. Let me just check in with you – how confident are you on a scale of 1 to 10 that you know how to build the trust you are looking for in that meeting?*	The TLA participant knows this stuff – he is telling the coach what he knows, which is good BUT it means there isn't really a gap.	Target/info/ using a calibration.
Participant	*9 – I'm pretty confident.*		
Coach	*Good – I can hear that. So what makes this challenging or tricky?*		Target – identifying gap.
Participant	*It's getting him to the meeting in the first place! I know what to do when I am in the meeting but it's actually getting him there that's the problem.*	The target is changing – the coach had no gap in the original part, so you are identifying the new, real gap.	

	The TLA Conversation	Commentary	Model
Coach	*Tell me more about getting him to the meeting.*		Info on the target.
Participant	*Well he has cancelled meetings in the past and he is very difficult to get hold of. He is a very busy man. We all are.*		
Coach	*Let me play back to you what I've heard: you are very confident that you know how to build trust with Pete when you are in the meeting you have arranged; the trick is getting him to turn up to that meeting.*		Summary of the gap/info gained.
Participant	*Yes – that's the problem.*		
Coach	*And shall we just check in – are you clear that the meeting is the best first step towards building this trust? Should we explore more options here?*	Checking on the gap – the coach could call it if he or she felt the need (see below).	Target.
Participant	*Yes – I'm clear that my best way forward is with the meeting.*		
Coach	*Good. So let's focus on getting him to the meeting. What could you do to get him to the meeting?*		
Participant	*I don't know – it's nearly impossible to get a meeting with this guy – I'm lucky he even put it in the diary but even when he's done that before for people he always cancels. What do you think I should do?*		Info.

	The TLA Conversation	Commentary	Model
Coach	*Sure – we can brainstorm and I can throw in some thoughts but really you are closer to the ground and know the business culture much better than I do... What's your gut feel, say, about what you could do to ensure that this is one meeting that Pete sticks to?*		Info/ options.
Participant	*I need to make it really worth his while.*		
Coach	*In what way could you make it worth his while?*		Info/ options.
Participant	*I need to make it really useful to him.*		
Coach	*And how could you do that? What might make it really useful to him?*		
Participant	*I could find out from Steve what's happening with the Acorn project that Pete is involved in at the moment and add that to the agenda. Also – one of our competitors released a report recently that no one else has seen internally – I could bring this to Pete's attention.*		
Coach	*Any other ideas – I just want to make sure we have left no stone unturned – what other options have you got for getting him to the meeting?*		Options.
Participant	*I could drop him a text the day before saying how much I'm looking forward to talking with him about the opportunities – that could peak his interest.*		

	The TLA Conversation	Commentary	Model
Coach	*Okay so we have two different ideas here – which of these are you going to commit to?*		Next steps.
Participant	*Both are good ideas – I'm going to do both.*	The coach can gauge the certainty here by using the structure of calibration… *'On a scale of 1 to 10 how confident are you on following through?'* – the coach will probably be able to tell confidence by the participant's voice.	Next steps.
Coach	*And what do you need to do to ensure that you follow through?*		
Participant	*I have time to give Steve a call this afternoon and I will diarize to send the text. Both are easy.*		
Coach	*Good – it sounds clear. You were clear anyway with what needed to happen at the meeting and now we have some actions that will ensure the meeting goes ahead. Anything else that we need to anticipate that might be good to plan around here?*	The coach adds a quick summary to remind the participant why he or she took that path.	Summary, check for additional gap in this area.
Participant	*No, I think that's a good solution.*		
Coach	*Great – so which goal shall we review now?*		Target.

References

Brinkerhoff, R O (2003) *The Success Case Method: Find out quickly what's working and what's not*, Berrett-Koehler Publishers Inc, San Francisco

Broad, M L and Newstrom, J W (1992) *Transfer of Training: Action-packed strategies to ensure high payoff from training investments*, Addison-Wesley, Reading, Massachusetts

Buckingham, M and Coffman, C (2005) *First Break all the Rules: What the world's greatest managers do differently*, Pocket Books, Simon & Schuster UK Ltd, London

Dweck, C (2006) *Mindset: The new psychology of success – how we can learn to fulfill our potential*, Random House, New York

Frankl, V E (1959) *Man's Search for Meaning*, Beacon Press, Boston

Gladwell, M (2005) *Blink: The power of thinking without thinking*, Little, Brown, New York

Kahneman, D (2011) *Thinking, Fast and Slow*, Penguin, New York

Kirkpatrick, J and Kirkpatrick, W (2011) 'The Kirkpatrick new world level 3', www.trainingzone.co.uk

Landsberg, M (1996) *The Tao of Coaching*, Harper Collins, London

Leimbach, M (2010) 'Learning transfer model: a research-driven approach to enhancing learning effectiveness', *Industrial and Commercial Training*, **42** (2), pp 81–86

McGregor, D (2006 [Annotated edition of the original book published in 1960]) *The Human Side of Enterprise*, McGraw-Hill, New York

Mintzberg, H (1975) 'The manager's job: folklore and fact', *Harvard Business Review*, **53** (4), pp 49–61

Naisbitt, J, Naisbitt, N and Philips, D (2001) *High Tech, High Touch: Technology and our accelerated search for meaning*, Nicholas Brearly, London

Phillips, J and Phillips, P (2008) *Beyond Learning Objectives: Develop measurable objectives that link to the bottom line*, ASTD Press, Alexandria, Virginia

Phillips, J and Phillips, P (2009) *Measuring for Success: What CEOs really think about learning investments*, ASTD Press, Alexandria, Virginia

Pink, D (2009) *Drive: The surprising truth about what motivates us*, Riverhead Books, New York

Prochaska, J O, Norcross, J C and DiClemente, C C (1998) *Changing for Good: A revolutionary six-stage program for overcoming bad habits and moving your life positively forward*, Avon Books, Inc, New York

Reichheld, F F (2003) 'The one number you need to grow', *Harvard Business Review*, OnPoint article, December

Saks, A M and Belcourt, M (2006) 'An investigation of training activities and transfer of training in organizations', *Human Resource Management*, **45**, pp 629–48

Wick, C, Pollock, R and Jefferson, A (2010) *The Six Disciplines of Breakthrough Learning: How to turn training and development into business results*, 2nd edn, Pfeiffer, John Wiley & Sons, Inc, Hoboken, New Jersey

Wood Daudelin, M (1996) 'Learning from experience through reflection', *Organizational Dynamics*, **24** (3), pp 36–48

Index

Note: *Italics* indicate a Figure or Table in the text.